soviet-american debate

1989 annual

David L. Bender, *Publisher*
Bruno Leone, *Executive Editor*
Bonnie Szumski, *Senior Editor*
Janelle Rohr, *Senior Editor*
Susan Bursell, *Editor*
William Dudley, *Editor*
Robert Anderson, *Assistant Editor*
Karin Swisher, *Assistant Editor*
Lisa Orr, *Assistant Editor*
Diana Shellenberger, *Assistant Editor*

greenhaven press, inc.
PO Box 289009
San Diego, CA 92128-9009

RILEY-HICKINGBOTHAM LIBRARY
OUACHITA BAPTIST UNIVERSITY

© 1989 by Greenhaven Press, Inc.
ISBN 0-89908-548-2
ISSN 0883-1270

contents

Editor's Note   *Opposing Viewpoints SOURCES* provide a wealth of opinions on important issues of the day. The annual supplements focus on the topics that continue to generate debate. Readers will find that *Opposing Viewpoints SOURCES* become exciting barometers of today's controversies. This is achieved in three ways. First, by expanding previous chapters with the most current opinions on the chapter topics. Second, by adding new materials which are timeless in nature. And third, by adding recent topical issues not dealt with in previous volumes or annuals.

Viewpoints

Afghanistan

1. **Communism Has Benefited Afghanistan** by *Najibullah* — 1
   Since Soviet troops were deployed in Afghanistan in 1979, the communist government of Afghanistan has worked to overcome the hardships of war. It has created a stronger economy and a more enlightened cultural life for the Afghan people.

2. **Communism Has Destroyed Afghanistan** by *Jeri Laber & Barnett R. Rubin* — 5
   The Soviet invaders and the Afghan communists have worked together to systematically destroy the people, culture, and country of Afghanistan.

3. **The USSR Is Relinquishing Control in Afghanistan** by *Stephen Sestanovich* — 11
   Having accepted defeat, the Soviets are trying to diminish their losses by withdrawing completely from Afghanistan.

4. **The USSR Is Retaining Control in Afghanistan** by *James A. Phillips* — 15
   The Soviet Union will never give up its control of Afghanistan. Even if the USSR withdraws its troops, it will find another way to dominate Afghanistan.

5. **Soviet Involvement in Afghanistan Will Continue** by *Lea Rehimi* — 19
   The Soviets will not remove their troops from Afghanistan. They will reduce their numbers to lull the West, while keeping control of Aghanistan.

6. **Soviet Involvement in Afghanistan Will End** by *Theodore L. Eliot Jr.* — 23
   The Soviet Union realized it could not win the war in Afghanistan. It will withdraw its troops and leave Afghanistan to the Afghan people.

7. **The Afghan People Should Determine Afghanistan's Future** by *Michael H. Armacost & Richard S. Williamson* — 27
   The US has supported Afghanistan's right to self-determination since the Soviet invasion in 1979. Afghanistan should revert to its nonaligned and independent status.

8. **The USSR Should Determine Afghanistan's Future** by *Workers Vanguard* — 31
   The USSR helped the Afghan government establish a freer, more open socialist regime. They should continue to aid the Afghan people in keeping their progressive new government.

9. **The US Should Continue Aid to Afghanistan** by *Henry Kriegel* — 35
   US aid to the Afghan rebels helped the rebels defeat the Soviet army. The US must continue aid to the rebels in order to pressure the Soviets to withdraw completely from Afghanistan.

10. **The US Should Not Continue Aid to Afghanistan** by The People & Carl Bloice — 39
    The US helped begin the war in Afghanistan and helped perpetuate it. The US should stop giving aid to the rebels and let the Afghan people live in peace.

Human Rights

11. The USSR Supports Human Rights *by Andrei Grachev* — 43
Human rights have become an important issue in the USSR. Improving human rights conditions is a vital part of the current Soviet reform program.

12. The USSR Does Not Support Human Rights *by Natan Sharansky* — 47
The current openness toward the West is a facade. It is intended to make Western leaders think that the USSR actually promotes human rights for its citizens and for people in Poland, Czechoslovakia, and other satellite nations.

13. Religious Freedom in the USSR: An Overview — 51
by Kenneth L. Woodward
The current reform program and the celebration of a millennium of Christianity in the USSR have raised questions about the extent of religious freedom in the Soviet Union.

14. The Soviet Union Represses Religion *by Andrew Sorokowski* — 55
The apparent easing of religious repression in the USSR is simply a propaganda campaign designed to pacify Western governments and human rights organizations.

15. The Soviet Union Does Not Repress Religion — 59
by Pimen, interviewed by World Marxist Review
Soviet citizens are free to practice their religions. The Soviet government and the church support each other's aims.

16. Repression of Jews in the USSR Is Easing *by George Perkovich* — 63
In order to keep the positive image glasnost projects, Soviet leaders have been forced to make some concessions to Soviet Jews. Jews have been allowed more freedom of expression and some have received permission to emigrate.

17. Repression of Jews in the USSR Is Continuing *by Thomas A. Idinopulos* — 67
While Christian religions in the USSR have a modicum of freedom, Soviet Jews continue to suffer deprivation of basic human rights, like the freedom to emigrate.

Glasnost

18. Soviet Reforms Are Genuine *by Robert Legvold* — 71
Mikhail Gorbachev has made bold and sweeping changes in the economics, politics, and military of the Soviet Union.

19. Soviet Reforms Are Not Genuine *by John Lenczowski* — 77
Gorbachev has not implemented revolutionary reforms and Soviet society has not changed. Gorbachev's "reforms" are merely a public relations ploy designed to improve the Soviet Union's image.

20. Soviet Reforms Are Easing Repression *by Abraham Brumberg* — 83
The reforms underway in the USSR have allowed and encouraged unprecedented freedom of speech and the press. The reforms have gained momentum and popularity, making their reversal nearly impossible.

21. Soviet Reforms Are Not Easing Repression *by I.F. Stone* — 89
Glasnost and perestroika have not eased religious or political repression in the USSR. In fact, the reform programs may provide propaganda that Gorbachev will use to cover increased repression.

22. Soviet Reforms Are Succeeding *by Jim Wallis* — 95
Previous repressive Soviet governments suspended basic human rights like freedom of speech and of belief. Soviet reforms under glasnost are allowing the Soviet people to begin to exercise fundamental rights.

23. Soviet Reforms Are Failing *by George Feifer* — 101
Gorbachev's reforms impress the Western media but only worsen the living conditions of the Soviet people. Without popular support, these reforms will fail.

24. Perestroika Benefits Ethnic Minorities *by Indrek Toome,* — 107
interviewed by Yekaterina Kozhukhova for New Times
The people of Soviet Estonia have used perestroika to improve their economic situation. Perestroika can ease national tensions by creating new economic opportunities for all the ethnic minorities.

25. Perestroika Harms Ethnic Minorities *by Workers Vanguard* — 113
Perestroika has caused extreme economic hardship among the ethnic minorities in the USSR. Strikes and protests have led to violent clashes. The Soviet military has suppressed these nationalist protests with force.

Bibliography — B-1

Index — I-1

"The revolution is still alive and developing, and the party is carrying on its constructive work [and] being quite a success at it."

viewpoint 1

Communism Has Benefited Afghanistan

Najibullah

Editor's note: The following viewpoint was written by the communist president of the Republic of Afghanistan. In the viewpoint, President Najibullah discusses some of the improvements the communists have implemented even while they fight a bloody war against the Muslim Afghan rebels whom they consider terrorists.

For years events in Afghanistan were first and foremost associated with reports from the battlefields of the undeclared war unleashed against the Republic of Afghanistan by the counter-revolutionary forces supported by the imperialist powers and their local accomplices. Today the name of our country ever more frequently brings to mind its peace-making efforts. The policy of national reconciliation declared by the People's Democratic Party of Afghanistan (PDPA) has the simple and concrete aim to put an end to the fratricidal war, which has been afflicting our land, the bodies and souls of millions of the Afghan people for nearly ten years now. The roots of this policy should be traced to the hearts of my compatriots. Our party carried on the aspirations of our people, formalising them theoretically and organisationally in what came to be called the *policy of national reconciliation.*

The PDPA first spoke of searches for an alternative to military confrontation at the 16th CC [Central Committee] Plenary Meeting in the autumn of 1985. But the task of implementing that policy called for a clear-cut concept of attaining peace and security, a concept that would take into account the entirety of Afghanistan's specific features and the situation in the region. It took shape in the course of numerous meetings and talks with party activists, scholars, elders and representatives of the most diverse strata of the population. We have gained much by studying the heritage of the founders of the scientific revolutionary theory and the experience of the fraternal parties.

The implementation of the national reconciliation policy began with concrete steps taken on January 15, 1987, when *our army initiated a unilateral ceasefire.* I can now safely state that this noble step has been discussed under the roof of every house in this country. The Afghan people are weary of bloodshed and no longer want to look at each other through the slit of a gun sight.

The Costs of War

War has inflicted enormous damage. The cost of things which had been blown up, burned out or razed to the ground exceeds 50 billion afghani. Hundreds of villages have been turned into ruins together with more than 2,000 schools and hospitals, the activity of many an economic project has been paralysed and agricultural production has fallen dramatically. Fourteen thousand kilometres of telephone lines and half the electric power lines have been destroyed. But how can we gauge thousands upon thousands of ruined lives, the suffering of those crippled and incapacitated or the tears of Afghan women mourning their fathers, husbands, sons and brothers. Mind you, the grindstone of war crushes primarily the flower of our people—their young, in this way depriving the nation of tomorrow.

The Western mass media often seek to present the Afghan people as victims of their own differences. *But this is not a civil war: it has been imposed on the people from without* by those, who, nurturing the counter-revolutionaries, hope to continue the massacre 'to the last Afghani man'. In the past years the U.S. and its allies spent a total of $4 billion to whip up hostilities in Afghanistan. It is precisely this 'gold rain' pouring into the pockets of the counter-revolutionary gang leaders that turned into a

Najibullah, "The Humane Idea of Reconciliation," *World Marxist Review,* January 1988. Reprinted with permission of *World Marxist Review* published by Progress Books (Toronto).

downpour of missiles and shells, death and destruction on our land.

The large-scale socio-political process is gradually gathering momentum, and the seeds of peace sown by us have already borne fruit. The course of the PDPA and the government towards renouncing the military means of settling problems, their readiness for dialogue and reasonable compromises, renunciation of monopoly of government and the passing of laws on political parties, a call for the establishment of a coalition government and the new Constitution are all the constituents of the integral and consistent programme that induced a considerable section of the opposition forces to go over, albeit slowly and cautiously, to negotiations.

"This is not a civil war: it has been imposed on the people from without."

During the latter period 2,300 villages have been liberated by peaceful means and people's rule is now in operation in more than 9,000 villages, 45 cities and towns, including all the 29 provincial centres, and in 214 districts and regions, that is, on a greater portion of the country's habitable territory. Back to their homeland returned 100,000 of our compatriots and the figure could have been much higher, had it not been for the obstacles raised by the Pakistani and Iranian authorities to the Afghan refugees. More than 30,000 rebels from nearly 200 formations have renounced armed struggle and, together with them, another 110,000 people returned to peaceful life. Over 6,000 former members of counter-revolutionary units are collaborating in bodies of local authority and national reconciliation commissions.

Statistics are, of course, incapable of demonstrating what matters most, namely, that the people have regained hope in the possibility of substituting implements of labour for arms, rebuilding ravaged villages and irrigation ditches and cultivating land which had for years been sown with mine and shell fragments rather than with grain and profusely sprinkled with blood rather than water.

As could be expected, our initiatives intensified divisions among the opposition, evoking ire among the extremist sections of the counter-revolutionaries. The ringleaders of the Peshawar Seven, the main anti-Afghan organisations entrenched on Pakistani territory, did not respond to the ceasefire call. They even intensified their fire raids especially in the east and south-east of the country and continue committing outrage and violence. These people are putting themselves outside the process of changes.

The national reconciliation course has, indisputably, had a favourable effect on reviving economic activity. In the past year industrial production growth rates exceeded by 40 per cent the mean annual figure of the post-revolutionary period.

Despite the difficulties caused by the complicated military-political situation and the enormous material loss mentioned above, the country has surpassed the pre-revolutionary level in key economic indicators. For example, in the past five years GNP [Gross National Product] grew by 18 per cent, national income by 10 per cent, while capital investment in the production and social spheres nearly doubled from 12 to 22.7 billion afghani.

A decisive factor of *industrial development* is Afghanistan's close cooperation with the socialist countries, above all the Soviet Union. Enterprises built with Soviet aid account for over 60 per cent of overall industrial output. Czechoslovakia, the GDR [German Democratic Republic], Bulgaria, Poland, Romania and Hungary are also giving us constantly growing help in economic development.

Attention to Agriculture

We pay special attention to *agriculture* which suffered most in the conflagration of war. The guideline here is the same—the abolition of feudal relations and the continuation of agrarian-irrigation reform in the interests of the mass of the peasants. As is known, the just solution of the agrarian problem has always and everywhere been pivotal to national democratic transformations. We believe that the improvement of socio-economic relations in the Afghan countryside and raising on this basis the peasants' living standards are the key condition of the success of the national reconciliation policy and of expanding the social base of the Saur revolution.

The party and the government show concern for *the needs of the people* by building new schools, hospitals, living quarters, libraries, museums and cinema halls. A special UNESCO (United Nations Educational, Scientific and Cultural Organization) medal has marked the fact that more than half a million people attend 25,000 courses to eliminate illiteracy. All this is undertaken in the conditions of war when we have to spend on defence three out of every five afghani of the state budget.

Our position on religion is consistent and clear-cut. We have always proceeded from the fact that the PDPA emerged and is acting on the political scene of a traditional Muslim country. Respect for Islam is graphically manifest in the emblem and national flag of Afghanistan. The documents of the people's government, first and foremost the Constitution of the republic, guarantee the believers all the conditions necessary for observing religious rites. Kabul University has a theological department and an Islamic research centre has been opened of late in the capital. In the years of the revolution 57 new mosques have been built and 527 old mosques and holy places restored in Kabul alone.

The experience of states, such as Lebanon, Iran and Iraq, forcefully demonstrates that the imperialist powers criminally exploit Islam for their own aims. Under its banner opponents of progressive changes in Afghanistan commit most godless atrocities. They are responsible for the destruction of more than 250 mosques and prayer houses and the death of hundreds of patriotically-minded representatives of the clergy.

It's a paradox that we representatives of the revolutionary government called by our enemies the 'infidels' are restoring and building mosques, showing respect for the clergy, while the 'fighters for Islam' glorified in the West are setting on fire and blowing up Islamic sanctuaries and killing imams.

Engaging in wishful thinking, the adversaries of the Saur revolution on countless occasions predicted its speedy demise and, together with it, the fall of the PDPA. Nevertheless the revolution is still alive and developing, and the party is carrying on its constructive work, being quite a success at it, to judge by the bitterness of our enemies.

Growing Ranks

The growing ranks of the PDPA are a convincing testimony of its viability and mounting influence. Veterans remember the times when the party numbered not more than several dozens. By the time of the revolution it had 15,000 and by the first all-party conference of 1982 nearly 90,000 members. The second conference held in October 1987 was attended by delegates sent by 185,000 party members. Incidentally, the declaration of the national reconciliation course triggered a sharp increase in the number of applications for PDPA membership. In the past five years party organisations in some provinces and the capital grew three-fold or so. The total number of grassroot party organisations reached 6,160, with 2,117 of them operating in the army units.

"The party and the government show concern for the needs of the people by building new schools, hospitals, living quarters, libraries, museums and cinema halls."

The following figures give an idea of the party's social structure: among the newly affiliated in the period between the two conferences workers accounted for 18 per cent, peasants for 26.5 per cent, artisans and handicraftsmen for 3 per cent and the representatives of the intelligentsia for 36.9 per cent. More than half the fresh forces were people under 30. Women account for one-tenth of the membership which the Central Committee considers inadequate and intends to change for the better.

The steady growth of the PDPA membership is not an aim in itself for us. The party shows strict concern for the healthiness of its ranks and will not tolerate neglect for inner party discipline or the principles of democratic centralism. The grim realities of our day demand that the style and methods of leadership should be changed as well as the bad habits of the past—passivity and reliance on instructions from above, tendency towards bombastic slogans not supported by deeds, lack of a principled attitude and exactingness towards both oneself and fellow party members. We have to renounce the evil practice of rotating loafers in high offices, while inculcating modesty among party members in all and everything.

We will continue combating red tape in the party and state apparatus. It is important that every leader should visit frequently villages and industrial shops, educational establishments and soldiers' barracks. A welcome fact is that many Central Committee and Political Bureau members spend most of their time touring provinces and meeting people rather than being confined to their offices.

I recall in this connection what a woman worker of the Kunduz province told me. She had been wounded when a bomb planted by bandits exploded, and I came to her place to give her an order for excellent work and participation in the defence of the accomplishments of the Saur revolution. Two of her sons were killed at the front and the remaining two were serving in the armed forces. I asked her if she needed any help and Malalai (that was the woman's name) answered: "I want only one thing—that you leaders always be in your element. And for a politician, the people are his element . . ."

Another duty of paramount importance for the party leaders was aptly expressed at the second PDPA conference by a worker called Rashid who urged the leaders invariably to hold their word and put all their promises into effect. The main thing, he said, is that the people want them always to tell the truth.

Faction Infighting

Like any political organisation, the PDPA finds it of vital importance to maintain the unity of its ranks. For many years the party was suffering from overt and covert faction infighting whipped up by rivalry among different groupings and their leaders who failed to abandon their coterie habits. The evolution of the national reconciliation process, the foundation of new parties in the country and prospects of a coalition government are increasingly attracting our attention to the problem of unity.

Advance towards democratising the life of Afghan society gives the existing parties and those in the making, which seek national reconciliation, an opportunity to act legally and freely express their opinion on all issues. The people's government has formalised it in a special law. The process of the PDPA's interaction with some left-wing democratic parties illustrates the gradual formation of the pluralistic system. The patriotically-minded clergy intends, too, to found an Islamic party in Afghanistan. There are prerequisites for the establishment of a peasant party. A compromise with other political forces is also being sought.

That is why the PDPA needs unity as never before. We should ensure the cohesion of our ranks in deed and not in word otherwise the party will lose its organising and mobilising role in society and find itself outside the political system. . . .

situation in the region and on the world scene. A key task facing the PDPA is to speed up this process and to create sound guarantees of peace.

Najibullah is the general secretary of the People's Democratic Party of Afghanistan and President of the Republic of Afghanistan.

"We regard our party as an inalienable part of the movement for the world without war or violence, for cooperation and mutual understanding."

We regard our party as an inalienable part of the movement for the world without war or violence, for cooperation and mutual understanding among nations, the movement which has swept the entire globe. We believe it our internationalist duty to our great and noble friend—the Soviet people—to ensure, among other things, the speedy return to their homeland of the limited Soviet troops contingent in Afghanistan. By working against the military confrontation in the country and the region and in defence of the sovereignty and independence, the PDPA is winning prestige on the international scene, as is borne out by its constantly extending international ties. We have signed cooperation protocols with 76 parties of different countries and maintain contacts with a total of 150 political parties, progressive organisations and movements.

The national reconciliation policy in Afghanistan has evoked wide interest abroad, for example, in Kampuchea and five Central American countries. The idea of reconciliation is in itself of *universal nature*. It has imbibed the historical experience of the revolutionary transformation of society and reflects people's eternal striving for eradicating wars, for progress and humanism. It reflects an attempt at mastering a new political thinking which has declared human life and peace on earth to be the highest values.

Peace and Socialism

Problems of peace and socialism are inseparable, the latter being unthinkable without the former. The national reconciliation programme is for us the only possible answer to the question how to stop bloodshed in Afghanistan, improving in this way the

"The people of Afghanistan have been defending their independence, their culture, and their very existence in a desperate battle with one of the world's great superpowers."

viewpoint 2

Communism Has Destroyed Afghanistan

Jeri Laber and Barnett R. Rubin

"A whole nation is dying. People should know." This terse statement befitted the speaker, Engineer Mohammad Eshaq, a resistance leader from Afghanistan's Panjsher Valley, a man of courage and conviction. Yet his eyes clouded over with tears when he told us about the fate of two men from his ancestral village of Mata—brothers, aged ninety and ninety-five. Old and blind, they stayed behind when the rest of the villagers fled during the spring offensive. "The Russians came, tied dynamite to their backs, and blew them up." He paused to collect himself, then added simply, "They were very respected people."

Afghanistan Remains Remote

For eight years now, in their remote, mountainous land in the center of Asia, the people of Afghanistan have been defending their independence, their culture, and their very existence in a desperate battle with one of the world's great superpowers. Yet the inherent drama of such a confrontation does not appear to have captured the world's imagination. Afghanistan remains remote.

There are many reasons for this. The Afghan government officially closed its doors to most of the major world media and to international humanitarian organizations, and the information it has released has been dictated by the needs of official propaganda. The few outsiders who have been allowed to visit the capital city of Kabul are shown only what the government wants them to see, and their movements are carefully watched. The Pakistan-based Afghan resistance parties, on the other hand, are hardly objective sources of information and are often at odds with each other as well. Independent investigation has involved entering the country illegally from Pakistan, trekking for weeks over forbidding terrain, and braving the dangers of a war without fronts. The largest group of victims consists of uneducated people who seem almost from another century and have no idea of how to tell their story to the modern world.

What little news we receive comes from a handful of intrepid scholars, doctors, and journalists who have taken the risk of "going inside," usually under the aegis of one of the resistance groups. Their reports, covering a variety of aspects of the Afghan conflict, have included numerous accounts of atrocities and other human rights abuses since the Soviet invasion of December 1979.

In September 1984 we made the first of several trips to the Afghan border—to Peshawar in Pakistan's North-West Frontier Province; to Islamabad, that nation's capital; and to Quetta in Baluchistan—to collect information about human rights violations in Afghanistan by interviewing some of the Afghan people who have sought refuge there. We went as representatives of Helsinki Watch and Asia Watch, human rights organizations based in New York. We had already interviewed Afghan refugees in the United States and Paris and had read extensively in preparation for our trip. Nothing, however, prepared us for what we were to see and experience during that visit and others that we made over the next few years.

The vast scale of the exodus—an estimated five million or more refugees in Pakistan and Iran, representing one-third of Afghanistan's prewar population—is immediately apparent in Peshawar, where the largest concentration of the more than three million Afghan refugees in Pakistan has settled. It is hard to imagine what Peshawar, always a colorful frontier town at the entrance to the Khyber Pass into Afghanistan, was like before this transfiguring, heartbreaking influx.

Everywhere there were Afghans, most of them Pashtuns, who have the same language and

Jeri Laber and Barnett R. Rubin, *"A Nation Is Dying": Afghanistan Under the Soviets.* Northwestern University Press, Evanston, IL 60201 © 1988 by Northwestern University Press. All rights reserved. Published 1988.

appearance as the Pakistanis of the North-West Frontier Province but who are ill suited to the summer heat of the city and to the passive life of the refugee. On the whole, they have not been assimilated into Pakistani life. They are waiting, as close to the border as possible—the women and children seeking food and shelter, the men seeking arms and support as they commute back and forth to the war inside Afghanistan. Their goal is to resume their lives in Afghanistan, the only country they have known.

"Just about every conceivable human rights violation is occurring in Afghanistan, and on an enormous scale."

The refugees arrive in a steady procession. They come on foot over the mountains on journeys that often take a month or more. Their children and possessions are carried by horses, mules, or camels; their caravans are helpless targets for Soviet bombers and helicopter gunships. They come from every province in Afghanistan, every walk of life. Those who left at the beginning of the war have been settled in refugee camps around Peshawar. Others, wounded by bombs, mines, shellfire, or gunshots, are being treated in hospitals. Tens of thousands of recent arrivals huddle into makeshift tents just over the border, filthy, hungry, and diseased. The Pakistani authorities have begun refusing to register new arrivals or to provide them with regular rations unless they agree to be relocated to other parts of Pakistan.

There are some refugees who have found homes and a purpose in Peshawar, often working with one of the many Afghan political parties based there or with one of the relief organizations that are trying heroically to cope with the crisis. But most are just waiting, lost and unhappy, bewildered by the unexpected devastation of their lives and by what they have experienced.

During four visits that we made to the Afghan border since 1984, including refugee camps in the tribal areas of North Waziristan and Bajaur, we interviewed some four hundred Afghans representing a cross section of Afghan society, old and young, men, women, and children. We met with educated people from Kabul—professors, doctors, teachers, students, lawyers, former government officials—and with Afghanistan's leading poet in the Persian language, Khalilullah Khalili, and its leading graphic artist, Ghausuddin. We spoke with villagers—farmers, shepherds, nomads—driven from their land. We visited hospitals where we met paraplegics and amputees, victims of antipersonnel mines left behind by retreating Soviet and Afghan forces or of the camouflaged plastic "butterfly" mines that are dropped from helicopters and intended to maim, not kill, the shepherd children and their flocks. We met with political leaders and resistance commanders. We interviewed deserters, Soviet soldiers barely out of their teens, themselves victims of a vicious war. We even met a defector from the Afghan secret police (KHAD), who described to us its inner workings.

Just about every conceivable human rights violation is occurring in Afghanistan, and on an enormous scale. The crimes of indiscriminate warfare are combined with the worst excesses of unbridled state-sanctioned violence against civilians. The ruthless savagery in the countryside is matched by the subjection of a terrorized urban population to arbitrary arrest, torture, imprisonment, and execution. Totalitarian controls have been imposed on institutions and the press. The universities and all other aspects of Afghan cultural life are being systematically "Sovietized."

Soviet personnel have taken an increasingly active role in the Afghan government's oppression of its citizens. Soviet officers are not just "advisers" to Afghan KHAD agents who administer torture, routinely and savagely, in detention centers and prisons; according to reports we received there are Soviets who participate directly in interrogation and torture. Moreover, because of the uncertain loyalties of Afghans who have been recruited into the army, Soviet soldiers have been led to adopt an increasingly aggressive military role. The Soviets have taken the lead in air and ground attacks on Afghan villages, looting, terrorizing, and randomly killing Afghan civilians, including women and children.

A Story To Tell

Just about every Afghan has a story to tell. Our interpreters, our guides, people we met accidentally, had personally experienced atrocities as great as those of the "victims" we interviewed. An Afghan doctor who had impressed us with his gentle kindness as he interpreted for us in a hospital for war victims had a sudden outburst as we were leaving. "What's the point of all this? People should know by now. There are no human rights in Afghanistan. They burn people easier than wood!" He went on to tell us that he had lost forty-two members of his family under the present regime and had just learned that two had been burned alive a few weeks before.

We talked to a group of refugees camped by the side of the road, peasants who had just arrived that morning from Nangarhar and Kunduz provinces. The stories they told were the same we heard over and over again: "The Russians bombed our villages. Then the soldiers came. They killed women and children. They burned the wheat. They killed animals—cows, sheep, chickens. They took our food, put poison in the flour, stole our watches, jewelry, and money." Two young women, encountered at random, had each lost five children in a recent attack. One of them, who had also lost her parents and sister, displayed the burns from bombings on the limbs of her remaining children, the three youngest, whom she had managed to take with her as she fled from her house when the troops arrived. "I don't know how the days become nights and the nights become days," she lamented, her eyes flashing in anger and desperation. "I've lost my five children. Russian soldiers do these things to me."

Villagers' Attitudes

The strategy of the Soviets and the Afghan government has been to spread terror in the countryside so that villagers will either be afraid to assist the resistance fighters who depend on them for food and shelter or be forced to leave. The hundreds of refugee families crossing the border daily are fleeing this terror—wanton slayings, reprisal killings, and the indiscriminate destruction of their homes, crops, and possessions. We were told of brutal acts of violence by Soviet and Afghan forces: civilians burned alive, dynamited, beheaded; bound men forced to lie down on the road to be crushed by Soviet tanks; grenades thrown into rooms where women and children have been told to wait.

Although the terror has desolated much of the countryside, it has failed to crush the resistance. None of the villagers with whom we spoke blamed the mujahedin for their troubles. How could they? The mujahedin are their husbands, sons, fathers, brothers. The resistance and the civilian population are inextricably entwined. "We need our people," a resistance commander told us. "But we are also responsible for them."

"The warfare against the population continues, with all its resultant suffering."

Refugees driven from their homes are also bombed and strafed on their way to Pakistan. "It's a ruthless policy," a Pakistani official told us. "They take away their lands. Then, when they leave, they bomb them. There's no logic, just cruelty." The Soviet and Afghan governments seem intent upon ending the exodus to Pakistan. Perhaps they are alarmed by the huge refugee population in Pakistan and the international attention it must inevitably attract. Certainly they are concerned by the support the resistance finds in Pakistan: a chance to rest, organize, rearm, and reenter—sometimes with foreign press, for the Afghan resistance has begun to grasp the importance of the press in enlisting outside support. We received reports that refugees on their way to Pakistan have been arrested by the Afghan militia or the KHAD, who turn them back, herding them toward their devastated villages or to the cities, already swollen with more than a million internal refugees. Those who persist in the trek to Pakistan risk attacks by bombers or the dreaded helicopter gunships. Along the arduous mountain trails used by refugee caravans are many tattered flags flying over hastily dug mass graves. The Afghan Air Force has made numerous incursions into Pakistani airspace, bombing public places and killing hundreds of Afghan refugees and Pakistani civilians. Pakistan is no longer a secure refuge.

At the same time, the Afghan government is now trying to lure refugees back to Afghanistan, promising monetary and other rewards as part of a new policy of "national reconciliation."

Prison or Exile

Most of the Afghan urban intelligentsia is either in prison or in exile. Professionals and academics have been killed, arrested, censored, or dismissed. University curricula require study of the Russian language, Russian history, and Marxist-Leninist philosophy. Book publishing and the press are under strict censorship. Tens of thousands of Afghan youths are being sent, sometimes against their will, to study in the U.S.S.R. Children of nine and ten are being trained in Pioneer groups to inform on their parents and infiltrate the resistance. State-controlled agents and informers watch every offfice and classroom. It is estimated that thousands of people are now in Afghan prisons, where they have been brutally tortured and subjected to vile conditions.

We interviewed a twenty-one-year-old student who had been released from Pol-e Charkhi Prison in Kabul just two weeks before. His eyes were bloodshot, his body tense, as he nervously fingered his "worry beads," telling us that if we mention his name in print his father and brothers in Kabul "will be finished." After his arrest for distributing "night letters" protesting the Soviet invasion, he was subjected to routine torture—he was hung by a belt until almost strangled, beaten until his face was twice its normal size, and his hands were crushed under the leg of a chair. He described an overcrowded prison cell with no windows, crawling with lice and with only one pot for a toilet. Others told us about prison cells with one toilet serving five hundred people. Still others described cells with no bathroom at all, in which prisoners were forced to defecate on the floor. Former prisoners told us about electric shocks, nail pulling, lengthy periods of sleep deprivation, standing in cold water, and other punishments. Many prisoners have been executed after summary trials.

Nor are women spared, a source of special torment to Afghan men as well, whose code of honor requires them to shelter and protect their women from the outside world. We heard of mothers forced to watch their infants being given electric shocks, and of men held in torture chambers where women were being sexually molested. A young woman described how she and others had been forced to stand in water that had been treated with chemicals that made the skin come off their feet.

One could feel his pain as an Afghan refugee, a former civil engineer from Kabul, described three women who were in the same prison as he: "In the night, many times, we could hear them crying. We did not know why—probably they were tortured. We could hear them crying many times."

"This mass destruction is dictated by the political and military strategy of the Soviet Union and its Afghan allies."

Many of the crimes already discussed are violations of the Geneva Conventions. There are other violations as well, such as the deliberate bombing of hospitals and the summary execution of prisoners of war. The resistance forces are also guilty of violations, in particular in their treatment of prisoners of war and in their training of young children to fight, spy, and assassinate. Whenever possible, we have documented these crimes as well. The Soviets and the Afghan government have accused the resistance of numerous crimes, but we were unable to investigate these allegations because the Afghan government has refused our requests to visit Kabul.

In 1987, however, as part of a new policy of reconciliation by the Najibullah government, the International Committee of the Red Cross, which has been operating medical facilities from outside Afghanistan, taking wounded refugees from the border to Red Cross hospitals in Pakistan, was invited to inspect prisons in Kabul. In addition, the Afghan and Soviet governments, which had previously refused to cooperate with the Special Rapporteur on Afghanistan appointed by the U.N. Human Rights Commission, in 1987 invited him to Afghanistan. Some Western journalists have also been permitted to visit, although their visits have been limited and controlled by the Afghan government. These moves go hand in hand with overtures in the Geneva peace negotiations to bring the conflict to an end.

Perhaps the Soviets really want to extricate themselves from Afghanistan; perhaps their concessions are merely aimed at improving public relations. Whatever the case, the warfare against the population continues, with all its resultant suffering. Whether the war ends tomorrow or stretches on into the distant future, we have a duty to try to preserve each victim's memory, name, and voice. "They killed many people, and this is a story people should not forget," said one refugee. Another added, "They were able to silence the people for the time being, but history cannot remain silent." . . .

People coming from almost every area of Afghanistan—Western scholars, journalists, doctors and nurses, as well as the Afghan refugees and resistance fighters themselves—tell of vast destruction: carefully constructed homes reduced to rubble, deserted towns, the charred remains of wheat fields, trees cut down by immense firepower or dropping their ripe fruit in silence, with no one to gather the harvest. From throughout the country come tales of death on every scale, from thousands of civilians buried in the rubble left by fleets of bombers to a young boy's throat being dispassionately slit by a Soviet soldier.

This mass destruction is dictated by the political and military strategy of the Soviet Union and its Afghan allies. Unable to win the support or neutrality of most of the rural population that shelters and feeds the elusive guerrillas, Soviet and Afghan soldiers have turned their firepower on civilians. When the resistance attacks a military convoy, Soviet and Afghan forces attack the nearest village. If a region is a base area for the resistance, they bomb the villages repeatedly. If a region becomes too much of a threat, they bomb it intensively and then sweep through with ground troops, terrorizing the people and systematically destroying all the delicate, interrelated elements of the agricultural system. The aim is to force the people to abandon the resistance or, failing that, to drive them into exile. . . .

Destroying Agriculture

The Soviet-Afghan forces have pursued a determined campaign of destroying agriculture in Afghanistan. The devastation includes significant portions of at least Badakhshan, Konarha, Parwan, Kabul, Nangarhar, Logar, Paktia, Kandahar, Herat, Laghman, and Kunduz provinces. They employ various tactics, from the killing of individual farmers to the destruction of the delicate agricultural infrastructure in the Afghan countryside. These tactics not only spread terror, but also destroy the food supplies in the villages upon which the resistance depends for sustenance. Farmers are killed; food is destroyed; the means of food production is disrupted. Whole regions of Afghanistan have become barren.

This is a far cry from the image of mechanized agricultural progress that is projected in Soviet literature and the press . . .

Louis Dupree, an anthropologist who lived in Afghanistan for fifteen years before the coup in 1978, has investigated the specialized weapons used to destroy crops in Afghanistan. He has described two types of bombs which, when exploded, scatter pellets of phosphorus over a wide area, increasing the amount that can be burned: One type, which is used to destroy wheat that has been gathered for threshing, drying, or milling, explodes and scatters incendiary material on contact with the ground. The other type, used to burn crops standing in the field, is dropped by parachute and explodes in midair, scattering pellets over a wide area.

We also received reports of how Soviet soldiers during offensives destroy other kinds of food—sheep, chickens, eggs, oil, and sugar. . . .

The Afghan regime and its Soviet allies maintain and enforce control in the cities through the fear of a terrorized population aware of the ever-present possibility of arbitrary arrest, torture, imprisonment, and execution.

> *"In order to maintain power, the Afghan government and its Soviet advisers have created a climate of fear."*

The system is enforced by the largest agency of the Afghan state, the State Information Services, known as KHAD. The KHAD has a larger budget than even the military and is reported to be directly financed by the Soviet Union. Organized in 1980 under the guidance of KGB advisers, it remains under close Soviet supervision. KHAD informers sit in almost every office and classroom in Kabul. A former high official of the KHAD told us in Peshawar that the KHAD aimed to have "a spy in every family."

House Searches and Arrests

The KHAD arrests people in a variety of ways. Sometimes the militia surrounds a house at night and proceeds to search it before making arrests, ripping apart pillows, tearing clothes, and going through all books and papers. In another common procedure, young men are stopped by street blockades and whisked away to join the army. Troops have been known to blockade an entire neighborhood while KHAD agents search the houses. Students have been called from libraries or classrooms only to find themselves in a jeep on the way to a torture center. . . .

The Afghan Communists and their Soviet allies have tried to construct a new Afghan society in the cities, especially in Kabul. It is a society in which all sources of information are directly controlled by the government and the ruling People's Democratic Party of Afghanistan (PDPA), which, in turn, are under the close supervision of Soviet "advisers." Criticism of the government is not allowed.

In order to maintain power, the Afghan government and its Soviet advisers have created a climate of fear. . . .

Those in Afghanistan who attempt to collect information about human rights abuses do so at great risk. If caught, they face arrest, torture, and imprisonment. Even those who have fled often decline to testify for fear they might cause harm to relatives or associates still in the country. . . .

Since the Soviet invasion, a third of the population of Afghanistan has fled, perhaps as many as a million have died, and even leaders of the resistance have feared that "a whole nation is dying." But Afghanistan is still fighting for its life, and it may yet prevail.

Jeri Laber is the executive director of the Helsinki Watch Committee, an organization that monitors human rights. Barnett R. Rubin is an assistant professor of political science at Yale University in New Haven, Connecticut. He is also a member of the board of Asia Watch, another human rights organization.

"The Soviets' ability to blunt the impact of defeat will depend on whether they can reassure their allies that Afghanistan is a unique case."

viewpoint 3

The USSR Is Relinquishing Control in Afghanistan

Stephen Sestanovich

With military victory in Afghanistan plainly out of reach, Mikhail Gorbachev is conducting the kind of high-pressure diplomacy that has become his signature: abrupt acceptance of the other side's most extreme demands, a fast pace to overcome last-minute hesitation, inflated claims that his is the only path to peace. It is an impressive performance, and so far it has almost obscured the principal meaning of the event: the Soviet Union is closer than ever before to the defeat that many experts said it could not endure.

There was good reason for this skepticism. As the first real breach of the Brezhnev Doctrine, defeat in Afghanistan is expected to unnerve allies, sow ideological doubt at home, expose a new leader to criticism from his rivals, and show the Soviet people (among them angry Armenians, Azeris, Tatars, and others) a loss of nerve at the top. Displaying weakness must seem especially unwelcome right now, for it coincides with growing domestic controversy over Gorbachev's reforms and pervasive anxiety about Soviet ability to compete with the West.

How, then, can the Politburo avoid becoming a "pitiful, helpless giant"? Not by banking on a decent interval between withdrawal and collapse: the sack of Kabul will be hard to schedule very precisely, and the terms that Moscow and Washington are still haggling over will not greatly affect it. Gorbachev's real job is to prevent the Soviet pullout from setting off much broader losses. It is a tall, even paradoxical, order—dodging decline by accepting defeat—but he has put together a plausible strategy for minimizing the repercussions of withdrawal both at home and abroad. And if he succeeds, he will leave the West with the same mixed feelings that the INF [intermediate-range nuclear forces] treaty has evoked: satisfaction at the Soviet Union's unprecedented step backward, disappointment at the lack of enduring restraints on its ability to challenge U.S. interests. Having invigorated Soviet diplomacy in Europe even while dismantling his SS-20s, Gorbachev seems to think that another retreat need not deal the Soviet Union out of an active global role. But it will be far harder to make his Afghan strategy work than it has been to turn the zero option to Soviet advantage.

Gorbachev's Political Environment

Nothing is more important to his chances than preserving the right political environment at home. Ordinarily the domestic aftershocks of a pullout might seem a fatal objection even to considering such a move. Yet so far Gorbachev has kept his colleagues in line. There has been no convincing public trace of factional disagreement over Afghanistan, as there has been on many other matters. Gorbachev himself has made little effort to cover his flank on the war issue. His speech last fall on the 70th anniversary of the Bolshevik Revolution was a striking case of indifference. Coming in the thick of the Yeltsin affair, when his political position looked suddenly shaky, Gorbachev's speech blended reformist ideology and patriotism but ignored Afghanistan. No one in the leadership spoke out to correct or exploit his omission.

Such silence suggests that at least for now the issue is not truly divisive. Perhaps not everyone is enthusiastic about Gorbachev's plan (General Yazov, the defense minister, gave it a conspicuously late and grudging endorsement), but there is some evidence of a deal to pacify the military by shielding it from blame. The much expanded coverage of the war in the Soviet media, even in the military press, stresses that the Red Army's difficulties are no fault of its own. One important article declared both that

---

Stephen Sestanovich, "Kabul Crunch," *The New Republic*, April 18, 1988. Reprinted by permission of THE NEW REPUBLIC, © 1988, The New Republic, Inc.

it was time to go and that there had been no defeat. "The army," it said, "is in excellent fighting form."

The media's message is that the Afghan Communists are simply beyond help, and that they never had any serious hopes of "building socialism." Here, as elsewhere, the purpose of *glasnost* is to strengthen the leader's hand and increase his political freedom of action. In a speech last year Foreign Minister Eduard Shevardnadze complained that there had been much bold media investigation of Soviet domestic problems, but not enough of foreign policy mistakes. Since then Gorbachev has let the Afghan war emerge as the kind of mess produced by the stagnant "old thinking" of his predecessors. There is even a claim circulating that when the decision to invade was made the members of the Politburo were drunk. With this kind of spin control the Brezhnev Doctrine starts to look like just another measure of Leonid Brezhnev's inability to cope with really hard problems. Retreat is supposed to show decisiveness, not weakness.

It was not only fear of domestic consequences that kept Gorbachev's predecessors from considering withdrawal. With Moscow's growing diplomatic isolation, the likely loss of international standing also seemed enormous. In early 1985, when Gorbachev took over, a pullout would have followed the worst Soviet foreign policy defeat in a generation: NATO's successful Euromissile deployments. Viewed against high East-West tensions (not to mention Soviet exclusion from the Middle East, the failure of efforts to court China, and other setbacks), a withdrawal would have symbolized the collapse of Soviet foreign policy on all fronts.

Gorbachev has sought to fashion a global Soviet posture that can cushion the impact of reverses. Policy toward the United States is perhaps the most important shock absorber, much as Nixon's détente policy toward the Soviet Union aimed to ease the pain of Vietnam. Once he has disposed of Afghanistan, he correctly expects a more sympathetic hearing in the West for proposals on arms control and trade. By sandwiching the start of an Afghan withdrawal between two meetings with Ronald Reagan, he has even introduced his own "linkage" policy. He clearly hopes to discourage any U.S. attempt to exploit Soviet vulnerability as the war winds down. Stiffer American terms for a settlement would only spoil the good summit atmosphere that both sides presumably want.

The Balance of Power

Soviet moves also show keen attention to the postwar balance of power in South Asia. Gorbachev has leased nuclear submarines to India, pursued a summit visit to China, offered increased economic aid to Pakistan, promoted joint ventures and doubled trade with Iran, rolled out the red carpet for the Saudi foreign minister, etc. He wants to be sure that after the war a hostile Afghan regime would find no support among its neighbors for "anti-Soviet" policies. Anti-Sovietism inside Afghanistan will be harder to control, but here too material inducements—economic agreements, walking-around money, bribes—will have their place. Moscow TV recently reported that one Afghan businessman who had just received a five million ruble credit is now an energetic supporter of the "national reconciliation" policy of Dr. Najib, the Afghan Communist leader. And Afghanistan will remain an arena of intense KGB covert activity for years to come.

"Gorbachev's real job is to prevent the Soviet pullout from setting off much broader losses."

In other regions, the Soviets' ability to blunt the impact of defeat will depend on whether they can reassure their allies that Afghanistan is a unique case. They have to show they are dropping an unprofitable product line, not going out of business. The hardest currency of superpower reassurance is, of course, weaponry. This explains why, despite doubts about the political prospects and ideological credentials of many of their clients, the Soviets have steadily increased military shipments to the Third World. According to PlanEcon, Inc., arms exports were up 25 percent in 1987 alone. The same desire to reassure will probably dispose Soviet diplomats to toughen their stands in other talks where their clients want support. Hence, for example, there have been criticisms in the Soviet media recently of American proposals to remove Cuban forces from Angola. As the foreign ministry spokesman puts it, all that Afghanistan and Angola have in common is that "both countries begin with the letter A."

New Thinking

Gorbachev has used his "new thinking" slogan to make his backpedaling diplomacy look innovative rather than beleaguered. Concepts like "interdependence" or "mutual security" are largely meaningless clichés in the West, but when used by a Soviet leader they do more than give him a reputation for dynamism and sincerity. They help him soften the appearance of failure, by redefining Soviet security goals in more attainable terms. In Gorbachev's withdrawal announcement in February 1988, he said lamely that the new thinking of the Afghan Communists "is not a sign of weakness, but rather of the force of spirit, wisdom, and dignity of free, honest, and responsible political leaders concerned about their country's present and future." In short, even if the Soviets end up leaving in helicopters from the embassy roof, all it will signal is the latest improvement in long-term planning.

Gorbachev may be able to soften the blow of defeat if his foreign policy as a whole is seen as a success. Nevertheless, he is running three risks that will not be easy to control. His approach may come unstuck first at home, where *glasnost* makes a public outburst of recrimination hard to prevent. Soviet journalists themselves warn that tough questions (Who got us into Afghanistan in the first place? Did we let our boys down once they got there?) have to be answered: "Today [these questions] are being asked in families and in private conversations, . . . tomorrow they will burst forth in the press." If so, Gorbachev will face a choice between a demoralizing debate about what really happened (in which military and Party leaders will openly accuse each other) and tightening the reins of media censorship. The Red Army's retreat may mean the retreat of *glasnost* too.

Second, a rapid collapse in Kabul will make it harder for Soviet clients to believe the reassurances from Moscow—and easier to hold Gorbachev up for ransom. The Cuban, Venezuelan, and other Latin American Communist Parties succesfully pushed Khruschev for more aid after the 1962 missile crisis, and the pattern can be repeated today in countless places. Clients who are unhappy with Moscow's response may start to explore Western options. If so, Gorbachev will face another choice—between seeing Angola and Vietnam go their own way, and paying more to keep them in the family.

"Even if the Soviets end up leaving in helicopters from the embassy roof, all it will signal is the latest improvement in long-term planning."

Finally, Gorbachev's strategy has tied Afghanistan more closely than at any time in the recent past (and more closely than he really had to) to other issues on the U.S.-Soviet agenda. If the Moscow summit produces a strategic arms treaty, it is the Soviets who will be most constrained by the linkage. Senate ratification will roughly span the proposed Soviet ten-month troop withdrawal period. If withdrawing from Afghanistan proves more chaotic and humiliating than the Soviets are banking on, Gorbachev will face a choice between using force and keeping ratification on track. How many more strategic arms agreements does Moscow want to sacrifice to Afghanistan?

In each of these cases, the unraveling of Gorbachev's Afghan strategy would force him to consider measures that, in effect, revive Brezhnevism: a clampdown on public debate, more expensive Third World commitments, a sacrifice of détente for considerations of "prestige." Gorbachev has made such responses synonymous with decline, and they are exactly what he wants to get away from. In this, of course, the West has an obvious interest. We don't want Brezhnevism back either.

Western Interests

Yet the unraveling of Gorbachev's strategy is also the only way he is likely to consider policies that even more clearly serve Western interests. Brezhnevism, after all, is just one response to the choices he may face. The alternative will be to push his own reforms even further—to radicalize them. This is in fact how Gorbachev has reacted to the failure of halfway measures in dealing with the economy, by pushing for deeper changes. A similar response to defeat in Afghanistan would mean opening up Soviet external goals as an issue of public controversy; a decision not to meet the demands of Third World clients just to assure their loyalty; and an acknowledgment that good relations with the West are more important than the Soviet Union's reputation for toughness. Failure radicalizes better than success.

Gorbachev's Afghan strategy aims to evade these choices in their sharpest form, and he may well succeed. Our interest is a little different: that he should succeed enough to keep making changes, and fail enough to have to.

Stephen Sestanovich is the director of Soviet studies at the Center for Strategic and International Studies in Washington, DC.

"Gorbachev clearly is attempting to salvage, not abandon, the huge Soviet political, economic and military investment in subduing Afghanistan."

viewpoint 4

The USSR Is Retaining Control in Afghanistan

James A. Phillips

The Soviet Union has failed to subjugate Afghanistan despite a brutal war of attrition that has claimed more than a million Afghan lives and created five million Afghan refugees....

Despite Gorbachev's soothing rhetoric, Soviet forces continue to fight brutally against the Afghan resistance. Moscow has staged sham "withdrawals" in the past and has ordered cosmetic changes in its Afghan puppet regime to defuse international opposition to its policies.

Gorbachev clearly is attempting to salvage, not abandon, the huge Soviet political, economic and military investment in subduing Afghanistan. Because of the rising military costs of the war and declining prospects of an outright military solution, Gorbachev is searching for a diplomatic solution that will perpetuate a pro-Soviet regime at the lowest possible cost to Moscow. Unable to eliminate the Afghan resistance through military means, he seeks to isolate it, deprive it of external support, divide it, demoralize it and eventually strangle it in a diplomatic "settlement."

Why the UN Has Failed

Efforts at finding a settlement in Afghanistan have been undertaken by the United Nations since 1983. These U.N. sponsored peace talks are seriously flawed because they: 1) exclude the Afghan resistance; 2) fail to address the central issue of the war, Afghan self-determination; 3) propose a drawn-out timetable for Soviet withdrawal which poses unacceptable risks to the resistance; 4) call for suspension of U.S. and other aid to the resistance at the start of the Soviet withdrawal; 5) fail to demand a reciprocal suspension of Soviet aid to Afghan communists; 6) create enormous loopholes; and 7) include weak provisions for verification of compliance....

The U.S. should:

1) *continue sending its military aid to the Afghans until the last Soviet soldier has exited Afghanistan.* The U.S. goal should be to force a total Soviet withdrawal from Afghanistan. Afghanistan is a strategic stepping stone to the Persian Gulf and a geopolitical lever for influencing and possibly dismembering Iran and Pakistan. It is not the U.S. goal simply to "bleed" the Soviets. This would only prolong the agony of the Afghans.

2) *work for a settlement that creates a neutral Afghanistan,* just as the 1955 Austrian State Treaty created today's neutral Austria.

3) *not allow Moscow to engineer a settlement that transforms Afghanistan into another Lebanon,* doomed by a lack of national consensus to chronic civil war. This would give Afghan communists the chance to subdue a splintered resistance. Worse, it could breed instability that invites Soviet re-intervention.

Approximately 120,000 Soviet troops, backed up by more than 30,000 support and combat personnel nearby in the Soviet Union, have failed to crush the elusive Afghan *mujahideen*—or holy warriors. The *mujahideen* are estimated at up to 200,000 strong. Always courageous and indefatigable fighters, in the long course of the war they have been bolstered by more effective organization, better training in some groups, modern arms, and growing foreign support. Gradually there has been improved operational coordination between the seven major resistance groups. A "natural selection" process has produced a class of battle-hardened field commanders whose claim to leadership is based on proven performance rather than traditional or tribal connections.

The *mujahideen* control more than 80 percent of Afghanistan and are supported by the overwhelming majority of the Afghan people. The Soviets control the major cities, air bases and primary roads.

James A. Phillips, "A US Agenda for an Afghan Peace Settlement," The Heritage Foundation *Backgrounder*, April 4, 1988. Reprinted with permission.

Though the *mujahideen* harass Soviet supply lines and besiege isolated garrisons, they have been unable to destroy major Soviet bases because of a lack of heavy weapons and mine clearing equipment....

Moscow now finds that it must pay a growing military price to contain, let alone defeat, the *mujahideen*. Pouring more troops into Afghanistan would strain what is surely an already overburdened Soviet logistical infrastructure dependent on Afghanistan's rudimentary road system.

To win the war in Afghanistan, Moscow has tried to make an end run through Pakistan, which has offered sanctuary to the *mujahideen*. Gorbachev buttonholed Pakistani President Zia ul-Haq at the 1985 Moscow funeral of Konstantine Chernenko and warned of dark consequences if Pakistani "aggression" persisted. Gorbachev then launched an escalating war of nerves against Pakistan. The Soviet press has castigated Pakistan as a "colonial creation." Pakistani separatist and terrorist groups have been armed and trained in base camps inside Afghanistan. The KGB-controlled Afghan secret police, the KHAD, has fomented uprisings among dissident Pushtun tribes straddling the border. Pakistani border towns have suffered increasing numbers of air attacks and cross-border artillery bombardments.

The KGB, through the KHAD, has orchestrated one of the largest state-sponsored terrorist campaigns ever mounted, assassinating Afghan exiles and planting bombs that have killed Afghans and Pakistanis alike. About 500 people have been killed by terrorist bombs in Pakistan since mid-1987. In addition to signalling the Afghans that they cannot escape communist terror, these terrorist bombings are meant to sap Pakistan's willingness to aid the *mujahideen*. Moscow and Kabul hope to strike a deal with Islamabad over the heads of the Afghans....

Buying Time

Gorbachev's latest peace gambit is a continuation of longstanding Soviet policy regarding Afghanistan—diplomatic initiatives aimed at defusing international criticism, reducing external support for the *mujahideen*, driving wedges between resistance groups, and buying time to crush the resistance. As early as February 1980, less than two months after their invasion, Soviet officials hinted that Moscow was eager to withdraw, but could not do so until "external intervention" had ceased. In the Soviet view the problem was not the Soviet invasion but resistance to the invasion. Soviet diplomacy consistently has attempted to deflect attention from the Soviet presence, reject the legitimacy of the *mujahideen*, and focus on non-Soviet "intervention" in internal Afghan affairs. The United Nations General Assembly has made it easier for Moscow to do so by refusing to condemn the Soviet Union by name for invading Afghanistan.

Gorbachev escalated the peace campaign in a July 28, 1986, speech at Vladivostok in which he promised to withdraw six Soviet regiments as a gesture of good faith in the U.N. peace process. His announcement came three days before the resumption of the Geneva talks and the "withdrawal" was executed with a flourish in October 1986, shortly before the U.S.-Soviet summit at Reykjavik. The much-heralded event, like a previous "withdrawal" staged before the 1980 Moscow Olympics, turned out to be a propaganda exercise. The units withdrawn, some of which had been introduced into Afghanistan shortly beforehand, were replaced by forces more suitably equipped to fight a guerrilla war....

A False Settlement

Although Western diplomats tend to conceive the Geneva talks as a diplomatic "endgame," the Soviets consider the negotiations to be "the first move in the next phase of that continuing game." Moscow is not merely seeking an exit. After all, the Soviet Union could withdraw its troops without an agreement. Instead, the Soviets want the U.S. and Pakistan to help create conditions in which Moscow can withdraw its overt military presence after "winning," while using its covert KGB/KHAD network to retain control over the government left behind. Warns a Western diplomat based in Kabul: "The Soviets want you by diplomatic means to help them stay in Afghanistan . . . Beware of a kind of Munich."

"Moscow can withdraw its overt military presence after 'winning,' while using its covert KGB/KHAD network to retain control over the government left behind."

Above all the Soviets seek an agreement that seals the Pakistani border and thus terminates foreign aid to the *mujahideen*, while leaving Moscow a free hand to bolster the Kabul government with aid and advisers. A cutoff of external aid would undermine the *mujahideen's* political unity and military strength. It would weaken the seven political parties based in Peshawar, Pakistan, that have served as conduits for aid, would increase the political independence of regional field commanders inside Afghanistan and would make it easier for Moscow to win through divide-and-rule tactics.

Najibullah already has appealed by name to eight *mujahideen* field commanders, offering to pull Soviet troops out of their sectors if they agree to a separate peace. Covert KGB/KHAD operations undoubtedly will be mounted to fan the flames of suspicion between rival resistance groups. The February 11,

1988, assassination in Peshawar of Professor S.B. Majrooh, a respected figure who worked tirelessly to promote Afghan unity, may have signalled the start of a campaign of assassinations to decapitate and fracture the resistance.

Moscow presumably is reckoning that a splintered resistance weakened by internal infighting and an aid cutoff would be unable to defeat decisively the Soviet-backed communist regime that controls the city-state of Kabul, but not much else. Moscow may attempt to enhance the survivability of a pro-Soviet "Kabulistan" by replacing Najibullah with an Afghan military figure similar to Polish General Wojciech Jaruzelski, who would head a relatively non-ideological regime that could hope to establish local alliances with dissident *mujahideen* groups. The short-term Soviet goal seems to be the "Lebanonization" of Afghanistan—plunging the country into anarchy by driving wedges between rival resistance groups in an effort to preserve a weak central government.

Moscow meanwhile will continue attempting to integrate northern Afghanistan into a Soviet economic and political sphere. Soviet influence is strongest in the north because the relatively flat terrain is ill-suited for guerilla warfare, a disproportionate number of the 2,000 Afghan children taken each year to the Soviet Union for "education" come from this area and many of the Soviet advisers stationed there are members of the Tajik and Uzbek ethnic groups that straddle the border.

Northern Soviet Security Zone

The Soviets are grooming a northern militia commander, Sayed Naseem Shah, as a regional leader who may be able to survive even if the Kabul regime collapses. In that event, Moscow may try to construct a northern security zone manned by local militias backed by long-range Soviet artillery and air power. Soviet military forces then could be inserted into Afghanistan covertly to stiffen the spine of pro-Soviet forces. There is a precedent for such a covert intervention: in 1929 Soviet troops disguised as Afghans were deployed to aid King Ammanallah. . . .

Since June 1982 indirect peace talks between Pakistan and Afghanistan have been held in Geneva under United Nations auspices. These talks have produced a framework for an agreement based on four "instruments": 1) "non-interference" in Afghan and Pakistani internal affairs; 2) international guarantees of the bilateral agreement; 3) the safe and honorable return of Afghan refugees; and 4) "interrelationships" specifying the linkage between the first three instruments and Soviet withdrawal. . . .

The most glaring flaw in the Geneva draft accord is that the Afghan resistance has been barred from the negotiations. Yet if Geneva does not address Afghan concerns, Geneva cannot end the war. The *mujahideen* will continue to fight the Afghan communists during any Soviet withdrawal, just as they fought them before the Soviet invasion. Moscow may use this as a pretext to halt its pullout or to intervene at a future date. If Moscow wants a cease fire during its proposed withdrawal, then it should talk directly to the resistance.

The Central Issue

The central issue of Afghan self-determination is ignored in the Geneva draft. In fact, the agreement favors the current communist regime by affording it tacit recognition, denying the *mujahideen* any political status, and ignoring the legitimacy of the resistance. By failing to link Soviet military disengagement to a political settlement, Geneva enables Moscow to retain control of the Afghan government. Moreover, the absence of agreement on a transitional Afghan government gives Moscow the opportunity to play one *mujahideen* group against another. Political, ideological, and personal rivalries long submerged by common hostility to the Soviets will emerge as the Soviets lower their profile.

"The short-term Soviet goal seems to be . . . plunging the country into anarchy by driving wedges between rival resistance groups in an effort to preserve a weak central government."

Pakistan's justifiable concern is that by ignoring Afghan self-determination, the Geneva draft would perpetuate the kind of turmoil in Afghanistan that would discourage the return of Afghan refugees from Pakistan. Already, Pakistan's economy and social fabric are strained from hosting almost four million Afghan refugees, with their three million head of livestock. They compete with Pakistanis for scarce water, grazing rights, firewood, and jobs. . . .

Although Soviet officials have promised to fight only in self-defense and to front-load the pullout by recalling half of its forces in the first three months, such pledges are of questionable value. The Soviet Union has taken an extremely elastic view of self-defense, as the devastating attack on Korean airliner KAL 007 confirmed. Furthermore most of the Soviet offensive operations are performed by the airborne, air assault, and *spetsnaz* (special forces), who comprise less than 20 percent of the Soviet occupation force. Such units might also be assisted by air and commando units stationed on the Soviet side of the border.

To make matters worse, the Geneva accords are vague on whether Soviet military and political advisers can remain in Afghanistan. The "second army," the 9,000 strong contingent of Soviet and East Bloc advisers that currently dominates the Afghan government, is an important lever of control that cannot be permitted to remain. It also is suspected that the giant military infrastructure that the Soviets have established would be turned over to the Kabul regime and would not be dismantled. Left unanswered too are such important issues as the return of Afghan children taken to the Soviet Union and the payment of war reparations. A particularly important question is the status of the more than 300 treaties that Moscow has signed with Kabul. If allowed to stand, the Soviets would have a "legal" pretext to remain involved at the "request" of the communist regime.

"Moscow already seems to have prepared to undermine the [Geneva] accords."

Any Afghan peace settlement must have strong and effective verification provisions. After all Moscow already has staged two false withdrawals. The Soviets could disguise their annual May rotation of troops, which normally involves one-fourth to one-third of the Soviet forces in Afghanistan, as the beginning of a pullout. Yet as soon as the world's attention strayed and the U.S. was distracted by its presidential election campaign, Moscow could halt the withdrawal and continue the war more covertly, assuming that Washington would lack the will to respond to violations of the agreement, just as it failed to respond to violations in Laos and Vietnam. Moscow already seems to have prepared to undermine the accords. In fact there are reports that Soviet personnel of Central Asian descent operate within the Afghan armed forces in Afghan uniforms. This indicates that the Soviets will seek to maintain a covert military presence after a "withdrawal." The Geneva draft agreement reportedly provides for only 50 observers to verify Soviet compliance. This is far too few—and they probably will have far too limited powers.

Resisting a Quick Fix

The U.S. must not be stampeded into a quick fix solution that allows Moscow to prop up the Kabul regime while weakening the *mujahideen*. The Soviet Union was wrong when it invaded in 1979 and its occupation remains unacceptable today. It should not be allowed to extract strategic advantages in return for vague promises to reduce its illegitimate presence....

After years of obstructing a negotiated settlement the Soviet Union suddenly wants to wrap up the Geneva peace talks in a rush. Moscow is pressuring Pakistan to agree to a one-sided deal, replete with loopholes, that would undermine the *mujahideen* by weakening their military strength and eroding their political unity. Pakistan is holding out for a neutral transitional government that would end the fighting, not just make it easier for Moscow to cut its losses while assuring it control over Kabul.

James A. Phillips is a senior policy analyst at The Heritage Foundation, a conservative think tank in Washington, DC.

"The Soviet agreement to withdrawal is so vague that experts on the war do not agree on what will happen to the Kabul regime and its army."

viewpoint 5

Soviet Involvement in Afghanistan Will Continue

Lea Rehimi

On April 14, 1988, in Geneva, Switzerland, representatives of the Soviet-installed Afghan regime and the government of Pakistan signed the UN-sponsored Accords on Afghanistan. Secretary of State George Shultz and Soviet Foreign Minister Eduard Shevardnadze signed on behalf of the United States and the Soviet Union as "guarantors" of the agreements. Despite the major media's hype concerning the proposed withdrawal of Soviet troops from Afghanistan, the Accords failed to specify the number and origin of the "foreign troops" to be withdrawn, and Moscow signed only the "Declaration of International Guarantees" that preceded the withdrawal agreement. Technically then, it is left up to broad interpretation how many troops will leave and the degree to which the Soviets are bound to this agreement. Point 5 of the second Bilateral Agreement, between the Afghan regime and Pakistan, states, "there will be a phased withdrawal of the foreign troops which will start on the date of entry into force mentioned above [May 15, 1988]. One half of the troops will be withdrawn by 15 August 1988 and the withdrawal of all troops will be completed within nine months."

The Accords and Pakistan

Western media have highlighted the Accords' positive points, such as the promised withdrawal of troops and return of refugees. Taken as a whole, however, the Accords severely restrict Afghanistan's neighboring state of Pakistan, which has until now provided a haven for the flood of refugees fleeing Soviet brutality. They also give the impression that Pakistan is the principal aggressor in the troubled region.

In the Bilateral Agreements, Pakistan and Afghanistan agreed to "noninterference and nonintervention" in each other's affairs, including a prohibition on "harboring in camps and bases or otherwise, organizing, training, financing, equipping and arming political, ethnic or any other groups . . . and the transportation of arms, ammunition, and equipment by such individuals and groups." This clear reference to the Afghan Mujahideen in Pakistan compels Islamabad to cut off all assistance to the Afghans short of expelling them from its territory. It also forbids the acceptance of U.S. aid for the Mujahideen, who rely on the Pakistani conduit for all assistance. Soviet Foreign Minister Shevardnadze hailed the agreement as a victory for Moscow, explaining that its terms oblige Pakistan to dismantle Mujahideen bases and training camps on its territory within 30 days.

The Geneva Accords will have four major effects:

(1) To prevent Pakistan from accepting supplies for the Mujahideen from any other country;

(2) To cut off outside aid to the Mujahideen;

(3) To provide the Kabul regime with international recognition as the legitimate government of Afghanistan; and

(4) To endorse Moscow's claim that Soviet troops invaded Afghanistan to protect Kabul's Communist revolution from "external enemies."

The Withdrawal

The *New York Times* reported on April 16, 1988: "The Soviet agreement to withdrawal is so vague that experts on the war do not agree on what will happen to the Kabul regime and its army. . . . The Geneva Accords do not clearly state what limits will be put on Soviet aid to the Government in Kabul. Soviet tactical and logistical aircraft flying from airfields in the Soviet Union may be able to continue to support the Government forces, and those forces may even be supported by [10,000] Soviet advisors and technical personnel." Moscow will also rely on the approximately 160,000 troops of the Afghan

Lea Rehimi, "Whose Side Are We On?" *The New American*, May 23, 1988. Reproduced with permission of the publisher.

Army, most of whom have been forcibly conscripted, and an unconfirmed number of border guards whose ranks undoubtedly include KGB agents.

The Mujahideen claim that the United States has stopped supplying Stinger anti-aircraft missiles in anticipation of a troop withdrawal. Mohammed Nabi Mohammedi, leader of the Harekat Islamic party, said during an interview on April 14, 1988 that the Mujahideen had not been receiving the shoulder-launch missiles for the past four to five months. "We are extremely worried," said Mohammedi, "We don't trust the Russians. They are deceitful and sly." Secretary of State Shultz suggested in January 1988 that aid to the Mujahideen would stop long before the final withdrawal of Soviet troops: "As withdrawal proceeds . . . you don't have the need for that continued support and it would cease."

In February 1988, leaders of the Islamic Unity of Afghan Mujahideen [IUAM], commonly known as the Afghan Alliance refused to meet with Under Secretary of State Michael H. Armacost, after learning that a slow-down in arms shipments would precede a Soviet pullout. "That is a shameful answer you gave us," Younis Khalis told Armacost in response to the U.S. refusal to grant the Mujahideen formal political recognition, thus denying them a part in the Geneva negotiations.

"The [Geneva] agreement is 'fundamentally flawed' because it fails to acknowledge even the existence of the Mujahideen."

Senator Gordon Humphrey (R-NH) argues that the agreement is "fundamentally flawed" because it fails to acknowledge even the existence of the Mujahideen. By signing the Accords, the Reagan Administration put the U.S. seal of approval on the Najibullah regime in Kabul and absolved the Soviets of blame for the nine years of genocide they have waged on the Afghan people. The document omitted mention of the 1.24 million Afghan civilians killed, the six million left homeless and the 10,000 Afghan children abducted to the Soviet Union for indoctrination. Abdul Satar of the Pakistan Foreign Ministry said that the UN-sponsored agreement could not promote peace in Afghanistan because political power remains in the hands of a government rejected by most of the Afghan people. The "moral issue" in the negotiations, he pointed out, is not necessarily an end to the war but "who is the legitimate government of Afghanistan."

The Afghan Alliance's formula for an interim government to replace the Kabul regime has been systematically ignored by all the governments involved in the negotiations. The Alliance's formula outlines the structure for a transitional government in Afghanistan, calling for a Shoora-i-Ali (Grand Council), which would be the supreme body of state, controlled by the seven-party Alliance. Pakistan's strong support for the interim government weakened in mid-March 1988, after Pakistani Prime Minister Mohammed Khan Junejo's meeting with Under Secretary of State Michael Armacost. Fourteen Islamic governments—including Saudi Arabia, Kuwait, Oman, Malaysia, and Sudan—had already extended diplomatic recognition.

Neutralizing Undesirable Elements

A UPI article, dated March 21, 1988, announced: "U.S. and Soviet officials, seeking an orderly withdrawal of Soviet troops from Afghanistan are sharing information on the radical Islamic rebels seen as a threat to agreement, administration officials say." The article explained: "A CIA source, speaking about the rebels, confirmed a shift in the U.S. position and said officials 'want to see some [mujahid] groups fed to other groups'—intelligence terminology for neutralizing undesirable elements."

Administration officials claim that "the war in Afghanistan has produced at least two factions of guerrilla leaders . . . whose clash of ideologies and ambitions is hampering negotiations for a Soviet troop withdrawal and eventual peace." The same officials, however, have consistently denied the Mujahideen a role in the Geneva negotiations. Gulbaddin Hekmatyar, current leader of the IUAM, acknowledged that there have been clashes, but denied that his party had ever been attacked by any other. "There is no internal fighting on the level of the [seven Mujahideen] parties. If there is an odd case, it is on the individual level."

The Mujahideen vehemently demanded that Pakistan not sign the agreement. Pakistani President Mohammed Zia ul-Haq concurred with the demand that the Mujahideen be included in the Accords. This "major obstacle" to the signing of the Accords was resolved in mid-March when Pakistan, at the urging of the Reagan Administration, abandoned its insistence that a transitional government be established in Kabul.

In 1985, three State Department officials—Robert Peck, Arnold Raphel, and Charles Dubar—sent a secret letter to the UN mediator Diego Cordovez. The letter outlined a plan to accommodate a Soviet withdrawal while allowing Moscow to continue its arm shipments to the puppet regime in Kabul. "Foreign interference," the letter assured, would stop—meaning that the United States would suspend its trickle of support to the Mujahideen. This scheme was known as the Day One Deal: Soviet aid to the Communist regime would continue uninterrupted, while U.S. support of the Mujahideen would stop on Day One of a year-long Soviet withdrawal.

Under the present Geneva Accords, the Reagan Administration and the Soviet Union have verbally agreed to suspend all arms deliveries to Afghanistan on the first day of a Soviet withdrawal. Nevertheless, Soviet Foreign Minister Shevardnadze stated in March 1988 that Moscow would "rule out" any cut-off of aid to the Kabul regime, claiming that "the Soviet Union has its obligations to the Afghan government . . . based on the status of a treaty, a treaty signed by the Soviet government and the Afghan government. Those are legitimate supplies and we are not going to review that treaty. We have had this type of relationship—such agreements—with Afghanistan since 1921."

"Moscow would 'rule out' any cut-off of aid to the Kabul regime, claiming that 'the Soviet Union has its obligations to the Afghan government.'"

After returning from a three-day visit to Pakistan in April 1988, Senator Humphrey called on President Reagan to reject the Accords. Humphrey warned that the terms of the Accords were unacceptable to the Afghan Resistance because they would keep the United States from living up to its obligations to support the Mujahideen. "If the Accord was signed in its present form," Humphrey lamented, "Pakistan would be violating the treaty if it allowed the U.S. to continue supplying weapons to the guerrillas across its territory as it is doing now." Humphrey termed the Accords a "slow-motion sell out" and said that he "found it hard to stomach the contradiction between Reagan's words and what the United States appears actually committed to do."

Conspiring with the Soviets

In an interview in the *New York Times* on March 18, 1988, Afghan Resistance leader Gulbaddin Hekmatyar of Hezb-i-Islami (Party of God) accused the United States of conspiring with the Soviet Union against Afghanistan. "[T]here are people in America who are against our jihad (holy war)," claims Hekmatyar; "they are in the government, in the parties, in the public." Hekmatyar, head of one of the strongest and most effective Mujahid groups of the seven aligned parties, was an engineering student at Kabul University before the invasion of Soviet troops. He is accused of being a radical Islamic fundamentalist determined to lead an Islamic revolution similar to the one under Khomeini in Iran. But such a revolution in Afghanistan, which follows the more moderate Sunni sect of Islam, is highly unlikely.

Former *New York Times* editor A. M. Rosenthal warns that the Kremlin has shown no signs that it intends to withdraw its troops from Afghanistan. According to Rosenthal, Gorbachev has a "plan to salvage political power from its military defeat in Afghanistan." The agreement signed in Geneva is designed to keep the Soviet Union in power as long as possible in Afghanistan, and to stop American aid as soon as possible, so that Moscow can deal the final blow to the Mujahideen without any interference from the United States. Not only has Moscow insisted that it will continue its arms shipments to the Kabul regime; it has also annexed two Afghan provinces in the northern part of the country, perhaps to use as a base from which to continue its bid for control over the country.

Afghan News, an Afghan Resistance newspaper published by Jami'at Islami, reported: "A news black-out will follow a Geneva agreement between Pakistan and the puppet regime. . . . The only news reaching the world will be propaganda presented by the Soviets. . . . A Geneva Accord will not bring peace to the country but the immediate effect would be to deprive the Afghans of the possibility of telling the truth to the rest of the world. Who will inform the world about massacres, the use of forbidden weapons, torture in prison, participation of Soviet combat troops against the strongholds of the Resistance, Sovietization measures, famine, epidemics and the thousand other things?"

Lea Rehimi is a contributor to The New American, *a conservative, weekly newsmagazine.*

"I am convinced that the Soviets are going to pull out their military forces."

viewpoint 6

Soviet Involvement in Afghanistan Will End

Theodore L. Eliot Jr.

Today the question is what kind of Afghanistan will emerge after the scheduled Soviet troop withdrawal? And what will be the policy questions that the new Afghanistan will pose for the region, for the United States, and indeed for the Soviet Union?

I undertake a reply to such questions with considerable trepidation. In the first place, it is as hard to believe that the Soviets are actually leaving Afghanistan as it is for a Red Sox fan to believe that his team won't fold in the clutch. In the second place, it is hard to understand a country so different from one's own....

One thing I do know: I am convinced that the Soviets are going to pull out their military forces. Soviet leader Gorbachev has correctly concluded that the war against the Afghans cannot be won. The Afghans are simply too tough (as Kipling could have told him; Kipling was so convinced of this that he never set foot in the country), and their friends have seen to it that they have the weapons they need. Perhaps even more important, Gorbachev's reform program at home and desire to win a period of less tension in the international climate have been jeopardized by domestic and foreign opposition to the Soviet war against Afghanistan.

So, the Soviets will pull back across the Amu Darya river.... As they have already demonstrated, they will not hesitate to strike hard at Afghan resistance forces who try to take advantage of their withdrawal while it is occurring. But they are going to leave.

The war will continue for a time. The resistance "holy warriors" or mujahideen will fight until the puppet government in Kabul of President Najibullah is overthrown. Since the Soviets are leaving an immense store of weapons and ammunition behind

Theodore L. Eliot Jr., "The Afghans' Next Ordeal," *World Monitor The Christian Science Monitor Monthly*, December 1988. Reprinted by permission from *World Monitor The Christian Science Monitor Monthly* © 1988 The Christian Science Publishing Society. All rights reserved.

($1 billion worth according to a Soviet general) and are still sending in new military supplies for the Kabul regime, the latter may be able to hold on for a while. Its ability to do so will be enhanced if the Soviets continue to mount air strikes against mujahideen positions even after Soviet forces have left the country.

The mujahideen are understandably reluctant to occupy towns which are then bombarded by Soviet air power at the cost of large numbers of civilian casualties. The mujahideen have adopted a strategy of taking the territory around the towns and waiting for the Soviets to leave before besieging them.

Najibullah Will Fall

The mujahideen will prevail, however, and the Najibullah regime will fall. In the meantime, the United States will continue to deliver military supplies to the resistance through Pakistan, having made it clear that we will do so as long as the Soviets supply the Kabul forces. Pakistan is likely to permit this supply operation across its territory, because it wishes the three million Afghan refugees it is sheltering to return home, and it knows they will not do so as long as the war continues and there is a Communist regime in Kabul.

Much less predictable is the shape of the next government of Afghanistan after the fall of the Najibullah government. The resistance is divided into seven groups whose leaders are in Peshawar in the Northwest Frontier Province of Pakistan and who have formed an uneasy Peshawar Alliance. In addition, there are four resistance organizations of Shia Muslims from the central mountain area of the country, a couple of which have offices in Pakistani Baluchistan....

The Peshawar Alliance parties agree only that the next government should be based on Islamic law. Two want the king, who has been in exile in Rome since 1973, to return. Those that are tribally based want a grand tribal assembly, a *loya jirgah,* to choose the next government. Others, from ethnic groups or regions where the tribal tradition is less important, reject this approach.

The military commanders inside the country will certainly have a voice in what happens. There may be a race between the commanders closest to the capital to take Kabul. There have been reports of arms stockpiling, not only for the final assault on the Kabul regime but also for the ensuing civil war that many expect. . . .

In addition to the three million refugees in Pakistan, there are perhaps another two million in Iran and maybe another three million who have moved into the towns from the countryside to escape the fighting. When these millions decide it is safe to return home, there will be an immense need for assistance to help them resettle. They will need seed, fertilizer, draft animals, and help in restoring ruined irrigation systems. They will need food and potable water to tide them over until the first crops can be brought in. Public health problems will require attention.

The First Problem

The first, immediate problem is the existence through the countryside of anti-personnel mines sown by the Soviets and by the mujahideen during the war. There are possibly millions of mines, ranging from large, sophisticated devices to small toys, dropped from the air by the Soviets along resistance supply routes. Clearing these mines will require an immense international effort. The Soviets claim they are clearing some they planted, but blame the resistance for most of them.

The United Nations has named the respected former High Commissioner for Refugees, Prince Sadruddin Aga Khan, to lead the resettlement and reconstruction effort. He estimates that Afghanistan needs almost $1.2 billion in assistance for the first 18 months of a resettlement program and another $840 million for a three-year reconstruction program. He has asked the international community to assist. Some pledges have been made. The United States is providing $119 million in the current fiscal year and hopes to provide about $142 million in direct aid in the next fiscal year. Washington insists that no assistance be provided through the Najibullah regime, and although the Soviets say they will help, they have as yet given no sign that they will be willing to channel their aid through the United Nations.

A major need is the training of Afghans to administer the relief and reconstruction programs. The Soviets continue to train some 2,000 Afghans each year in the Soviet Union, but many of these will not be welcomed, at least initially, by the new non-Communist government. Western countries need to mount major efforts to train Afghans in reconstruction as well as persuade trained Afghan exiles to offer their services.

What is clear is that an international effort to assist Afghanistan is going to have to be a major and sustained one over several years.

There are also important international implications for the region following a Soviet withdrawal and the establishment of a new Afghan government.

"There are also important international implications for the region following a Soviet withdrawal and the establishment of a new Afghan government."

The Soviet Union will continue to have a strong interest in assuring that Afghanistan is a non-aligned state posing no threat to Soviet interests. The Soviets will no doubt try to maintain some of their civilian advisers in the country. They will also want to continue to have access to Afghan raw materials, such as the natural gas of northern Afghanistan which they have been exploiting for years, even having the metering system on their side of the border.

For its part, any new Afghan government will eventually have to restore some *modus vivendi* with the USSR, despite the bitter struggle of the last ten years. Afghanistan will continue to need to use Soviet transit facilities for some of its imports; it will want to market many of its exports to the USSR; and it will want Soviet assistance in developing its economy.

Two Neighbors

Any reconciliation between these two neighbors that share a long, common border is, however, likely to take several years. The Afghans will have to overcome their rage at what the Soviets have done to their country. The Soviets will not only have to swallow some pride; they will also have to get rid of their overbearing ways toward their poorer neighbor. I remember, for example, Soviet Ambassador Puzanov, whom my British colleague called the "gauleiter" of Afghanistan (after the old German term for the chief of a territory under Nazi control), trying to ply Afghans—good Muslims—with forbidden vodka and pork.

Afghanistan will also have to establish a comfortable relationship with Pakistan and put aside its longstanding dispute over the allegiance of its fellow Pushtun tribesmen across a border it has refused to recognize. For its part, Pakistan will have to resist temptations to interfere in internal Afghan politics. One hopes these two nations which have established a new, brotherly relationship over the past ten years will put aside old differences in the interest of regional security and stability.

The same can be said of Iran and Afghanistan. Here again, longstanding cultural and historical differences need to be put aside. Iranians have tended to look upon Afghanistan as some sort of underdevelolped "Appalachia," whereas the Afghans have regarded Iranians as hopelessly effete. Pakistan can help in the process of Iran-Afghan reconciliation because it is a friend of both.

The Soviets can, as a result of their withdrawal, expect improved relations with the United States and with China. They will no doubt attempt to improve their relations with Pakistan by offering assistance and by taking advantage of what is likely to be a changing US-Pakistan relationship.

India has severely damaged its potential for influence in a post-Communist Afghanistan by its refusal to condemn the Soviet invasion. It was one of only 30 nations not to vote against the Soviet invasion in the United Nations. India clearly hopes to continue its close relations with the USSR and to have its adversary Pakistan occupied on the Afghan as well as the Indian front. If this Indian attitude continues, it will further motivate Pakistan both to strengthen its relations with the new Afghanistan and to seek a rapprochement with the Soviet Union.

"The Soviets can, as a result of their withdrawal, expect improved relations with the United States and with China."

Afghan-US relations will return in due course to their pre-1978 (Communist coup) norm. The United States supports an independent, nonaligned, developing Afghanistan living in peace with its neighbors. Budgetary pressures and competing priorities will inevitably mean that American aid will not fully meet Afghan desires. But the American aid program should be sizable at least through the first few years of Afghan reconstruction.

US Relations

US relations with Pakistan are likely to undergo a significant change as their mutual interest in Soviet withdrawal from Afghanistan is achieved. Inevitably, Americans will begin to focus on other aspects of the bilateral relationship such as Pakistan's nuclear program, human rights and democratic political development, drug production and trafficking, and Pakistan's relations with India and attitude on the Arab-Israeli question.

This changing focus will affect the relationship, and it will take skillful diplomacy to move it smoothly into a new era. The United States will have to continue to be cognizant of Pakistan's exposed strategic position and its important role in the security and stability of the Gulf region and Southwest Asia. Washington will have to bear in mind that a supportive American policy is the best means for the United States in dealing with bilateral issues.

For its part, Pakistan, which had certainly learned this lesson in the period prior to the Soviet invasion of Afghanistan, will have to have modest expectations of American assistance while relying more heavily on strengthened relations with the nations of the region in meeting its security needs. . . .

Whatever ensues, it is good news that the Soviets are leaving Afghanistan and that that war-ravaged country will be free again. It will be up to the Afghans to set their future course. It is up to the international community not to interfere in their politics but to help them rebuild their country.

Theodore L. Eliot Jr. was US Ambassador to Afghanistan from 1973 to 1978. He currently is the senior research fellow at the Hoover Institution on War, Revolution, and Peace at Stanford University in Stanford, California.

"Afghanistan's future political course must be left to the Afghan people themselves to decide."

viewpoint 7

The Afghan People Should Determine Afghanistan's Future

Michael H. Armacost and Richard S. Williamson

Editor's note: The following viewpoint consists of two parts. Part I is by Michael H. Armacost. Part II is by Richard S. Williamson.

I

I welcome this opportunity to discuss our Afghanistan policy. . . .

Our aims in Afghanistan have been consistent since the Soviets invaded that small, traditionally nonaligned nation in December 1979. They were, and remain:
- Rapid and complete withdrawal of Soviet troops;
- Restoration of Afghanistan's independent and nonaligned status;
- Return of the refugees in safety and honor; and
- Self-determination for the Afghan people.

These objectives have been widely shared by other nations, as demonstrated by the overwhelming majorities which have each year supported the Pakistan-sponsored UN General Assembly resolution calling for their implementation. Even more importantly, they represent the goals of the people of Afghanistan themselves. The valiant struggle of the Afghans, with the support of their friends, is what has made our policy achievements possible.

Withdrawal of Soviet Forces

The successful conclusion of the Geneva accords on April 14, 1988 provides a framework for attaining our policy goals. Above all, it calls for the complete withdrawal of the Soviet occupying army. . . . This, in turn, will remove the principal impediment to achievement of other goals, particularly the safe return of refugees and the creation of a broadly based government representing the Afghan people.

The significance of this accomplishment cannot be overstated. The 1979 invasion marked the first time

Michael H. Armacost and Richard S. Williamson, "Status Report on Afghanistan." Statements made before the Senate Foreign Relations Committee, Washington, DC, June 23, 1988.

since their occupation of Eastern Europe in the final months of World War II that the Soviets had seized territory by military force. A blatant violation of Afghanistan national sovereignty to salvage communist rule in Kabul, it brought Moscow's army and air force to the borders of the Indo-Pakistan subcontinent and to within striking distance of the Persian Gulf. It was an affront to Afghan self-determination and a challenge to the peace, stability, and security of the region. The reaction of the United States, and of the overwhelming majority within the community of nations, was strong opposition to the Soviet actions and support for the Afghan resistance.

The withdrawal of the Soviet forces is, perhaps, an even more historic milestone. Its implications go well beyond the restoration of the strategic balance of the region and the rebirth of an independent Afghanistan, important as these are. It strengthens the cause of self-determination everywhere. It could also lend impetus to efforts to resolve other regional conflicts.

You will recall that when we agreed in principle in December 1985 to Pakistan's request that we serve as a coguarantor with the U.S.S.R., we did so on condition that the accords be satisfactory to us. It was only when we were so satisfied that we took on the coguarantor role and, with the Soviet Union, undertook to respect the agreements arrived at by Pakistan and Afghanistan. We insisted, moreover, that the obligations of the guarantors must be balanced and symmetrical. We were prepared to accept a joint U.S.-Soviet moratorium on further military supplies to Afghan parties during the period of their withdrawal and several months thereafter. The Soviets refused such an arrangement, insisting on their right to continue providing military supplies to their client government in Kabul. We consequently insisted that the United States would retain and exercise the right, consistent with its own obligations as a guarantor, to provide military assistance to parties in Afghanistan. Should the Soviet Union exercise restraint in providing military assistance, the United States similarly will exercise restraint....

We believe that Afghanistan's future political course must be left to the Afghan people themselves to decide. The United States has no blueprint for Afghanistan. Nor do we favor any group or individual. The experience of the British in the 19th century and the Soviets in this one suggests that the Afghans do not take kindly to efforts by outsiders to choose a government for them.

We hope that the Afghans will be able to develop a process for selecting a government representative of Afghan society. We support the efforts of UN Under Secretary General Diego Cordovez to promote a dialogue among the Afghan parties. His aim is to work out a transitional arrangement as a step toward self-determination. We do not know if his efforts will be successful.

"We hope that the Afghans will be able to develop a process for selecting a government representative of Afghan society."

We continue to urge the resistance to overcome its factional differences. We are heartened by evidence that the *mujahidin* are making efforts to increase cooperation both among commanders in the field and among the resistance parties. I have noted the better coordination of the resistance military effort within Afghanistan, particularly since the Soviet withdrawal began. The resistance alliance has recently announced both a cabinet for its proposed interim government and plans to hold elections within the next few months. These plans are tentative and may be modified over time, but they do show that the resistance recognizes the need for greater cooperation and is attempting to bring this about.

We do not know what kind of government the Afghans will choose. But I am confident that a free Afghan government will eventually emerge with which the United States will enjoy the friendly relations which characterized U.S.-Afghan ties before the communist coup of 1978 and the Soviet occupation which followed.

As part of our ongoing effort to keep in close touch with the resistance and the refugees, we have sent periodic special missions to supplement our regular staff in Islamabad and Peshawar. Our current plans include the assignment of a very well-qualified, language-trained officer to serve as Ambassador [to Pakistan Arnold] Raphel's special assistant for Afghan affairs. He will be spending much of his time in contact with resistance figures in Peshawar and elsewhere.

In line with our objective of promoting a peaceful and stable Afghanistan, the United States expects to play a role in helping the Afghan people get back on their feet and rebuild their war-devastated country. Refugee resettlement and rehabilitation will be a major challenge. Approximately 3 million Afghans fled to Pakistan in the years following the Soviet invasion; another 2 million are estimated to be living in Iran. In addition, several million have been displaced within Afghanistan itself. In fact, population distribution within the country has been dramatically altered, putting significant pressure on Afghanistan's fragile infrastructure and the slender food resources of many regions of the country. The widespread sowing of literally millions of landmines has added an ominous new dimension to the rehabilitation effort. The refusal, thus far, of the U.S.S.R. or the Najibullah regime to help locate and remove these mines is a moral outrage and inconsistent with their commitment in the Geneva accords to facilitate the return of the refugees.

We have been actively engaged with the United Nations and other governments in planning for the repatriation of the refugees and the resettlement of these people and of displaced persons within Afghanistan.

II

For years the safe and honorable return of the Afghan refugees has been a major objective of the United States and the international community. Their return, as well as that of the displaced persons, will enable them to participate in the political and economic reconstruction of their country. It will help carry forward the process by which the Afghan people exercise their right of self-determination and establish their own government.

As the Afghan people return home, they hope to begin rebuilding their lives after enduring almost 9 years of Soviet occupation and the destruction of much of their country. However, as Prince Sadruddin Aga Khan, the newly appointed UN Coordinator for Humanitarian and Economic Assistance in Afghanistan, has pointed out, this expectation of better things to come can turn into a crisis of hope. As he notes: "Unless the essential needs of normal life can be quickly met, hope may be just as quickly followed by despair and renewed suffering."

Refugee Issues

The refugee and related issues pose a daunting challenge to the international community. The demands for expertise, experience, and finance compel an international response to which the United Nations and its technical and development agencies must provide leadership. This is one of the principal functions for which the United Nations was created—to help put into place the building blocks of peace and create the conditions "to give peace a chance."

The Afghan people are hardy and capable. Their valor and self-reliance are impressive. But despite their resilience, self-reliance, and downright toughness, the Afghan refugees need our help. The international community must rise to the occasion to assist the refugees as they return to homes in rubble, fields laced with mines, and destroyed irrigation systems—so vital in an arid country such as Afghanistan.

> *"[The return of refugees] will help carry forward the process by which the Afghan people exercise their right of self-determination and establish their own government."*

We have put a great deal of energy and effort into assuring the creation of a UN relief and resettlement program for the Afghan people that runs efficiently, effectively, and without duplication. Beginning in March 1988, I spoke with the Secretary General on several occasions, urging him to appoint a special coordinator who could organize and manage this type of UN effort and obtain the necessary contributions from the donor nations. Secretary of State George Shultz raised the issue with UN officials when he signed the Afghan accords in Geneva on April 14, 1988. We continued to campaign for such an appointment right up to the announcement on May 11 that Prince Sadruddin Aga Khan had been selected as the special coordinator. We strongly applauded his selection.

We have already had extensive contact with Prince Sadruddin. I spoke with him immediately following his appointment and consulted with him in Geneva at the end of May following his visit to Afghanistan, Pakistan, and Iran. At that time, I shared with him our ideas on the UN assistance effort and ascertained how his thinking was evolving. On June 13, 3 days after the Secretary General announced the UN appeal, Prince Sadruddin came to Washington for meetings with President Reagan, Vice President Bush, and Secretary Shultz—an indication of the importance which we place on Prince Sadruddin's role and coordinated UN action. On June 14, I attended the first donors' meeting in New York, which was chaired by Prince Sadruddin.

Because Prince Sadruddin's office is in Geneva, we have appointed Ambassador Petrone, U.S. Permanent Representative to the UN offices in Geneva, to serve as his principal U.S. Government interlocutor with that office. As his work progresses, Prince Sadruddin is committed to provide frequent briefings to us and other donors on his planning and interaction with the various UN agencies. . . .

Prince Sadruddin has moved with record speed in developing a coordinated UN program. Less than a month after his appointment, the Secretary General was able to issue his appeal to donors and supply them with an outline (to be refined later) for the cooperative work of the various UN agencies. Other meetings will be scheduled after donors have had time to study the relevant documentation. . . .

The report emphasizes that, as the refugees return home, the focus must be on immediate and basic support—e.g., providing food aid and agricultural supplies (seed and tools), repairing local irrigation canals, and delivering basic health care. . . .

A Humanitarian Effort

The report explicitly states that the relief effort must be seen as being a humanitarian effort and notes that the Secretary General has clearly distinguished it from his political good offices.

The report states that it would be unrealistic to attempt a nationwide rehabilitation effort at the present time. Rather, program efforts will be focused at the regional level as conditions permit.

Aid will be channeled directly to the refugees as they return.

In summary, the report states that "the fundamental purpose of this programme is to link people back to their homes and engender self-reliance in order to avoid institutionalizing relief." We could not agree more.

There are basic principles that must underlie the UN effort to ensure the success of its program. The United States opposes UN financial assistance flowing through the Kabul regime. It must not be administered in a way that permits that illegitimate regime to enhance its political standing within the country. This position is firmly held by the United States. Secretary Shultz has emphasized this point on several occasions. . . . "The UN assistance should be provided directly to the refugees and displaced persons as they return home, that the agencies involved must ensure that the aid indeed gets to the intended recipients and that humanitarian goals alone drive the effort." Other donors, such as Great Britain, the Federal Republic of Germany, and Japan, also voiced on that occasion their opposition to the Kabul regime obtaining any control over UN financial assistance.

Prince Sadruddin and other senior UN officials have assured us that they understand the strength of this shared concern and that they hold a similar view. We have made clear—and will continue to do so—that we will be watching this matter very closely. Working with Prince Sadruddin, we are confident that the UN effort will be directed in ways supportive of the interests of the Afghan people.

Let me now turn to our contribution and role in this relief effort. In fiscal year (FY) 1988, the United States budgeted $119 million in humanitarian assistance to the Afghan refugees. Approximately $49 million of this assistance goes through multilateral channels—specifically, the UN High Commissioner for Refugees and the World Food Program—to assist the more than 3 million refugees in Pakistan: The remainder, consisting of food and agricultural equipment, medicine and medical supplies, and educational training and materials, is provided bilaterally, primarily to people still within Afghanistan.

Not only does the bilateral program assist needy Afghans, it has encouraged them to remain in their country rather than fleeing to Pakistan and placing an additional burden on the Pakistani Government and people. Throughout the years of conflict in Afghanistan, Pakistan has earned the admiration of the world for its courageous stand against Soviet intimidation and the provision of refuge for millions of homeless Afghans. Our bilateral program, initiated with strong and bipartisan congressional input and support, has been generously funded....

"The fundamental purpose of [US aid] is to link people back to their homes and engender self-reliance."

We are encouraging other donors to contribute substantially to the Afghan assistance effort. In our appeals, we point out that we are by far the largest donor of humanitarian assistance to Afghans and that others should now assume a major share of the new burden as the refugees begin their return home.

We are making clear to the Soviet Union that it should make a major financial contribution to the special international assistance effort. It destroyed the country of Afghanistan; it is obligated to pay a major part of the bill to rebuild it. But its contribution to the United Nations must come without strings or any requirement that the funds be used to bolster the illegitimate Kabul regime. Soviet and UN officials understand our position clearly.

The U.S.S.R. should certainly assist in eliminating the danger to the refugees of the millions of mines Soviet and Kabul forces have sown across the roads and fields throughout most of Afghanistan. No humanitarian task is more important than the removal or destruction of these mines. They are a major obstacle to permitting the safe return of the refugees and allowing them to begin cultivating their land. We and the United Nations are pushing the Soviets to stop laying mines, remove the mines they can, and provide information on minefield locations so that any remaining mines can be removed quickly.

The United Nations

I mentioned at the onset my profound belief that the United Nations must lead the international community in meeting the challenge of the Afghan refugees. I am convinced it will succeed and, in doing so, help advance interests of major importance to the United States. There are legitimate grounds for criticizing some of the failings of the United Nations. I have done so when I believed such criticism was warranted, as have many Members of Congress. But, even as we seek to criticize constructively, we must not forget the indispensable work the United Nations does—work essential to global peace, stability, and development; work that benefits directly our national and international interests.

More specifically, the UN system is uniquely placed to lead the multinational effort to aid the Afghan refugees. It has the capacity to coordinate and pool resources. Contributions made in isolation by small nations with limited aid programs, for example, would be much less effective and productive than when channeled through the UN system. The specialized agencies also have had decades of experience managing the various issues associated with major refugee programs (e.g., distributing food aid and providing health care). Finally, the United Nations can undertake refugee programs in countries such as Iran where individual nations cannot. For all these reasons, the UN effort on behalf of the Afghan refugees is important and should be supported.

In conclusion, the international community faces a major challenge. We will not relax our vigilance until the last Soviet troops are gone, until all the refugees who want to return are able to do so, and until the proud Afghan people have established, through self-determination, a representative government that serves their needs and sustains their traditions.

Michael H. Armacost is the former under secretary for Political Affairs and Richard S. Williamson is the former assistant secretary for International Organization Affairs under the Reagan administration.

"Moscow's intervention both defended the Soviet Union and posed the possibility of a revolutionary transformation of this hideously backward country."

viewpoint 8

The USSR Should Determine Afghanistan's Future

Workers Vanguard

When the Soviet Red Army went into Afghanistan on 27 December 1979, we Trotskyists of the international Spartacist tendency declared "Hail Red Army in Afghanistan!" and called to "Extend Social Gains of the October Revolution to Afghan Peoples!" Propping up a shaky national-reformist regime on the USSR's vital southern flank against CIA-backed Islamic reactionaries, Moscow's intervention both defended the Soviet Union and posed the possibility of a revolutionary transformation of this hideously backward country. The Soviet troops brought with them literacy, doctors, and the first taste of liberation for Afghan women from the enslavement and seclusion symbolized by the *chadori*, the smothering veil covering them in yards of heavy cloth from head to toe.

A Peace Deal

Now, in the hopes of striking a "peace" deal with Ronald Reagan, the Kremlin Stalinists are opening the door to a bloody Islamic *jihad* (holy war) against every form of social progress in Afghanistan. In Kabul Soviet foreign minister Eduard Shevardnadze announced to the Afghan press: "We would like the year 1988 to be the last year of the presence of Soviet troops in your country." That would mean leaving in the lurch the Afghan women, teachers, leftists, workers and soldiers who have fought for the last ten years to drag their country into the 20th century! The price for this obscene bid to placate U.S. imperialism is to hand over hundreds of thousands of Afghans to be tortured, flayed alive, beheaded and dismembered as infidels by the mullahs, tribal khans and feudal landlords. This is treachery!

The imperialist press is rubbing its eyes in disbelief. "Light in the Khyber Pass?" asked the *New York Times* (9 January 1988). "Could it really be true? A Soviet-free Afghanistan" editorialized the *Philadelphia Inquirer* (10 January 1988), saying that "If Mr. Gorbachev has truly made up his mind that the burdens of occupation outweigh the costs of defeat" there should be no problem. For that is what they're after: not a deal but *defeat*, to install an anti-Soviet regime in Kabul and complete the encirclement of the USSR by hostile regimes all along its southern border. As we wrote in "Afghanistan and the Left: The Russian Question Point Blank" (*Spartacist* No. 29, Summer 1980):

> Afghanistan is a flash of lightning which illuminates the real contours of the world political landscape. It has exploded the last illusions of détente to reveal the implacable hostility of U.S. imperialism to the Soviet degenerated workers state.

We warned then:

> It is possible the Kremlin could do a deal with the imperialists to withdraw, for example, in return for NATO's reversing its decision to deploy hundreds of new nuclear missiles in West Europe. That would be a real counter-revolutionary crime against the Afghan peoples.

A Soviet withdrawal now will embolden the deeply discredited Reagan regime, encouraging it to step up its murderous contra wars against Nicaragua, Angola and Kampuchea as well. Not withdrawal but victory! Red Army—Finish the job!

Target of Cold War II

To mark the eighth anniversary of the Soviet intervention, thousands of Afghan counter-revolutionaries in Pakistan rallied around burning effigies of Gorbachev, chanting "Death to Russia! Death to Communism!" That same day TASS reported that Afghan thugs invaded the Soviet mission in the Iranian city of Isfahan. The U.S.'s Afghan "freedom fighters" have vowed to kill all Communist collaborators. They mean it. Already, they have assassinated more than 2,000

Workers Vanguard, "Russia Must Win Afghan War," January 15, 1988. Reprinted with permission.

schoolteachers for trying to bring literacy to a country where, before, 90 percent of the population was illiterate. The *mujahedin* have also justified shooting down an airliner taking Afghan children to study in the USSR, claiming they were being "brainwashed" by Satan. These feudalist reactionaries want to return to a 7th-century society based on the cruelest social parasitism, criminality and slavery.

"These feudalist reactionaries want to return to a 7th-century society based on the cruelest social parasitism, criminality and slavery."

Emancipated women in particular are threatened by the Islamic reactionaries. The vice president of the All-Afghanistan Women's Council went to university in Kabul with Gulbaddin Hekmatyar, now one of the top Afghan contras. "In 1971, when women came out in public with no veil, Gulbaddin's supporters sprayed acid in their faces," she said. "When women wore stockings, they shot at their legs" (London *Guardian*, 5 January 1988). As one Islamic fanatic declared at the anti-Communist orgy in Pakistan "We are Afghans and we do not allow women to come out. Women have no opinion in determining the future of Afghanistan." (*New York Times*, 28 December 1987). Today a majority of students at Kabul University are women, and 15,000 women serve as soldiers and commanders in the Afghan army. The withdrawal of Soviet troops would mean they face the prospect of hideous slaughter.

Not only Afghans will die. For Washington, Afghanistan was the opening shot of the second Cold War, a global drive to "roll back" supposed "Soviet expansionism." Democrat Carter's "national security" czar Zbigniew Brzezinski stood at the Khyber Pass in a U.S. Army jacket and pointed an automatic rifle at Afghanistan. Republican Reagan took aim at Sandinista Nicaragua and soon was bankrolling contra mercenaries from Central America to Southeast Asia. In his second term this became the "Reagan doctrine" of attacking the Soviet "evil empire" on its fringes. Journalist Bob Woodward reports of his conversations with CIA chief William Casey:

> He was interested in taking one back from the Soviets—a visible, clean victory.
> "Where can we get a rollback?" Haig had asked.
> "I want to win one," the president had said.
> —*Washington Post Magazine*
> 27 September 1987

Even after the Iran/Contragate fiasco the Reaganauts are hoping to "win one" in Afghanistan. But they can't unless the Kremlin hands it to them.

Reaganites and Democrats alike have insisted on the withdrawal of Soviet troops from Afghanistan as *the* key test of sincerity for Gorbachev's "peace" drive. Nowhere is the futility and danger of trying to appease the war-crazed U.S. rulers clearer. While the Soviets were talking of pulling out, Reagan was in the Oval Office promising his Afghan contras that U.S. aid will *increase*. In the aftermath of the Washington summit, the White House decided to turn up the heat:

> Administration officials . . . have concluded that a tough stand by the United States can probably force further compromises from the Soviet Union on the timing and manner of its proposed troop withdrawal.
> —*New York Times*
> 15 December 1987

Now that the Soviets have promised to be out by the end of the year, Secretary of State George Shultz is demanding that they also *cut off all aid* to their erstwhile Afghan allies, while insisting that U.S. arms and aid to the Afghan rebels will continue until the Soviets are gone.

Mop Up the Mullahs

On ABC News' "This Week with David Brinkley," Soviet foreign ministry spokesman Gennadi Gerasimov proclaimed: "We are going to withdraw, and the process of national reconciliation will take place, and you will have a nonaligned Afghanistan; nonsocialist, also" (*Washington Post*, 14 December 1987). The idea of "Finlandizing" Afghanistan is pure illusion. The most minimal bourgeois-democratic measures, such as a modest land reform, provoked a savage feudalist backlash. Even bringing back the king, deposed in 1973, as the Soviets are seeking, won't restore a stable, pliant buffer regime. As for the program of "national reconciliation" with the *mujahedin*, it would have been easier for Lenin's Bolsheviks to form a coalition government with the tsarist Black Hundreds, who look downright liberal compared to the Afghan cutthroats!

The possibility of bringing this land of feuding tribes, opium smuggling, bride price and religious obscurantism out of the Middle Ages is directly tied to the achievements of Soviet Central Asia. Many of the initial Soviet troops were in fact Tadzhik, Turkmen, Kirghiz, Uzbek and Kazakh soldiers from just across the border. The Toronto *Globe and Mail* (5 February 1987) noted, following some nationalist riots in Kazakhstan, that the threat of Islamic fundamentalism in the USSR "is limited by relative economic comfort in the central Asian republics. While religious commitment and population trends ring ominously, the memory of what life without the Soviets was like is on their side." But as the Kremlin has restricted social reforms in Afghanistan, U.S.-armed *mujahedin* (holy warriors) have even begun to strike across the border into Tadzhikistan.

At Moscow's urging, the authentically Afghan People's Democratic Party of Afghanistan (PDPA) regime has tried to conciliate the rebels. Agrarian reform was cut back, all ceilings on land ownership for the feudal landlords and Islamic clergy were lifted, the mullahs were exempted from taxation. Education for girls was made "voluntary" instead of compulsory. In November PDPA leader Najibullah called a *loya jirgah*, bringing in tribal and religious chiefs. In the name of Allah and "Islamic consciousness," the red star was removed from the Afghan national seal and the country was renamed the Republic of Afghanistan, dropping the "Democratic" because of Communist connotations. As Najibullah was appealing for a "political solution" by holding out the prospect of Soviet withdrawal, the guerrillas responded with rocket blasts that shook the meeting room.

The only "political solution" that will benefit the Afghan masses is for the Soviet army to intensify and finish the war by mopping up the Afghan contras. This sentiment is evidently shared by many in the Soviet Union, notably within the army. According to the *Los Angeles Times* (5 November 1987), recent issues of the Soviet defense ministry newspaper *Krasnaya Zvezda* (Red Star) have featured articles complaining that the unilateral cease-fire declared by Kabul last year allowed the rebels to regroup and rearm, shooting down civilian airliners "right and left" while Afghan troops returned to their bases and Soviet troops were made to hold their fire.

Over the past year, the U.S. has shipped more than 600 Stinger surface-to-air missiles to its Afghan mercenaries. While some were sold to the Iranians and used against the U.S. in the Persian Gulf, the imperialists claim the Stingers together with British Blowpipes are taking down an average of one Soviet helicopter gunship a day, while making it impossible for Soviet fighter jets to fly close support. Referring to the Soviet MI-24 helicopters which were key in wiping out guerrilla strongholds in Afghanistan, one *mujahedin* leader boasted: "For nine years the dragon ruled the skies over Afghanistan. Now the dragon is dead." The solution is simple, and McDonnell Douglas has it—the "Black Hole Infrared Suppression System." As advertised in the December 1987 issue of *Scientific American,* the Black Hole system makes helicopter exhaust "so cool it is ignored by heat-seeking missiles."

Internationalist Duty

The real barrier to Soviet victory in Afghanistan is not on the military front. As one senior Reagan official admitted, even armed with Stingers "a possibility of a resistance victory . . . there never has been." An article in the *Philadelphia Inquirer* (22 December 1987) noted that the Soviet military "knows that the Red Army cannot be defeated by the mujaheddin," and "there has been a sharp improvement in the [Afghan] army's performance." This was demonstrated at the end of December in the successful drive by Soviet and Afghan troops to break the guerrilla siege of Khost, just a few miles from the Pakistani border, disrupting a key arms route and killing over 2,000 rebels. A U.S. government official carped: "The Soviets are showing they still have the firepower to go anywhere they want." So they do. The obstacle is political.

Gorbachev has called Afghanistan a "bleeding wound." But it has been the Kremlin Stalinists' efforts to strike a deal with the mullahs and their imperialist godfathers which have needlessly prolonged the war, allowing the U.S. to keep the blood of Soviet soldiers flowing. Much is made of opposition to the war within the Soviet Union, turning a tiny protest in Moscow (eight protesters carrying signs demanding "Withdraw Soviet Troops from Afghanistan") into a major event. But the most common demand reported in demonstrations of Afghan war veterans and letters to the Soviet press is not for withdrawal but *recognition* of the valiant internationalist contribution by Soviet youth.

"The only 'political solution' that will benefit the Afghan masses is for the Soviet army to intensify and finish the war by mopping up the Afghan contras."

There have been increasing demands to build a monument in Moscow to commemorate Soviet soldiers fallen in battle against the CIA's Afghan contras. In a letter to *Pravda,* the father of Sergeant Yuri Shevchenko, who died in Afghanistan, asked why his son's heroic sacrifice could not be inscribed on his gravestone: "Why can't it say that he died carrying out his international duty in Afghanistan? What are we ashamed of?" (*Pravda* monthly English edition, October 1987). Beholden to the Stalinist dogma of "socialism in one country," Gorbachev & Co. are "ashamed" of anything that smacks of revolutionary internationalism, because it stands in the way of pursuing their reactionary illusion of "détente" with the imperialists. At the 27th Communist Party congress in 1986, Gorbachev denounced any concept of "revolutionary war" as "Trotskyite" heresy.

Meanwhile, the war-crazed psychos in the White House are exporting counterrevolutionary wars around the globe, and the Afghan rebels have received the biggest subsidies. Over the past year they were reportedly bankrolled to the tune of $660 million—six times what the Nicaraguan contras got—and in 1988 this is scheduled to rise to $1 billion. The Democrats have out-Reaganed Reagan in boosting the cause of the bloodthirsty Afghan "freedom fighters," for here they see a perfect opportunity to bleed the Russians without the overhead of direct U.S. intervention and the dread spectre of "another Vietnam." ...

No Peaceful Coexistence

Any hope of peacefully coexisting with this crew of Cold Warriors is ludicrous. A *Wall Street Journal* (8 December 1987) editorial argued that Gorbachev's intentions to pull out of Afghanistan could not be honorable because "he hasn't said much about getting out of Eastern Europe"! Now there is recollection of the claim that Wrangell Island, right off the Soviet Arctic coast, belongs to the U.S. because 14 Americans for the Lomen Reindeer & Trading Co. were trappers on the island more than 60 years ago! In 1924 they were removed from the island by the Soviet ship Red October and sent back to Seattle. Now Jesse Helms is claiming Wrangell and four other nearby islands as property of the U.S. of A.—next thing you know, they'll be claiming Sakhalin island and the Kurils for Japan, and Kamchatka Peninsula and Vladivostok to seal off Russia in the Far East. And where would this stop? Where did it stop in 1918—nowhere! The Soviet Red Army stopped it.

"Only total Soviet victory over the mullahs can bring peace and the prospect of national and social liberation for the peoples of Afghanistan."

The U.S. imperialists seek to destroy and dismember the Soviet Union not through ludicrous land claims but by economic pressure, destabilization and war, to overturn the revolutionary gains of the 1917 Bolshevik Revolution and restore "free market" capitalist exploitation. The USSR is too strong militarily and the loyalty of the Soviet peoples too deep to risk a direct assault right now. So they attack on the periphery of Soviet power. Pledging to pull Soviet troops out of Afghanistan, Gorbachev & Co. are not only sacrificing the lives of millions of Afghans on the altar of "détente" but leaving the Soviet Union open to imperialist provocation and attack on this crucial southern flank.

Total Victory

Only total Soviet victory over the mullahs can bring peace and the prospect of national and social liberation for the peoples of Afghanistan. To carry out what many in the Soviet Union, homeland of the October Revolution, rightly see as their internationalist duty in Afghanistan requires a proletarian political revolution in the USSR against the Kremlin oligarchy to restore the revolutionary internationalist traditions of Lenin and Trotsky's Bolsheviks.

Workers Vanguard is the biweekly newspaper of the Spartacist League, an organization that advocates a revolution of the working class to establish socialism in the US.

"Although the Reagan Administration would like to convince conservatives that its policy in Afghanistan helped attain the victory, the war is far from over."

viewpoint 9

The US Should Continue Aid to Afghanistan

Henry Kriegel

The decision of the Soviet Union to withdraw from Afghanistan is hailed in the 1988 Republican Platform and by the Administration as a victory for the Reagan Doctrine. However to call the situation in Afghanistan "a victory" is at best premature. The Geneva Accords, hurriedly signed on April 14th, will not bring peace to Afghanistan. They have, on the other hand, jeopardized what the mujahideen, their supporters, and President Reagan have fought for during the past eight years. The Soviets, through their clever *glasnost* campaign and their well-publicized "withdrawal" from Afghanistan, have successfully convinced most of the American public, the media, and our government that the war is over. As a result, support for the mujahideen has decreased and deliveries of key weapons to the freedom fighters have been cut off.

According to Pakistani officials, the Soviets consider the Geneva Accords on Afghanistan as important as the ratification of the Intermediate Nuclear Forces Treaty. Although this might be debated, the Soviets clearly gained through these accords, and were allowed to cut their losses and perhaps even effect a triumph for themselves in Afghanistan. Through the Geneva Accords, Gorbachev helped to change Western perception of the Soviet Union. As Georgi Arbatov boasted just prior to the Moscow Summit, "We are going to do something terrible to you—we are going to deprive you of an enemy." No longer recognizing the tactics of the enemy, this Administration has vigorously involved itself with détente, nuclear-arms pacts, and trade agreements.

The Geneva Accords helped to facilitate the Senate's ratification of the INF Treaty, guaranteed a successful Summit in Moscow, and paved the way for the resumption of high-tech trade with the Soviet Union. In fact, one day after the accords were signed, Secretary of Commerce C. William Verity travelled to Moscow with 500 U.S. businessmen to negotiate contracts with their Soviet counterparts. During the May 1988 Summit in Moscow, several of these contracts were consummated, including a multibillion-dollar deal with Armand Hammer's Occidental Petroleum.

A Failure

Several key issues make these accords a political and legal failure. When you consider that Gorbachev hailed this agreement as a model for settling regional conflicts around the world—*i.e.*, Angola, Cambodia, and Nicaragua—and that the State Department is pursuing these settlements, the global implications are disastrous. The Geneva Accords legally recognize the Kabul regime as being the legitimate government of the "Republic of Afghanistan," and prohibit U.S., Western, Chinese, and Arab "interference and intervention" in its affairs. This translates to a prohibition of aid to the mujahideen, who are referred to as mercenaries.

The unilateral statement attached to these accords by the U.S. has no legal weight; it was not a part of the agreement. In essence this statement says that although the U.S. has committed itself to act as a guarantor to the accords, the U.S. does not respect or give legitimacy to the Kabul regime and reserves the right to assist the mujahideen as long as the Soviets continue aiding the communist Afghans. The latter principle, known as "positive symmetry," was an idea cooked up by Secretary of State George Shultz and Assistant Secretary Michael Armacost as a way to defuse intense criticism from the U.S. Senate and grass-roots conservatives and to convince the President that his policy of aiding the resistance would continue unabated.

The U.S. Senate initially opposed these accords. The Senate passed a resolution (on a 77 to 0 vote)

Henry Kriegel, "Bear Appeasement in Afghanistan," *Conservative Digest*, November 1988. Reprinted with permission.

which called for continued assistance to the mujahideen until "it is absolutely clear that the Soviets have terminated their military occupation, that they are not redeploying their forces. . . ." The resolution was sponsored by Senators Byrd, Dole, Humphrey, and Symms and produced some fiery floor discussions. Senate Majority Leader Robert Byrd threatened to hold up ratification of the INF Treaty until the Senate read and approved the accords, to prevent, as he put it, the State Department from "unwittingly selling the Afghans down the river."

However, this proved to be bluff. The State Department delayed delivery of the accords until 10 p.m. of the evening before they were to be signed in Geneva by Shultz. Senator Byrd did not express any opposition and quickly relented. Congress had no chance to review the accords or to offer any dissent. The President's decision was made in a political vacuum; it was made public early Monday morning, April 11th, just after Congress returned from its Easter recess. To add insult to the injury done, the President casually announced his decision to sign the accords as he introduced the NCAA basketball champs from Kansas on the White House lawn. A matter of grave international importance, referred to by one French diplomat as another "D-Day," was handled disgracefully.

President Reagan was convinced to sign the agreement, despite it being contrary to his rhetoric and record of support, largely as a result of pressure from Cabinet members who fed him intelligence information that some Pentagon officials characterized as "wishful thinking." The assumptions, passed off as intelligence, were that the Soviets would withdraw from Afghanistan, that the Kabul regime would eventually collapse, and that the mujahideen would then take over. This author, during an April 12th, 1988 meeting among conservative activists (led by Paul Weyrich) and President Reagan, tried but failed to convince the President otherwise.

"International lawyers I consulted agreed that the [Geneva] accords were fatally flawed."

You don't sign binding international agreements based on assumptions; you sign them on the basis of what they legally mean. (International lawyers I consulted agreed that the accords were fatally flawed.) One legal scholar said, "It could not have been written better by Soviet lawyers." Now the Afghans and their supporters are stuck with this outrageous document. They are left with only words of assurances from the President that the aid will continue despite Soviet and KhAD (Afghan secret service) pressure on Pakistan to stop serving as a conduit.

The Kremlin's Assertions

The Administration and the media have accepted almost unquestioningly the Kremlin's assertion that it withdrew its troops on August 15th [1988]. Yet, there have been several reports of Soviet troop *deployments* to Kabul. On April 11th [1988], the Soviets sent 10,000 troops to Kabul "to assist in the withdrawal process." On July 23rd [1988], President Zia charged that another 10,000 troops were sent to Kabul. He was forced to retract the charge after his Foreign Minister visited high-level officials in Washington, D.C.

In its Foreign Report for May 26th, 1988 the *Economist* cited "intelligence sources" as indicating that "in the months before the start of the Soviet military withdrawal from Afghanistan on May 15th, substantial numbers of Uzbeks, Tadjiks, and Turkmen from the Soviet Union were secretly enrolled in the Afghan armed forces." These reports have been substantiated by a number of mujahideen sources.

The bottom line is that it is nearly impossible—based on a maximum of 45 U.N. monitors in Afghanistan, satellite photographs, or reports from diplomats stationed in Kabul—for us to determine whether the Soviets have fulfilled their withdrawal obligations. Lastly, there is no agreement between the U.S. and the Soviets as to how many troops they had deployed in Afghanistan: The State Department used a low figure of 117,000 Soviet troops; the Soviets only admit to 103,000. If we don't agree on the total numbers of troops, how can we be certain the Soviets have withdrawn half of them?

As a result of the accords, there is a noted reduction of public support for the mujahideen. After all, it is reasoned, if the Soviets are leaving Afghanistan there is no need for more aid to the freedom fighters. Further eroding public support is an assertion by State Department officials that the mujahideen are "sufficiently supplied." But with what? Even if the Soviets do completely withdraw, the many Soviet HIND helicopters and air fighters left behind are still a menace if the mujahideen do not have adequate air defenses.

It must be remembered that it was not the U.N. accords that forced the Soviets to begin withdrawing. It was due to their utter humiliation by the mujahideen on the battlefield. President Reagan's decision to send Stinger anti-aircraft weapons in late 1986 turned the tide of the war. Soviet losses of one aircraft per day prompted reconsideration of their Afghan adventurism.

Although State Department officials today insist that the mujahideen are sufficiently supplied, the fact remains that Stingers have been cut off since

May 1988. According to congressional sources, the State Department, in a secret deal with the Soviets negotiated by Assistant Secretary Armacost, agreed to cut off sophisticated weapons (including Stingers and Spanish 120mm mortars) to the mujahideen in exchange for a Soviet agreement not to launch offensives during their withdrawal period.

True to Form

True to form, the Soviets have violated this secret agreement. Just one day after the freedom fighters captured Konduz in northern Afghanistan and several other provincial capitals, they were driven out by combined Soviet aerial and ground attacks. The reason: The mujahideen no longer have sufficient supplies of Stingers and are hoarding those they do have. The Soviet attacks on Konduz, it should be noted, were launched from the Soviet Union. This is a clear violation of the Geneva Accords. The U.S. response was predictable. We filed a complaint with the United Nations and the State Department's Mr. Armacost discussed the issue in a meeting with Soviet Deputy Foreign Minister Voronstov in Moscow.

"Assistance will... force the Soviets to fulfill their promised withdrawal."

To this date, the freedom fighters, although they have captured a large number of garrisons, have not captured a major city or town. The Communists, in an effort to bolster Kabul and other major cities, have abandoned garrisons in outlying districts. They realize that whoever controls Kabul rules Afghanistan; so Gorbachev will continue to bolster Kabul with 25,000 advisors. And Najibullah, the puppet Communist Afghan leader, has approximately 110,000 to 125,000 troops at his command in and around the Kabul area; many of them, like the KhAD and the police, are highly trained and loyal. The fall of the capital is not imminent.

Islamic experts like Dr. Louie Dupree of Duke feel that if necessary the Communists would evacuate Kabul and go to Mazir-i-Sharif, a more easily defended northern city. This would dovetail with Soviet plans to annex the mineral-rich northern provinces of Afghanistan which produce two million cubic meters of natural gas annually, gems, and other resources.

The mujahideen desperately need Spanish 120mm mortars because they are highly accurate and will allow rocket attacks on Soviet and communist Afghan garrisons, airports, and depots; Stingers because they provide needed air defense capability against Soviet counterattacks; and "Lightfoot" mine-breaching equipment because they will help defuse millions of Soviet mines dispersed throughout the country. This assistance will, in turn, force the Soviets to fulfill their promised withdrawal.

Although the Reagan Administration would like to convince conservatives that its policy in Afghanistan helped attain the victory, the war is far from over, and it is much too early to tell if the mujahideen can win it. If they do, it will be in spite of constant State Department opposition and bureaucratic bungling of military and humanitarian aid, as well as the President's acquiescence to manipulation and deception.

Henry Kriegel is the executive director of the Committee for a Free Afghanistan in Washington, DC.

"The continued flow of deadly U.S. Stinger missiles to the extremist Afghan armed opposition. . . .'[takes] the lives of innocent people."'

viewpoint 10

The US Should Not Continue Aid to Afghanistan

The People and Carl Bloice

Editor's note: The following viewpoint is in two parts. Part I is by The People. *Part II is by Carl Bloice.*

I

Only the most jaded defenders of imperialist rule—East or West—could refer to the April 14, 1988 Geneva accords on Afghanistan as a "peace agreement." Indeed, only ruling-class officials, accustomed to overseeing the waste of human lives in war and the papering over of conflicts through "diplomacy," could have come up with such a thoroughly disingenuous and meaningless set of accords.

The Soviet Union, the United States and Pakistan joined the Soviet-installed Afghan government in signing the accords, solemnly pledging to respect Afghanistan's sovereignty and to refrain from intervening in Afghanistan's internal affairs "in any form whatsoever."

Yet each of these nations has publicly declared that it would continue to do just the opposite, as circumstances warrant. A more pointed example of the worthlessness of ruling class diplomacy would be hard to imagine.

The surest result of the "peace agreement" is that the war will continue. The rebels have vowed to continue fighting until the pro-Soviet Najibullah regime is replaced by an Islamic regime. The Najibullah regime will only accept peace and reconciliation on its own terms.

The Soviet Union will not accept an Islamic regime on its borders and maintains that its treaty obligations to Afghanistan permit it to continue arms shipments there despite the accords. The United States and Pakistan insist that they retain a right to continue their own military aid to the rebels.

The People, "Afghan 'Peace Agreement' An Imperialist Fraud," May 7, 1988. Reprinted with permission. Carl Bloice, "Soviets Issue Firm Warning on U.S.-Pakistan Interference," *People's Daily World,* September 30, 1988. Reprinted with permission.

The only accomplishment of the accords is that they supposedly allow the Soviet Union to save face as it pulls its own troops out of Afghanistan. In a manner similar to the "peace with honor" nonsense that President Nixon used to extricate the United States from Vietnam, the Soviet Union will presumably stop the shedding of Soviet workers' blood and have more Afghanis shed theirs instead.

Initial Intervention

Just as the initial interventions in Afghanistan by the superpowers were prompted by material and related strategic reasons, so too was the signing of the accords. Hopes for peace or a truly sovereign Afghanistan have nothing to do with it.

It is impossible to ascertain which factors weighed most heavily in the Kremlin's decision to invade Afghanistan in December 1979. But one of them was the fear that a successful Islamic rebellion in Afghanistan might stir up a resurgence of nationalism in the Central Asian republics of Tadzhikistan, Turkmenistan and Uzbekistan—regions with large Islamic populations that remain largely undeveloped and not fully assimilated into Soviet economic, political or cultural life.

A second factor was the internal economic instability of the Soviet Union. The Soviet ruling class at that time used the invasion of Afghanistan as a pretext for introducing administrative measures intended to improve labor discipline.

A third factor, no doubt, was protectiveness. Though not well known in this country, CIA [Central Intelligence Agency] infiltration and funneling of arms to Islamic rebels began in 1978, *before* the Soviet invasion. The prospect of the United States gaining a new forward base and listening post on the border, just after losing control of the same assets in Iran, surely raised alarms among the Soviet ruling class.

Soviet opposition to either an Islamic or a pro-U.S. regime in Afghanistan will prompt it to keep the Najibullah regime alive—or possibly even invade again. But for now, the Gorbachev government wants to reduce the economic and political costs of maintaining an unpopular war with Soviet troops—about 20,000 of whom have been killed. Those costs include strained relations with a number of Middle East countries.

U.S. ruling-class motivations for its own intervention in Afghanistan are clear enough: to weaken its chief imperialist rival economically and politically. For that purpose, it has no compunctions against arming to the teeth Islamic fundamentalists very similar to those it condemns in Iran.

For the U.S. ruling class, the accords change nothing. Yet, like the Soviet government, the Reagan administration is claiming a diplomatic victory over nothing.

> *"[The US] has no compunctions against arming to the teeth Islamic fundamentalists very similar to those it condemns in Iran."*

In addition, a separate, private "gentlemen's" agreement with the Soviets to maintain "symmetry" in arms shipments to each side was reportedly reached, which could reduce the costs of the war for both superpowers while ensuring its continuation.

Of course such an agreement is inherently unstable. But that the two superpowers could even contemplate making such a calculated decision to maintain a "cost-contained" war—on top of fomenting and sustaining that bloody war for nearly nine years already—testifies to the degree to which both capitalism and Soviet state despotism elevate material interests over human life and all humanitarian concerns.

II

The latest Soviet warning about developments in Afghanistan could not have been clearer: the situation in the region could take a serious turn for the worse if the current obstinate violations of the Geneva agreement continue.

"We have the means to make things fall into place," Soviet Foreign Minister Eduard Shevardnadze told the United Nations General Assembly. Soviet and Afghan officials have said repeatedly that the bold violation of the Geneva accords by the Reagan administration and the government in Pakistan would not be allowed to continue long.

On Sept. 21, 1988, the Soviet news agency TASS said that Washington and Islamabad are involved in "an unworthy and dangerous game," and declared, "Under these conditions the Soviet Union and Afghanistan reserve the right to take coordinated measures which would be dictated by the developing situation."

The Same Message

The same message was contained in a Sept. 22, 1988 joint communique issued following a meeting between Soviet and Afghan leaders.

Soviet spokespersons have made it clear that the government considers the four-party Geneva agreement on Afghanistan as a general model for solving other regional conflicts, and that failure to implement it would cast a pall over prospects elsewhere.

While Shevardnadze was addressing the United Nations, Soviet leader Mikhail Gorbachev was telling a Kremlin audience that current actions by some in the West reflect "a desire to use the current situation for selfish interests ignoring possible baneful consequences for international cooperation."

Gorbachev said it appears that the present leadership in Pakistan has decided to try to install a government of its choosing in Kabul, "ignoring the will of the Afghan people and the real alignment of social and political forces."

Speaking at a Sept. 27, 1988 luncheon honoring visiting Laotian head-of-state Kaysone Phomvihane, Gorbachev also drew attention to the continued flow of deadly U.S. Stinger missiles to the extremist Afghan armed opposition. He noted that these weapons "take the lives of innocent people, among them women and children, almost every week."

The Soviet leader called upon U.S. and Pakistani leaders to "come to their senses and give up adventurist actions." He stressed that those who violate the Geneva accords "undertake a grave responsibility before the international community."

The sharper tone to warnings of this kind came amid increased involvement of Pakistani military forces in attacks on Afghan territory, and amid signs that Islamabad may be preparing to employ its U.S.-equipped air force in strikes inside Afghanistan. This conclusion is suggested by the coordinated Washington-Islamabad propaganda campaign alleging violations of Pakistan air space by Afghan planes.

Real Concern

Another cause of real concern is the Reagan administration's abrupt rejection of the USSR's call for immediate four-power talks on the situation involving itself and the United States (the guarantors of the Geneva accords), Pakistan and Afghanistan, as well as a representative of the U.N. Secretary General. Islamabad has also turned thumbs down on an Afghan proposal for a mixed commission to investigate the alleged air space violations.

Since the Geneva agreements came into force May 15, 1988, Pakistan has violated nearly every provision. Contrary to the pact, military training and staging areas are maintained in Pakistan, attacks are launched across the border and obstacles are placed in the way of Afghan refugees seeking to return home.

On the other hand, the Soviet Union has been sticking to its commitment to withdraw its contingent of troops from the country, and the Kabul government is actively pursuing a policy of national reconciliation.

Agreements cease to be agreements if they are honored by only one side, said Gely Batenin, military expert for the Soviet Communist Party Central Committee Aug. 5, 1988. "This cannot go on indefinitely," he told an interviewer.

For the time being, Batenin said, the USSR is not reconsidering the schedule of its troop withdrawal, although that seems to be what Islamabad is seeking. Batenin said Moscow would continue to take political actions, including efforts through the United Nations. "But if interference is not stopped," he said, "despite the measures taken, and if the political efforts made by the USSR jointly with the United Nations do not succeed, we will find a means to meet our obligations as a guarantor of the Afghan settlement."

"Soviet and Afghan officials have said repeatedly that the bold violation of the Geneva accords by the Reagan administration . . . would not be allowed to continue long."

Contrary to the conclusions drawn in most western media reports, the new dangers may well have arisen not because of any weakening of the Afghan government's position, but because of its staying power. With the exception of the terror rocket attacks on population centers which do not alter military balance, the government forces appear to remain in control of the situation, the policy of national reconciliation is gaining acceptance, the international legitimacy of the Kabul government has been increasingly recognized internationally, and the Afghan armed forces have been strengthened. . . .

The extremists, or Dushmans, have yet to seize sufficient territory to proclaim a "government" on Afghan soil as they pledged to do months ago.

But not everything has gone well for government forces. The battle for the important city of Kunduz came close to being a major disaster. In August 1988, following the departure of most of the Soviet troops from the provincial capital, the city fell to the counterrevolutionaries. . . .

The situation around Kunduz appears to have reflected not so much a military problem as remaining persistent political problems and divisions among some government forces. "The past weeks also set a bitter lesson for us," Afghan President Najibullah said Aug. 28, 1988. "The developments in Kunduz demonstrated to the whole country what indecision, lack of consideration of security issues, conflicts between heads of provinces, alienation from the people and readiness to yield positions lead to."

Gorbachev described Afghan Prime Minister Mohammad Hassan Sharq as a leader representing very broad sections of Afghan society. The Soviet leader praised Sharq for agreeing to lead the country during the current "crucial phase."

In talks that proceeded with a "forthright and very frank exchange of opinions," Gorbachev and Sharq agreed on the need to push national reconciliation in Afghanistan more energetically.

Mutual Trust

The two leaders put emphasis on the mutual trust between the Prime Minister and President Najibullah, who also heads the leading People's Democratic Party of Afghanistan. The official report of the meeting said Gorbachev and Sharq agreed that the PDPA's role and place "depend on its constructiveness which is needed in the new conditions, with regard to the new nature of the system of power that will shape up in the course of political settlement."

Meanwhile Indian Prime Minister Rajiv Gandhi has expressed serious concern over Pakistan's actions toward Afghanistan. He warned that any attempt to install an Iran-type fundamentalist regime in the region with outside help would doom peace in Afghanistan and generate new tensions in the entire region.

"The future of Pakistan and the peace process in the region largely depend on whether Islamabad has enough will and determination to stop this war," said the Soviet Communist Party newspaper Pravda Sept. 15, 1988.

"It is at the bidding of the United States that Pakistan is building up tensions on the border with Afghanistan. There is ample evidence that, contrary to logic, Pakistan is getting bogged down in a direct military confrontation fraught with unforseen consequences for all nations in the region."

The People *is the biweekly newspaper of the Socialist Labor Party of America. Carl Bloice is the associate editor of the* People's Daily World, *a communist newspaper.*

"The profound democratic restructuring of our society compels us to raise and resolve human rights issues."

viewpoint 11

The USSR Supports Human Rights

Andrei Grachev

Only recently the term human rights as such did not appear in our press or political treatises without being placed between inverted commas or being preceded by the attribute "so-called." Hearing the words pronounced in debates with their foreign counterparts, our representatives would "recoil," preparing to give a resolute rebuff to "attacks on socialism" and attempts "to interfere in the internal affairs" of the socialist countries.

This defensive reaction reflected the misinterpretation of socialism widespread in the years of stagnation and in large measure inherited from the previous decades coloured by the personality cult. Karl Marx associated these views with the idea of crude communism everywhere repudiating the human personality and identifying it with "the preconceived minimum." The minimum of well-being, the minimum of social justice, the minimum of democracy.

Now, along with other truths of Marxism-Leninism, we are discovering for ourselves the correct attitude to the human rights problem.

Having defined the objective as building a self-governing democratic society, we are justified in striving to develop a community where each member is entitled to say, after Louis XIV: "L'Etat, c'est moi" (I am the state).

Accordingly, we urgently need to produce a mechanism that will ensure the realization of a socialist pluralism of opinions, guarantee the interests and protect the rights of each individual, consider the stands, opinions and views of all members of society and coordinate them with the public interest.

Unfortunately, due to our accumulated negative experience, we must now, to a great extent, in a sense rediscover the maxim expressed by V.I. Lenin: "Whoever wants to reach socialism by any other path than that of political democracy, will inevitably arrive at conclusions that are absurd and reactionary, both in the economic and the political sense." It goes without saying that the democratization of society is inconceivable without the guarantee and protection of human rights.

The new interest in the problem of human rights, the thorough and profound analysis of it with regard to all aspects of present norms in our society is in no sense to be understood as a concession to pressure from the West. The need for development and the profound democratic restructuring of our society compels us to raise and resolve human rights issues. In doing so, we do not intend to copy and blindly follow Western standards. Yet, at the same time, it would be wrong to ignore the democratic experience accumulated by bourgeois society. Socialism has no ambition to build an anti-world or anti-universe that in its every feature confronts the capitalist society from which it emerged and with which it severed itself as a result of the socialist revolution. The socialist system is a step forward that promotes everything genuinely humane and common to all mankind, everything amassed by previous forms of social organization.

Eliminating Stalinism

Socialism, with its genuine democratic and humanitarian vision regained, suggests its release from the gross distortions and deformations that were forced on it during Stalin's rule. What is at issue is not just the setting up of an impregnable barrier to safeguard us from the threat of any recurrence of the monstrous lawless practices and trampling on human rights perpetrated at that time but also the need to break down the administrative and command system we inherited from it. This system exists not only in the form of the

Andrei Grachev, "I Am the State," *New Times*, 1988, No. 34.

bureaucratic superstructure but also lives on deep in the collective consciousness in the shape of garbled ideas about the relationship between the individual and the state in a socialist society.

A concept has evolved in the minds of many people that civil and socio-economic rights are not a sovereign and inalienable attribute of each individual but something of a "gift" from the state and party leaders. The reverse of this mentality is social apathy, indifference and that form of parasitism where each believes that the government and state are there to take care of him.

This idea of how the machinery of socialist democracy works undermines the civic initiative of the masses and the social activity of each member of society and severs the interaction between rights and obligations which can be the only basis on which to ensure the fulfillment of the individual.

We also need to restore another integral whole that has been brutally torn apart—the whole consisting of socio-economic, civil and political rights of the individual. The artificial fragmentation of the human rights complex brought about a situation where the individual in a socialist society, "in return" for guaranteed social security, was alienated from the political process and participation in the mechanism of government.

Civil and political rights must assume a real and concrete, "fulfilled" character as has happened in the sphere of socio-economic rights. This must be underpinned by legal guarantees through the elaboration of the relevant laws furthering and concretizing some clauses and principles of the Soviet Constitution. This process has already begun and will be expedited according to the special resolution on legal reform adopted by the 19th Party Conference.

Impeccable Laws

However, the elaboration of the most impeccable laws and the more precise definition or even review of some constitutional provisions cannot ensure the complete solution of the problem that has been posed. In 1936 the country received a fairly democratic constitution which was, however, powerless to stand in the way of the orgy of repressions. It is necessary to establish a mechanism that will guarantee the application of the law and abidance by it as a fundamental rule governing the whole of public life. This can be achieved through the legal education of the population, "learning democracy," comprehensive compulsory instruction that must embrace both the administrative personnel of different Soviet institutions, party and public organizations (who make vital decisions related to living conditions), and the broadest strata of the ordinary people. We still do not know how to use the laws already in existence and are unable to claim protection of our rights, being accustomed only to grumbling about negligent managers or overzealous petty tyrants.

Belief must be restored in the effectiveness of democracy, the conviction that the individual's actions, opinions, and voice can influence both the further development of perestroika and concrete living and working conditions for each and all. The inability to resolve the problem of the democratic and civic education of the masses, and win back the citizen to active membership of socialist society will once again bog us down in that mire of social apathy and historical fatalism which is the breeding ground for personality cults.

"Civil and political rights must assume a real and concrete, 'fulfilled' character."

A socialist state governed by law is inconceivable without the assertion of the reciprocal responsibility of the state and its citizens for the observance of the law, the maintenance of public order, and guarantees of the whole spectrum of the citizen's political and civil freedoms and socio-economic rights.

Particular interest is also attached to the human rights issue in the broader sense of humanitarian cooperation, in the sphere of international relations. Such discussions arise in the course of diplomatic negotiations and other government and public contacts between East and West.

In recent years these spheres have been burdened with reciprocal propaganda considerations. The temptation was too strong on both sides to exploit human rights as a tool to gain an albeit short-lived but dazzling propaganda victory over the opponent.

There are objective factors, however, that stand in the way of dialogue and mutual understanding. Human rights issues are tied up with ideological confrontation, with often irreconcilable philosophical and political differences, and the desire to prove the superiority and advantages of one's own social system and one's own choice to the detriment of that of the opponent. Broadly speaking, specific human rights policies come under the jurisdiction of respective states and governments and these polemics, therefore, can very often be interpreted or presented as an attempt to interfere in each other's internal affairs.

There are also a great many artificial obstacles. For too long diplomats, followed by the press as well as the representatives of public organizations, have interpreted discussions raised in the West solely as an attempt at the ideological erosion of our social system or a topic of vicious propaganda campaigns. It should be admitted, however, that the West gave ample ground for such suspicions.

At the same time, the restrictive factor in our foreign policy was unquestionably our underestimation of the organic connection that nowadays exists between security and humanitarian cooperation. Having signed over 13 years ago, together with other European countries, the U.S. and Canada, the Final Act of the Helsinki Conference on Security and Cooperation in Europe, we treated it largely as a document consolidating the territorial-political realities of postwar Europe, ignoring the "third basket" and questions relating to humanitarian cooperation. And this was to a great extent because the West, in its turn, saw the document as the diametrical opposite, as it were, of our interpretation, regarding the Final Act as a document on human rights.

In a sense humanitarian cooperation is as much a part of the process of political détente as control systems are part and parcel of any disarmament accord. In both instances, what is at issue is strengthening the mutual understanding without which it is impossible to achieve understanding on issues of mutual security.

In an open society the state's foreign policy and its strategic intentions are predictable. Silent practices, however, and unnecessary secrecy give rise to suspicion on the part of partners and opponents alike, playing into the hands of forces opposed to the relaxation of tension and mutual understanding in their efforts to justify the buildup of tension and the arms race.

The paradox now is that whereas the Soviet Union is revising its backward approach to the issue of humanitarian contacts, the West, particularly the United States, is coming out with bitter ideologically-coloured appeals to free "the nations enslaved by communism," and whip up pressure on countries that have opted for socialism with a view to bringing them back to the realm of freedom.

Is cooperation between East and West possible in the sphere of human rights? Or is it doomed to remain a constant battleground for propaganda warfare, especially at a time when wars with the use of other weapons are, fortunately, becoming less and less likely? I should like to hope that cooperation in the humanitarian field is a reality. To achieve this, several simple conditions must be observed. We shall try to formulate them.

Commitment to Human Rights

First and foremost is the commitment to ensure human rights and their genuine implementation in one's own country. "Charity begins at home," as the familiar saying has it. The same goes for the sincerity of any foreign policy, or highly moral appeals to the other side, which must be underpinned by scrupulous and real work in putting one's own house in order.

Both sides should abandon attempts to reshape the other after its own likeness against the former's will. They should also give up the temptation to see in the opposite side a hangover from a past obsolescent world which is about to disappear. The experience of seventy years of coexistence shows that they will still be on this planet for a long time and this is why they should work out civilized rules for competition and the juxtaposition of their political and social experience.

"First and foremost is the commitment to ensure human rights and their genuine implementation in one's own country."

Both East and West have accumulated a great deal of experience in resolving the vital problems their societies encounter. Neither can claim to be perfect, and neither possesses the ultimate truth, or indeed, has a monopoly on it. Naturally, the foreseeable future does not and simply cannot hold out hope of doing away with the profound socio-political differences in approach and social practice that characterize the situation of how human rights are in reality ensured in the East and the West. This is, clearly, why the exchange of criticism on these aspects of social life should not be halted.

At the same time, humanitarian cooperation, different ways of resolving social issues, ensuring the political and civil rights of man, and creating the most favourable conditions for the realization of his individual abilities and creative potential could become an area for cooperation between states and people living in countries with different social systems the world over.

Andrei Grachev is a contributor to New Times, *a weekly Soviet newsmagazine.*

"Gorbachev's reforms are not, then, intended to lead to the democratization of Soviet society or to any true pluralism."

The USSR Does Not Support Human Rights

Natan Sharansky

Mikhail Gorbachev is a huge success in the West. Viewed as more honest, more talented, and more courageous than his predecessors, he has induced a euphoria in the media, in the public, and among politicians. He regularly bests Western leaders in public-opinion polls. He, not Ronald Reagan, is the hero of the arms-control agreement and his *glasnost* and *perestroika,* now securely ensconced in our language, are viewed as harbingers of even better things to come. The conventional wisdom is that he is on the right track, that while he cannot change everything at once ("he has opposition in the Kremlin and in the bureaucracy, you know") he will, given time and Western support, bring democracy and renewed vigor to the Soviet Union and peace to the world. Concomitantly, most seem to believe that the Soviet people, like a sleeping princess now awakening to the kiss of *glasnost,* are pining for Western-style democracy and ecstatically relish the daily broadening of their horizons.

There is something very winning in this optimistic view. But it fails to consider the genesis, purpose, and depth of Gorbachev's reforms, and it underestimates what generations of coercion, negligence, tyranny, and brutality have done to the soul of the Russian people.

Not that the reforms have been insignificant. Some have been dramatic and, in the context of Soviet society, even revolutionary. But a comparison with the upheaval which led to Nikita Khrushchev's rise to power in the 50's is instructive. Then, the KGB chief was executed, and the KGB's iron grip on the government and the populace was noticeably weakened. Hundreds of thousands were released from the gulag, exonerated, and rehabilitated.

Under Gorbachev the KGB may be more subtle and sophisticated, and careful to keep a low profile.

Natan Sharansky, "As I See Gorbachev." Reprinted from *Commentary,* March 1988, by permission: all rights reserved.

But there is no sign that its powers have been curtailed. With its blessing, and using *glasnost* as a license, Nazi-like anti-Semitic gangs have been allowed to organize and grow, to distribute *The Protocols of the Elders of Zion* freely, and to assault Jews in the streets, thus doing the KGB's dirty work without reflecting directly on the regime. Jailed refuseniks, known as "prisoners of Zion," and a few score of dissidents, mostly "celebrities" famous in the West, have been released, but there have been no admissions of error by the regime, and none of the falsely convicted has been rehabilitated. (The privilege of rehabilitation is now reserved for figures from the 20's and 30's who were murdered by Stalin and have been non-persons ever since.)

Unfortunate Victims

The less publicized victims have been less fortunate, however. Anatoli Marchenko and Alexsei Niktin, proponents of free trade unions, have died in prison, and Vladimir Klebanov, another labor activist, is lost somewhere in the psychiatric gulag. Vazif Meilanoff, who spent seven years in an isolation cell for the crime of protesting Andrei Sakharov's exile, is himself still in exile, and Leonid Lubman, who was arrested on trumped-up charges very similar to those used against me, and sentenced to the same term—thirteen years—is still in prison. The number of such prisoners is estimated at anywhere between 2,000 and 15,000, but only 500 of their names are known to Amnesty International. When Robert Bernstein, chairman of Helsinki Watch in America, asked Gorbachev why, after two-and-a-half years in power, he did not simply release all political prisoners, he replied, furiously, with a harangue about Americans shooting at Mexican "wetbacks."

Khrushchev, as it turned out, did indeed have strong opposition in the Kremlin—the KGB and other elements whose wings he clipped never forgave him.

But until he was finally toppled, rumors of rifts in the leadership were vehemently denied by the Kremlin. Now news of opposition to Gorbachev, a KGB protégé, usually *originates* in the Kremlin and is disseminated with great fanfare. The purpose, it seems, is not only to aver that unless he is supported abroad he will be overthrown at home, but to impart the impression that the Kremlin is just like any other government, with hawks and doves vying for influence.

Useful Comparisons

Another useful comparison can be drawn in the area of emigration—this time between Gorbachev the "reformer" and Brezhnev the "ruthless dictator." Under Gorbachev the number of Jewish applicants granted exit visas jumped from 1,000 in 1986 to 8,000 in 1987. Under *glasnost*-less Brezhnev, almost 300,000 Jews left the Soviet Union in the 1970's, 51,000 of them in the peak year of 1979.

It is testimony to Gorbachev's skill that the sudden but far from impressive increase in exit permits, accompanied by hints, winks, and veiled promises by Soviet officials to visiting Jewish leaders, gave rise to hopes of massive Jewish emigration. In the general euphoria, many failed to realize that the new Soviet emigration law enacted under Gorbachev is not designed to facilitate emigration but to terminate it. It limits eligibility for emigration to those who can receive invitations from blood relatives of the first degree living abroad—parents, children, or siblings. It thus excludes over 90 percent of the 400,000 Jews who have indicated their desire to leave.

"It is testimony to Gorbachev's skill that the sudden but far from impressive increase in exit permits . . . gave rise to hopes of massive Jewish emigration."

The Soviet authorities, now in a post-summit mode and flush with Gorbachev's popular success, are stringently enforcing these draconian restrictions. The new regulations also stipulate that of the 10 percent eligible to apply, those who possess "state secrets" would automatically be turned down. (The Soviets have applied this restriction to, among others, a seventy-four-year-old widow whose mathematician husband died seventeen years ago, under the pretext that he might have left her "state secrets.")

Not surprisingly, the number of would-be emigrants now refused visas on these grounds has drastically increased, and some old-time refuseniks have been notified that previous reasons for rejecting their applications have been canceled only to be replaced by "security considerations." Even relatives of such refuseniks, known in the dark humor of Jewish activists as "genetic security risks," are thus excluded. And since applying under these conditions courts being branded a traitor willing to compromise state secrets, a potential applicant would have to contemplate the possibility not only of being fired and harassed and of living in limbo for many years but imprisonment for treason. The few who succeed in getting through this sieve are required to provide an affidavit from all relatives, including in-laws and ex in-laws, that there are no financial claims against them. A brand-new regulation stipulates that they must pass a psychiatric examination to ascertain their sanity before they can exit.

The Universal Declaration

Lest it be forgotten, the Universal Declaration on Human Rights, reaffirmed in the Helsinki accords, to which the USSR is a signatory, clearly states that the right to leave any country, including one's own, is a basic human right. Contracts obviously mean different things to different people. Or, as the Communist party spokesman put it in Washington, "Your suit wouldn't suit me and my suit wouldn't suit you."

The one area in which *glasnost* has had to "give" more is the field of communications and the arts. Even seventy years of primitive conformism have not completely destroyed the Russian genius in literature, music, and dance, or suppressed the ferment among the intelligentsia and artistic community. To assuage the envy with which the Soviet intelligentsia view the freedom their colleagues in other Communist countries have been enjoying for decades, creative editors have been appointed at newspapers and magazines, and such subjects as crime, drug addiction, corruption, the Afghan war, and even—though rarely—anti-Semitism, all hitherto virtually taboo, are now discussed. Some banned dead writers, including Boris Pasternak, Mikhail Bulgakov, and Vladimir Nabokov can now be read, and even a live émigré, Nobel-prize-winner Joseph Brodsky, is being published. Marc Chagall's paintings, previously considered prime examples of "bourgeois decadence," were exhibited in Moscow, albeit without mentioning his Jewishness, and the movie *Repentance*, a potent denunciation of Stalinist terror, though still cautious enough never to mention him by name, is a big hit. The restless energies of Soviet youth, for whom anything Western is a seductive symbol of liberty, have been placated by the legitimizing of rock, jazz, and jeans.

Other foreign influences, however, have not fared so well. At [1987's] Moscow book fair, forty English-language books and twenty Russian books published outside the USSR were confiscated, and foreign artists of whose affiliations and sympathies the Soviet Union does not approve, including such luminaries as Leonard Bernstein, Zubin Mehta,

Itzhak Perlman, and Daniel Barenboim, cannot perform there.

The traditional fear of foreign influence is matched by the traditional horror of demonstrations and rallies, and of the uncontrollable momentum they might create. When a large group of Tatars, a people exiled by the Soviet authorities from their land during World War II and never allowed to return, tried to demonstrate in front of the Kremlin, they were forcibly packed into buses and driven away. When a hundred refuseniks gathered in Moscow on the day a quarter of a million Jews marched in Washington to demand free emigration for Soviet Jews, they were roughed up by 200 agents of the KGB and dispersed. Peaceful protests of Jewish women in Moscow and Leningrad, by Latvians in Riga, and Kazakhs in Alma Ata, were also forcibly put down.

> "When a hundred refuseniks gathered in Moscow on the day a quarter of a million Jews marched in Washington to demand free emigration for Soviet Jews, they were roughed up by 200 agents of the KGB and dispersed."

What is discouraging about these incidents is not that they were suppressed, but that the grabbings at the crumbs of freedom have been so few. Almost all have been expressions of national and ethnic aspirations by minorities, not a surge for liberty by the majority. This tends to confirm the pessimistic view that the apathy, fatalism, and cynicism that permeate the Soviet Union make a groundswell for greater liberty—something like the momentum for liberalization which occurred in Poland during the heyday of Solidarity—quite unlikely. Alexander Zinoviev describes the new Soviet man as an empty vessel unable to think or revolt, ignorant of the world and his own history, and conditioned to believe not that what the authorities tell him is *true* but that it must be accepted as an inevitable part of life, the way one accepts rain. And, indeed, not only the authorities consider citizens cogs in the wheel of the state, the people so consider themselves too. The Western notion that the government is subject to the constraints of law is alien to the Soviet citizen. The government *is* the law. It can grant rights to its subjects and it can take them away. It can be benevolent and it can be cruel. But, by definition, it cannot violate the law. Gorbachev has not changed this principle, nor can he do so within the framework of the system. All he has done is to increase the number of gifts the government is currently willing to bestow.

The "credit" for creating such passivity and conformity should perhaps not be given exclusively to the Communist regime. The czars, although far more liberal in allowing foreign contacts and emigration, deserve at least part of it. A decade before the Bolshevik takeover, the Stolypin reforms encouraged peasants to emerge from feudal "collectivism" and adopt free-enterprise methods. The reforms were an abysmal failure because, among other reasons, those who established successful independent farms were assaulted by fellow peasants who considered the communal tenure of the feudal village the only just and egalitarian system.

The Prospects of Perestroika

This kind of attitude puts the prospects of Gorbachev's *perestroika* into question. Gorbachev wants to introduce a modicum of free enterprise, create new incentives to prod people of talent and intelligence, and allow efficiency and productivity, rather than bureaucratic inertia, to determine the survival of plants and factories. He wants to do this without giving up the power to dictate, without a real decentralization of economic planning, and, needless to say, without allowing market forces of supply and demand into play. His reforms, at least initially, will mean more work and less vodka, higher prices and lower wages, and the dislocation of workers and unemployment. They will require enthusiasm, enterprise, and a lot of popular trust in the party-created ruling class, which is just as remote from the masses and just as privileged as the czars and noblemen who preceded them. It is a tall order.

The generalizations about the Soviet populace do not usually apply to Jews. Perhaps because they have always been considered outsiders, or because their own cultural heritage served as a powerful counterinfluence, the Jews never quite accepted enforced conformity and the obliteration of individualism. Ever since emerging from the ghetto they have tended to push for change, and the number of Jews who participated in revolution and upheaval was always grossly disproportionate to their percentage in the population. But in times of retrenchment, their effervescence was deemed dangerous, and they have never been considered loyal Soviet citizens. Much is being said about the possibility, the logic of which is seemingly unassailable, that Gorbachev will attempt to make life in the USSR so attractive for Jews that they will not want to leave. For most, the freedom to study Hebrew and worship in a synagogue is less important than the prospect of attending a good university and attaining a high professional position. But it is doubtful that they will be given these opportunities.

Gorbachev's reforms are not, then, intended to lead to the democratization of Soviet society or to any true pluralism. As he himself told the French-USSR Friendship Society, "We openly say that nobody will be allowed to act against socialism."

"The reforms are dictated, rather, by the need to invigorate the Soviet economy, now in one of its worst slumps since the 1920's, and to reverse its decline."

The reforms are dictated, rather, by the need to invigorate the Soviet economy, now in one of its worst slumps since the 1920's, and to reverse its decline. International factors, like the crash in oil prices, which has caused Soviet indebtedness to the West to rise to $40 billion (it may reach $60 billion by 1990), as well as industrial inefficiency, corruption, backwardness and sloth, and a lopsided defense and space-exploration budget, threaten to make the economic gap between the USSR and the West unbridgeable. Even if *perestroika* succeeds beyond expectations, the modernization of the economy cannot be achieved without Western help. The official bluster about the inevitability of socialist victory over capitalism notwithstanding, the Soviet leaders know that the limitations inherent in the Soviet system preclude successful competition with the West. But the West, wary of dark dictatorships, must be assured of Soviet benignity. As Gorbachev put it on the 70th anniversary of the October Revolution, "[Our reforms] are eliminating the fear of the 'Soviet threat.'" . . .

The West's Response

Many conclude from this recent history that the Western response to Soviet reforms and gestures of rapprochement should not be one of conciliation and assistance, but of rejection and boycott, and that the troubled Soviet economy should not be rescued again the way it was salvaged in the 20's, 40's, and 70's by Western assistance, but allowed to collapse. Only thus, the reasoning goes, can today's totalitarian threat to the democracies be removed.

But to expect the West to launch a successful boycott of the Soviet Union in today's world is not realistic. The Soviets have managed to circumvent even so watertight a constraint as the Stevenson amendment, which prohibits the U.S. Export-Import bank from granting Moscow taxpayer-subsidized trade credits. By going directly to major banks, they have received billions of dollars at ridiculously low interest rates in untied loans, not linked to any specific trade deal or project. The question is not whether or not there will be deals with the Soviets but under what conditions and with what results.

Gorbachev is the most pragmatic and most realistic of all Soviet dictators. As his reversal of the Soviet attitude to arms negotiations following the positioning of American Pershing missiles in Europe showed, he has more respect for facts than for doctrine, and if an initial idea fails, he will cast about for others. Skillful in gauging and manipulating the public mood in the West, he can become more dangerous than his predecessors. But his realism also gives room for hope, for it should enable him correctly to assess his regime's weaknesses and the real power of his adversaries. That is why it is vitally important to expose his deceptions and demonstrate massive opposition to his policies. The march of 250,000 Jews in Washington before [the] December [1986] summit, decrying Soviet violations of human-rights treaties and the ongoing refusal to allow Jewish emigration, aimed at doing just that. It also showed that the gut reaction of people is sometimes healthier than that of politicians.

Natan (formerly Anatoly) Sharansky is a Jewish leader and human-rights activist who spent nine years in Soviet prisons. His book, Fear No Evil, *was published in 1988 by Random House.*

"Gorbachev is wooing long-suffering believers... with hints and promises of greater religious freedom."

viewpoint 13

Religious Freedom in the USSR: An Overview

Kenneth L. Woodward

It was like a medieval fresco suddenly come to life: Byzantine archbishops in conical caps, bearded bishops in tubular headdresses of black and white, cardinals from the Vatican shouldering crimson capes—plus evangelist Billy Graham in his best Baptist threads. All converged on Moscow to celebrate the moment, a millennium ago, when Prince Vladimir of Kiev introduced Christianity into what is now the Soviet Union. Although Pope John Paul II was absent, his secretary of state delivered a letter from the Roman pontiff to party Secretary Mikhail Gorbachev, who recently signaled a new era of tolerance for religion by meeting publicly with Russian Orthodox Church leaders. There was a concert at the Bolshoi theater attended by Mrs. Gorbachev and a lengthy liturgy at the Cathedral of the Epiphany which tired many non-Orthodox guests. "I can't stand for four hours," said Roman Catholic Bishop Vilhelms Nukss of Latvia. "It's not in our tradition."

The Least of Paradoxes

That all this ecclesiastical pomp took place in the world's first militantly atheistic state was the least of [the] paradoxes. Despite seven decades of systematic oppression and control by the state, religious faith is more vital in the Soviet Union than it is in England, Sweden or any other unfettered democracy of Northern Europe. An estimated 40 to 60 percent of the nation's 285 million citizens are believers. But except for the elderly, who have nothing to lose, most stay away from church—other than on major feast days—for fear of jeopardizing jobs and careers. Of these largely secret believers, between 50 million and 90 million are Russian Orthodox; an additional 10 million are Catholics—more than half of them members of the underground church in the Ukraine—and roughly 4 million adhere to various Protestant churches. Among non-Christians, about 60 million are Muslims.

At the same time, there are strong signs that atheism in the Soviet Union has decayed into the anemic agnosticism typical of the secularized West. Dialectical materialism, the philosophy on which Marxist atheism is based, has lost its power to command intellectual assent. Courses in Scientific Atheism, required of all university undergraduates except science majors, are widely dismissed by students as simplistic, antireligious apologetics. Participation in the atheistic Young Communist League (Komsomol), once considered indispensable for any young man or woman with career ambitions, has fallen off.

None of this would be so evident to outsiders if the Soviet economy were not a shambles and *glasnost* the order of the day. To help rally popular support for his economic restructuring, Gorbachev is wooing long-suffering believers—and their coreligionists in the West—with hints and promises of greater religious freedom. "There can be no economic success without democratization and no democratization without freedom of conscience," says Alexander Nezhny, a journalist whose specialty, religious affairs, for the weekly *Moscow News*, is itself a symbol of change. But for all the signs of change, some facts remain the same: "We cannot say that the church is free in this society," says Nezhny.

The Communists

In truth, the communists were not the first to shackle the Russian church to the state. In 1721, Czar Peter the Great reduced the church to a department of the government; the bishops reported to a lay "overprocurator" (overseer) who reported directly to Peter. Catherine the Great, in turn, confiscated the church's estates. In this century, Lenin allowed the church a brief moment of

Kenneth L. Woodward, "Can Glasnost and God Coexist?" From *Newsweek*, June 20, 1988. © 1988, Newsweek, Inc. All rights reserved. Reprinted by permission.

independence in 1917, then nationalized church property and declared war on religious faith as "a kind of spiritual gin in which slaves drown their human shape." In the '30s, Stalin killed, imprisoned or exiled an estimated 66 million clergy, nuns and lay believers, and closed all but a handful of churches. When Hitler invaded in 1941, Stalin allowed thousands of churches to reopen as a way to build up morale. Beginning in 1964, Nikita Khrushchev again suppressed organized religion by closing 15,000 churches.

Today religious activities are still governed by draconian statutes promulgated by Stalin in 1929 and administered by the ubiquitous Council for Religious Affairs (CRA). Although the Soviet Constitution guarantees freedom of religion, atheism is the only creed that enjoys the full protection of law. Under the Stalinist statutes, the separation of church and state has become in reality the separation of church from society, and religion from child rearing. "A child from a religious family," observes a Komsomol deputy in the Ukraine, "soon feels alone at school when he sees that his classmates are happy without believing in God."

In essence, believers are allowed only the freedom to pray—by themselves at home or together at services inside a church. Clergy are forbidden to hold religion classes in or outside church buildings for children under 18 years of age. Ministers may visit the terminally ill but only with the permission of local government authorities. Pilgrimages and religious funerals away from church buildings are prohibited. Religious proselytizing is unlawful though atheist propaganda is encouraged. Recently, churches have been allowed to import Bibles, but in 70 years, only 350,000 copies have been printed in the Soviet Union.

The CRA controls the nation's 6,800 Russian Orthodox churches from above and from below. Appointments and other major decisions of the hierarchy are cleared in advance with CRA officials; activities of individual bishops are monitored closely and each is rated according to his willingness to cooperate with the state. At the same time, each individual religious congregation—whether Christian, Muslim, Buddhist or Jewish—is subject to control by local CRA officials. Effective preachers or pastors who prove too popular with the young are routinely reassigned. And in small cities and towns infested with gossips and other informers, workers who attend church risk retribution from their superiors.

Secret Societies

Religious dissidents have for decades exposed the state's routine suppression of the church and criticized the highest-ranking bishops as toadies of the government. "In the Soviet Union we have two secret societies—the KGB and the Russian Orthodox Church," says Alexander Ogorodnikov, 33, a prominent Russian Orthodox layman who edits a dissident news bulletin. Orthodoxy's leaders continue to deny the dissident's accusations—but unintentionally buttress the critics' charges in their actions. In a rare interview with Izvestia, Patriarch Pimen of Moscow, head of the Russian Orthodox Church, recently praised the programs of Soviet socialism as "close to Christian ideals" and denounced dissident priests and laymen. "As a rule," Pimen said, "these people criticize the church leadership and take upon themselves the right to express outside what they assume to be the true interest of all believers, and pit themselves against the entire church."

"Religious dissidents have for decades exposed the state's routine suppression of the church and criticized the highest-ranking bishops as toadies of the government."

But now, to the embarrassment of Orthodoxy's hierarchs, even government officials admit that they have tried to choke religious faith by controlling the clergy. In a surprisingly frank speech to teachers at a Communist Party school, CRA chief Konstantin Kharchov declared, "We cut off the priest from believers but this did not make believers trust local authorities any more, and the party and the state are losing more and more control." He was especially critical of party officials who harass believers in their private lives and refuse to allow the reopening of churches. There are, he said, 1,000 communities pleading for permission to open a church.

In his rambling lecture, which was surreptitiously taped, Kharchov expressed considerable contempt for the tamed Russian church and fears about the advent of others. "Despite the fact that the activities of the Russian Orthodox Church are controlled and restricted, and its initiative is no cause for fear— although even a kicked-around mongrel's patience is not boundless—there is concern about the strengthening of other churches," he said. "In the past we suppressed the Russian Orthodox Church and did not curb the sectarians since we were afraid they would go underground and we would lose control of them altogether. But after all, Catholics, Protestants, Adventists and others have centers and administrative bodies beyond the reach of Soviet rule, and therefore their rapid growth is fraught with unpredictable consequences."

Among Protestants, the Baptists have proved to be the most aggressive in claiming religious rights. At the Baptist church in Leningrad, which serves 5,000 faithful, the elders circumvent the law against religious instruction by holding Bible classes for children and Wednesday-night dialogues with atheists in their basement tearoom. Until recently churches were also forbidden to do charity work. But in Moscow, women Baptist volunteers wearing religious insignia already work with elderly patients in a state hospital.

Soviet Jews

Soviet Jews, by contrast, have no national organization, no seminary to train rabbis or cantors and, given the Soviet's attitude toward the State of Israel, no formal ties to a religious center outside the U.S.S.R. Although Soviet Judaism is Orthodox—about 10 to 20 percent of the 2.5 million Jews are believers—strict observance of Jewish law is virtually impossible. For instance, there are 100 synagogues scattered across the U.S.S.R. but only two ritual slaughterers, both in Moscow. Studying the Bible is possible, if you can find one, but not in Hebrew: Jews are not permitted to study Hebrew, although Gentile scholars are free to do so.

For the Soviet government, the most troublesome Christians are in the Ukraine, where Vladimir brought his message of good news 1,000 years ago and the fires of faith and nationalism still burn with fierce intensity. Two-thirds of all the Orthodox churches are in the Ukraine and they supply 85 percent of Orthodox seminarians. Half the Baptist churches are also in the Ukraine. In the western end of the republic some 7 million Catholics identify with the underground Uniate Church, which combines Orthodox rituals with loyalty to the papacy. Many of these Ukrainian Catholics worship in Orthodox churches, but only because the state refuses to grant their own church legal status. "Besides, the Russian Orthodox bishops will never allow it," says dissident Orthodox editor Serge Naboka of Kiev, "because they would lose half their people to the Catholics."

Nonetheless, Gorbachev's call for greater democracy has given believers of all kinds reasons to hope. Under his reformist regime, four monasteries have been returned to the Orthodox Church, religion is openly discussed in the media and party leaders say that universities will no longer require applicants to produce proof of membership in the Komsomol when they take entrance exams. Still, believing parents remain wary—for themselves and for their children.

Aleksei Zolessky, 51, is one of the many unheralded heroes of Russian Christianity who have quietly put religious faith ahead of personal ambition. A professor and translator of French and German for 15 years, Aleksei resigned from the intelligentsia when he became an Orthodox Christian. Now he works as a manual laborer. His rationale: "The risk of faith depends on where you work. As an intellectual, they can manipulate you but as an ordinary worker, they can do nothing to me."

Aleksei's wife, Tina, is a psychologist in Moscow and at the age of 40 is pregnant with their sixth child. Their eldest son, Aleksei, 12, says that most of his classmates have been baptized but do not go to church as he does. When the son was discovered wearing a cross around his neck in class, the teacher called to find out if this was something his babushka (grandmother) had made him do. Grandmothers are renowned as the mentors of religion in Russian families, but with young Aleksei the opposite is true: his babushkas were raised as atheists under Stalin and worry that their believing grandchildren will become social pariahs. Aleksei's father explained that he was raising his children as Christians, and the teacher backed off, asking only that Aleksei not display his cross lest other children be influenced by his example.

"Gorbachev's call for greater democracy has given believers of all kinds reasons to hope."

Katya B. (the family does not want its name used) is luckier. Her father, a convert to Orthodoxy, has risked imprisonment by organizing a neighborhood Sunday school in which his daughter has not only learned the basics of her religion but also acquired friends whom she can look to for support. "We are a Christian family," Katya's mother says, "but we live in a society that thinks that because of this we are disloyal." Her mother worries about what will happen when Katya goes away to university, and harbors fears about a mixed marriage: what if Katya falls for an atheist?

For Soviet believers, the test of *perestroika* is whether Gorbachev can make good on his pledge to pass a substantive law guaranteeing freedom of conscience. Legal scholar Yuri Rozenbaum, a member of the prestigious Soviet Academy of Sciences and the Institute of State and Law, has drafted such a law. It would give religious organizations juridical status which, he argues, would allow Sunday schools for children, permit believers to publish books and broadcast religious programs and thus exercise real separation from the state. But Rozenbaum, an atheist himself, warns that representatives of the Soviet Council of Ministers have drafted a counterlaw, now being debated behind closed doors, which leaves current restrictive statutes essentially intact.

Indeed, Gorbachev's strategy seems aimed at producing just enough democracy to win the political allegiance of believers while keeping the churches firmly in check. As Kharchov explained it to party loyalists, "whether we like it or not, religion . . . is driving in like a train on a track. And since power belongs completely to us, I think we are capable of pointing this track in whatever direction is in our interest."

In the Soviet Union, the body politic will undoubtedly remain officially atheistic. But after 1,000 years, the soul of Russia—and many other Soviet republics—is still animated by religious faith. To millions of believers, icons remain windows to the transcendent, the liturgy the collective voice of redeemed humanity and the church the one sacred oasis in a dreary work society where the spirit can clap hands and rejoice.

Kenneth L. Woodward is a senior writer at Newsweek, *a weekly newsmagazine.*

"Despite the massive release of prisoners of conscience, Soviet persecution of religion remains widespread."

viewpoint 14

The Soviet Union Represses Religion

Andrew Sorokowski

It was Christmas eve in Kalynivka, a village in the Lvov region of the southwestern USSR. The church was packed with some 250 worshipers attending the midnight service. Father Petro Zelenyuk, a Ukrainian Catholic priest, celebrated the mass long into the early morning hours as the congregation sang the responses. At about 3 A.M. there was a commotion. Someone began shouting to the people to disperse. Several men made their way to the altar and tried to stop the service. The parishioners recognized them as local Communist Party officials, schoolteachers, and antireligious activists, led by the regional plenipotentiary of the state Council on Religious Affairs. One of the activists started trying to jostle people out of the church. A young man pushed him, and a scuffle broke out. The activists called the police, who reportedly made several arrests.

One morning a month later Nijole Sadunaite, a well-known Lithuanian Catholic and former prisoner of conscience, was trying to make a call at a telephone booth in Vilnius. She was planning to attend a service that day in memory of Fr. Juozas Zdebskis, a priest who died two years ago after being hit by a car. Suddenly a man came up and began to abuse and threaten her. Sadunaite walked away, but later that morning two men attacked her companion. One of them punched her hard in the stomach. Passers-by intervened, but Sadunaite suffered ill effects for some time after. Official involvement is suspected.

Such scenes hardly enhance the liberal image that the Soviet government is so anxious to project. It is particularly inappropriate this year, when massive celebrations of the millennium of Christianity in the East Slavic lands are to be held in Moscow and other Soviet cities.

Andrew Sorokowski, "Millennial Propaganda Hides Soviet Repression." This article appeared in the June 1988 issue and is reprinted with permission from *The World & I*, a publication of the Washington Times Corporation, copyright © 1988.

Yet these are not isolated incidents. Sadunaite is one of many Lithuanian Catholic activists who continue to be persecuted. Among them are Fr. Alfonsas Svarinskas, who was reported [in] February [1988] to be among the 100 prisoners confined in corrective labor colony VS 389/35 in Perm, deep in the Russian interior, and his fellow-prisoner Fr. Sigitas Tamkevicius, whose whereabouts were not certain. While not illegal, the Catholic Church in Lithuania is severely restricted. The highly popular Archbishop Steponavicius has been confined for some 27 years to an isolated village. During the recent observances of Lithuania's 600th anniversary as a Christian nation, priests were forbidden to travel to or from Rome.

Zelenyuk's parish belongs to a church that the Soviet authorities brutally attacked in 1945-46 and whose existence they have refused to recognize ever since. The Ukrainian Catholic Church has 10 bishops, several hundred priests, and possibly four million faithful. Yet since the church cannot legally function, every religious gathering is fraught with danger. Priests are regularly fined or arrested for conducting services, and several have been murdered.

Persecution Remains

Despite the massive release of prisoners of conscience, Soviet persecution of religion remains widespread. It also varies in kind and degree. Near one end of the spectrum are violent incidents like those described above, and the confinement of believers in prison camps. Konstantin Kharchev, head of the Soviet Council on Religious Affairs, promised that all Soviet "prisoners of belief" would be released by November 1987. But at an informal human rights consultation in the Netherlands in January 1988, Western representatives claimed that there were as many as 260 religious prisoners still left in the USSR. Keston College, a British research center that monitors religious life in the USSR and Eastern Europe, reports that as of November 1988, 255 persons were imprisoned in the Soviet Union for their religious beliefs; a more recent estimate counts 220. Among them are inmates of Perm labor camp VS 389/35 such as Orthodox deacon Vladimir Rusak, and those sent into "internal exile," like Orthodox lawyer Lev Lukianenko, a veteran of 25 years of religious and political imprisonment who is now living in the Tomsk region of Russia.

Petty Harassment

At the other end of the spectrum of persecution is the petty harassment of individuals like Baptist Anatoli Ivashchenki, who was recently refused permission to emigrate. In between is a whole range of discriminatory practices in education, employment, and housing.

At the Netherlands consultation, Soviet representatives did admit to having imprisoned 18 believers for violating the laws on religion. However, the USSR has never admitted imprisoning anyone solely on the basis of his beliefs. When confronted with a well-documented case, they claim that the individual in question either violated the laws on religion or was engaging in proscribed political activity.

The latter charge is typically made against members of national minorities like Lithuanians or Ukrainians, whose religious convictions are often bound up with their belief in national self-determination. But the alleged political activity usually consists of oral statements or writings—the sort of conduct protected by the Universal Declaration of Human Rights, the International Covenant on Civil and Political Rights, and the Helsinki Final Act.

As for the allegation that religious prisoners of conscience have violated the laws on religion, often this is literally true. As Soviet representatives are fond of pointing out, religious belief pure and simple is not illegal in the USSR. Certain kinds of religiously motivated conduct, however, are forbidden. This, of course, is the case in every country. The question is to what degree the practice of religion is restricted, by law and in fact. Countries vary considerably in this respect; the Soviet Union is still among the most repressive.

In Violation

Zelenyuk, for example, was apparently in violation of the law because neither he nor his parish is registered with the authorities, as required by the Law on Religious Associations. However, there is nothing in the law to compel the authorities to register a parish or even to give reasons for their refusal to do so. The Soviet authorities have consistently refused to register Ukrainian Catholic parishes. This comports ill with the declarations of freedom and conscience and religious practice, of separation of church and state, and of the prohibition of religious discrimination enshrined in the USSR Constitution. In effect, the Law on Religious Associations permits abuses that are inconsistent with constitutional law.

"The law actually contradicts the constitutional guarantee of freedom of conscience."

Furthermore, the law actually contradicts the constitutional guarantee of freedom of conscience. Article 17 specifically bans a whole range of activities in which many religious believers are conscience-bound to engage, such as charitable and educational work. A religious association may not even organize a Sunday school, a reading-room, or a sewing club. The apparent intent of this law is to contain religion as much as possible, preventing it from exerting any influence on society. Originally, Article 17 was aimed at evangelicals, to whom proselytizing is a principal Christian duty. In fact, today many evangelical congregations refuse to register under this statute, preferring constant harassment to compliance with what they believe to be anti-Christian laws. However, many Orthodox and Catholics also consider the Law on Religious Associations as unduly restrictive of normal religious activity.

Criminal laws, too, are frequently applied against religious believers. These are often vague in their wording and unconscionably broad in their application. Two articles of the Criminal Code are specifically aimed at religious believers—one on "violation of the legislation on separation of Church and State and School from Church" and the other, originally intended for use against Pentecostals, on "infringement of the person or rights of citizens under the guise of performing religious rituals." In other cases, articles of the code concerning crimes against the state are applied—particularly the prohibition of "anti-Soviet agitation and propaganda" and "slandering the Soviet state and social order." Such broad notions of criminality cannot easily be reconciled with international standards of civil liberties.

Hinting at Reform

Having had this pointed out to them at various international forums, Soviet representatives have been hinting lately at reform or repeal of these statutes. They have also indicated that the Law on Religious Associations would be amended this year. But until this happens, they can continue to claim that their religious prisoners are mere lawbreakers.

Unfair laws are not, of course, the whole problem. De facto discrimination against religious believers is a common feature of Soviet reality. Furthermore, the Law on Religious Associations leaves the local authorities considerable opportunity to manipulate church life. Using their supervisory powers and their influence over the personnel and finances of parish executive committees, the local Soviets of People's Deputies can and often do carry on "effective atheist work" by sowing discord in religious communities, weakening them to the point of extinction. By covertly placing an atheist on a parish committee, they can, for example, arrange for the appointment of a weak or dissolute priest, thus demoralizing the congregation and undermining its faith.

Before there can be a reasonable degree of religious freedom in the USSR, Soviet practices as well as Soviet legislation will have to change.

A curious feature of the Soviet laws on religion is that they do not actually recognize any church as such. The recognized entities are "groups of believers" and "religious associations," and the Law on Religious Associations also mentions religious centers and eparchial (diocesan) administrations. But no church has legal standing as an institution—not even the Russian Orthodox Church. . . .

"Before there can be a reasonable degree of religious freedom in the USSR, Soviet practices as well as Soviet legislation will have to change."

That the Orthodox Church's privileges have no basis in law, but are entirely dependent on the good will of the state, belies their purpose. For they are contingent on the good behavior of the Russian Orthodox hierarchs, as monitored by the Council on Religious Affairs. Good behavior involves frequent pronouncements in support of Soviet foreign policy, particularly its "peace" initiatives, as well as praise of Soviet religious liberty, condemnation of the United States and other Western countries for escalating the arms race, and close contacts with Orthodox and other churches in the West. It means taking advantage of the ecumenical movement and particularly the World Council of Churches in order to extend Soviet influence. Good behavior at home means restraining overly active or popular priests and believers and ensuring that religion remains confined to the rites performed in registered church buildings. In return, the hierarchs are permitted to survive—a privilege richly appreciated by those who, like the present Patriarch Pimen, can remember the antireligious terror of the twenties and thirties.

The Russian Orthodox hierarchs can speak before an international forum. . . . They will center on the first council that the Russian church has been allowed to hold since 1971, and only the third since the Bolsheviks consolidated their rule. In anticipation of the event, the Soviet government has returned the Danilov Monastery in Moscow to the church. Lately, a number of articles favorable to Russian Orthodoxy—some even written by clerics— have appeared in the Soviet press. Churches are being renovated and reopened. Bibles are being printed. Even the persecution of ordinary Russian Orthodox believers seems to have abated. . . .

Historical Claims

To establish their historical claims, the Soviet state and the Russian Orthodox Church must eliminate their rival claimants. The Byelorussian and Ukrainian nations are rather more convincing successors to Kievan Rus'—particularly the Ukrainians, whose capital is none other than Kiev. Their churches, both Orthodox and Catholic, perpetuate the Byzantine traditions developed in the Kievan realm.

As it happens, these churches are banned in the USSR, and the Moscow Patriarchate has taken over their parishes. The final act in their tragedy was the official liquidation of the Ukrainian Catholic Church—the only one surviving underground today—in 1945-49. Not surprisingly, the Moscow Patriarchate, itself resuscitated by Stalin only two years earlier, played an important role in this travesty, and it continues to congratulate itself on its success. . . .

The Soviet government understands the power of history. It knows that obliterating the memory of a people or its church is an effective tool in their neutralization. The Moscow Patriarchate has long served to eliminate political opposition to the regime by russifying the non-Russians and converting the non-Orthodox. Now it is helping the party to rewrite history, erasing from memory the sources of contemporary challenges to Soviet legitimacy.

Andrew Sorokowski is a writer who specializes in Soviet religious history and current affairs.

"Facts of our everyday life bear witness that the claims about the Church being oppressed in the USSR are not objective."

viewpoint 15

The Soviet Union Does Not Repress Religion

Pimen, interviewed by *World Marxist Review*

Could you describe the relations between the Orthodox Church and the socialist state, and the concrete areas and forms in which cooperation has proceeded, whether at home or in international affairs? How true are the claims that the Church in the USSR [Union of Soviet Socialist Republics] is being persecuted and the rights of the faithful are being violated?

I should say that the relations between our Church and the state are now quite normal. The decree on the separation of church and state, and of school from church is now 70 years old. We regard that as being natural, because church and state differ in nature. We have every opportunity for the pursuit of our ministry in accordance with ecclesiastical tradition.

The state has, at the same time, done everything necessary to ensure the vital activity of the Church, and has met its daily needs, such as the appropriation of funds for the building and restoration of churches, made available premises and materials for the making of church utensils, newsprint and printing works for its publications, and so on.

In response to our request, the Soviet government transferred to us in 1983 St. Daniel's Monastery in Moscow, on whose territory a monastery has been restored and the administrative and spiritual centre of the Russian Orthodox Church is being created. Two other cloisters were recently transferred to us: The Novovvedenskaya Optina hermitage in the Kaluga Diocese, an outstanding centre of spiritual life in Russia, and the Tolgsky Convent in the Yaroslavl Diocese, which is to be the home of priests and other members of the clergy who are advanced in years and who are in need of care and nursing.

These and many other facts of our everyday life bear witness that the claims about the Church being oppressed in the USSR are not objective. Cases of breaches of the rights of believers do occur, but these are, as a rule, the result of departures from legislation by individuals or local authorities. Breaches of the law on the part of religious organisations likewise occur. The central press has reported on these conflicts and has given them due assessment.

Normal Relations

The observance of religious legislation is the concern of the Council for the Affairs of Religions under the USSR Council of Ministers, and it also conducts relations between the Church and the state, which are normal businesslike relations. We have always met with mutual understanding and support on the part of the Council for the Affairs of Religions.

As for the cooperation between believers and atheists, I should like to note, first of all, that, while the Church is separated from the state, believers are full-fledged citizens of our state and are involved in various aspects of their country's life on a par with other citizens.

This cooperation is multifaceted. Believers, the parishes, the dioceses, the Supreme Church Administration and the entire Church have always actively responded to the problems faced by society, they have not kept aloof from the solution of vital problems, and are daily involved in the country's affairs—morally, through material donations, and by their labour.

The Russian Orthodox Church is an active participant in many social organisations. The Soviet Peace Committee, the Soviet Peace Fund, the Soviet Committee for European Security and Cooperation, the Union of Soviet Societies for Friendship and Cultural Relations with Foreign Countries, the Culture Fund, the Soviet Children's Fund and other bodies have among their members many dignitaries

Pimen, "The Church, Freedom of Conscience, Peacemaking," *World Marxist Review*, June 1988. Reprinted with permission of *World Marxist Review* published by Progress Books (Toronto).

and clerical and lay members of the Russian Orthodox Church, who have been making a fruitful contribution to their activity.

Our readers would like to know about the attitude of the Orthodox Church to the socialist way of life and to the materialist world outlook. What do you think of the perestroika in Soviet society? Can religion help create a new moral and psychological climate and educate men and women with the loftiest moral qualities? Is there a dialogue between those who take the religious and the atheistic world view?

Let me stress, first of all, that the freedom of conscience principle is a legislated part of the Constitution of the USSR. We do not impose our views on anyone, and our churches are open to all who want to go in. We are prepared, at the same time, to carry on a dialogue on ideological matters. The main thing is that such a dialogue should not divide people, but should help them to gain a better understanding of each other.

The Good of Every Individual

As for the Church's attitude to the socialist way of life, our point of departure is that the purpose of socialism is to serve the good of every human individual. Ministering to man is our purpose as well. In some ways we take different views of this ministry, and in others they are identical. That is why cooperation is possible in many concrete spheres of life. The role and place of such common endeavour tends to grow especially when every aspect of life in society is being renewed.

In the past few years, the processes of glasnost and democratisation have given the country what could be called a second wind. We sense imaginative and purposeful creation in the economy, politics, morality, science and culture. The demands on the purity of the moral atmosphere of society have been raised, and spiritual life is becoming more diverse and profound. Truthfulness, responsibility and exactingness are being asserted with fresh vigour. Believers feel that this beneficial process is consonant with their own Evangelical ideals and welcome the government's course of the country's further economic and social renewal and perfection of socialist democracy.

Creative Labour

The Soviet people's peaceful creative labour has the blessings of the Church, whose pastoral activity is largely devoted to fostering the civic activity and sense of responsibility of the children of the Russian Orthodox Church, their conscientious attitude to work, and their unflagging pursuit of high ethical norms in personal and social life. In this sense, the Church is undoubtedly making a contribution to creating a sound moral and psychological climate in Soviet society. That is why, as religious people, we take especial note of the high purpose assigned to morality in the new system of orientations, and of the fact that the renewed system of values is centred on man as a socially active personality open to the perception and creation of great spiritual values.

Together with our fellow citizens who are not religious-minded we are imbued with a profound concern for the future aspect of our homeland. Our Christian activity is designed to serve the true well-being of our compatriots and all other people, and to help everyone to fulfil their high predestination of seeking "after the things which make for peace, and things wherewith one may edify another" (Romans, XIV, 19).

"The freedom of conscience principle is a legislated part of the Constitution of the USSR."

Reflecting on this mission, we note that its spiritual essence is immutable, while its forms are determined by the circumstances of the day and by the specific religious needs of our flock. We bear witness with profound satisfaction, for instance, that the perestroika has been having a positive influence on the development of church life as well, creating a more favourable atmosphere for its ministry. In the new conditions many of the questions and problems relating to the life of our parishes and dioceses have been solved to the satisfaction of all the parties concerned.

The changes under way in the country have extended the limits of cooperation between believers and non-religious citizens. The Russian Orthodox Church now maintains fruitful contacts with wide circles of workers in culture and science, and has the use of the mass media. It is now commonplace for dignitaries of our Church and for members of other churches and religious associations in the country to take part in various press conferences and public meetings, which gives everyone who is interested an opportunity to receive at first hand exhaustive answers to some of the questions which it was not the custom to air publicly in the recent past.

What are the relations between the Orthodox and the followers of other religions in the Soviet Union and in the world?

Throughout the entire thousand-year history of its existence, the Russian Orthodox Church has, in one way or another, come into contact with other religions, both at home and abroad. And today we have close cooperation with their adherents in our works for the good of our Homeland and for the strengthening of peace among the peoples.

The first Conference of the Churches and Religious Associations in the USSR was held at the

Troitse-Sergiyev Monastery in Zagorsk in 1952, at the time of a dramatic increase of international tension, for the purpose of consolidating their efforts in strengthening peace throughout the world. Even then one could draw the conclusion that the kindred religious and moral positions of the various creeds, despite their doctrinal differences, could unite believers for fruitful cooperation in peacemaking. Since then such meetings have been traditional. Today, no one can any longer deny that the followers of the various creeds are united in their ministry to their neighbours, near and distant, in their common civic and human striving to ward off the danger of war.

Inter-Creed Cooperation

Our inter-creed cooperation with the churches and religious associations in the USSR has been steadily growing wider and stronger. We have also joined in peacemaking efforts with our numerous brothers who are followers of other creeds abroad. Our wide-ranging and frank discussions have led us to the unanimous conclusion, which abounds in hope and optimism, that there is now in all the creeds an urge for cooperation in serving the good of mankind and in solving its vital problems. We believe that this common effort is based on the recognition by the various creeds that the ideas of brotherhood, justice and peace are the supreme principles of human relations. There is also the inherent tendency of religious people to comprehend the meaning of human being, an effort which cannot be separated from putting these ideas into practice.

What is the view of the Russian Orthodox Church of the problems in the defence of peace today? What has the Orthodox Church been doing? What is your view of the future of civilisation?

Our view of the moral problems of war and peace today was most fully expressed in the epistle of the Holy Synod of the Russian Orthodox Church 'On War and Peace in the Nuclear Age' of February 7, 1986. Without commenting on that document in detail let me merely say that we are now most keenly conscious that the idea of peace can no longer remain an abstract ideal; it must acquire the degree of reality which is inherent in life itself. For the time has already come when without peace there can be no life either. The time has come, accordingly, when the very idea of war must be totally excluded from international relations. The global threat to life demands of mankind global solutions as well. It is now more timely than ever before to replace the baneful mistrust and the barren rivalry by a coordination of all the efforts and of all the resources to create more favourable conditions both for the material and for the spiritual perfection of people.

In this situation we, believers, guided by our religious principles, are led to multiply our efforts to avert the danger of a universal nuclear holocaust. Evil demonstrates its power in dehumanised human relations and neglect of the ethical and moral values of civilisation. But evil has met and will continue to meet with resolute rejection on our part, because for us, Christians, peace is a supreme good.

Peace is the word used in the language of the Church to express the wish of every kind of good, the totality of good. It is also the concept used by the Bible to designate just relations between people, their cooperation and their right to enjoy the gifts of nature and the results of their own labour. We flatly reject hostility, exploitation and murder as a violation of divine law and regard peacemaking as its fulfillment. In other words, our Church regards the ministry of peacemaking as a form of its being, as the basis of its manifestation, as a necessary condition for fulfilling this precept of Christ's: "Blessed are the peacemakers: for they shall be called the children of God" (Matthew, V, 9).

A Moral Atmosphere

True to this commandment, our Church has worked hard in its daily activity to create a moral atmosphere in which any infringements on human life and dignity will become impossible. The Russian Orthodox Church, preaching and carrying profound and inalienable peace from its spiritual depths, continuously prays for the granting of peace to the whole world, and inculcates the ideas of peace in all believers. In this peacemaking, our Church is at one with the entire Soviet people, with all people of good will.

> *"Our inter-creed cooperation with the churches and religious associations in the USSR has been steadily growing wider and stronger."*

The forms of the Church's peacemaking ministry are now highly diverse. Divine service and sermon are outwardly the simplest, but also the most profoundly effective and never flagging form. The rule of our Church contains no divine service without prayers for 'the peace of the world'. Indeed, there is hardly a sermon or archipastoral epistle that does not in one way or another, directly or indirectly, enjoin the Christian to gather peace within himself, peace with his neighbours, peace in the collective, peace in society, peace between nations and peoples. This divine service and homily, in which the word 'peace' may sometimes not even be mentioned, helps to create in the congregation what is best and most important for the cause of peace: an atmosphere of active yearning for peace, for its preservation and consolidation.

Cooperation with Orthodox and other Christian churches and religious associations, and participation in the ecumenical movement, which is also expressed in efforts to strengthen peace, is an important element of the peacemaking activity of the Russian Orthodox Church, whose representatives have been making a considerable contribution to implementing the peacemaking programmes of the World Council of Churches, the Christian Peace Conference, the Conference of European Churches, and other ecumenical organisations of which the Russian Orthodox Church is a member.

The world conference 'Religious Leaders for Saving the Sacred Gift of Life from a Nuclear Catastrophe', which was held in Moscow in 1982, was the most significant of recent events in the peacemaking history of our Church.

It was attended by representatives of the Christian, Muslim, Hindu, Judaic, Buddhist and Shinto creeds, and of Sikhs, from almost 90 countries, and adopted a number of documents stressing the need for cooperation of all the religions and all people of goodwill for the establishment of peace on earth. By arranging the conference, the Russian Church imparted a fresh impetus to religious peacemaking activity on all the continents of the globe.

Round Tables

In pursuance of the ideas of that conference, round tables of theologians and experts, which are attended by prominent Soviet scholars and public leaders from our country and from abroad, are now held in Moscow every year, and there have been five such conferences up to now.

Numerous bilateral contacts with various Christian churches and organisations are a special page in the present record of the Russian Orthodox Church, and the important thing to note is that in all these meetings and conversations with representatives of these churches and organisations the most diverse aspects of peacemaking activity are always an important element of the dialogue.

"Much needs to be done to create a world without international conflicts."

Let me emphasise in conclusion that we are profoundly convinced of the ultimate triumph of the ideas of good and peace over the forces of evil and destruction. The religious views underlying this conviction induce us to raise our voice in protest against nuclear war, which could lead mankind to self-annihilation, and to call on all people of goodwill to brand war and the arms race as a crime against God and mankind.

I mentioned earlier some, perhaps the most important, facts, initiatives and tendencies in the activity of the Russian Orthodox Church aimed to preserve and strengthen peace in our unstable and eternally quavering human society. We are clearly aware that people of goodwill still have a long and hard way before them. Much needs to be done to create a world without international conflicts, a world in which the peoples will build their relations with each other exclusively on the principles of trust, friendship and brotherhood.

Pimen is the head of the Russian Orthodox Church of Moscow and all Russia. World Marxist Review *is a monthly journal of Communist and Workers' Parties.*

"Jewish activists say conditions have significantly improved under Gorbachev."

viewpoint 16

Repression of Jews in the USSR Is Easing

George Perkovich

More than any other minority in the world, Soviet Jews have won the attention and interest of U.S. foreign policymakers and the American public. Every U.S. president since Richard Nixon has made Soviet Jewry a key topic at summit meetings and other bilateral discussions. Congress, through the Jackson-Vanik, Stevenson, and Byrd amendments, has restricted trade and credits to the U.S.S.R. to protest Soviet limits on Jewish emigration. American Jewish organizations, in conjunction with Israel, have made their presence felt in the U.S. political process, skillfully gaining support in Washington for Soviet Jewry. And Soviet Jews themselves stage protests and demonstrations in the Soviet Union that are well reported by the Western media, especially in cases when police suppression makes clear the Soviet system's determination to control the aspirations of its minorities....

The fate of Jews in the Soviet Union is such an important and complex issue—both in terms of human rights and in terms of its impact on the superpower relationship—that an adequate policy cannot be based on the perspective of any one group. The challenge that U.S. policymakers face is to frame an effective human rights policy that is also part of an overall strategy for improving Soviet-American relations. This will require familiarity with and consideration of the positions of all parties involved....

It is the emigration movement that is primarily responsible for making Americans aware of Soviet Jewry. The plight of refuseniks—people whose applications to emigrate have been denied—is told frequently through the Western media, often in heart-rending terms. Jewish communities across America demand, "Let My People Go!" U.S. political leaders pass resolutions, enact trade restrictions, and visit refuseniks to further the emigration cause.

Partly in response to American pressure, but more to serve Soviet domestic interests—particularly the state's desire to rid itself of newly activated malcontents—Soviet leaders have allowed over 275,000 Jews to leave the U.S.S.R. since 1968. This emigration occurred in two waves, with a potential third wave beginning in 1987....

Thousands of Applicants

The thousands of applicants who have been refused the "privilege" of emigrating (it's not a recognized right in the U.S.S.R.) face different and frequently tragic circumstances. Refusals are usually without foundation and not subject to appeal. When a rationale is given, the most common is that the applicant or a member of his family has been privy to state secrets. Subsequently, refuseniks experience Kafkaesque horrors—the loss of work, the contempt of neighbors, intimidation by the police.

A small core of these refuseniks become disruptive and confrontational. With nothing to lose, they demonstrate, protest, and petition—attempting to attract Western attention and thus to pressure the state into letting them go. In response, the state has tended to cut refuseniks' phone lines, intercept mail, and make threats of more dire action, such as imprisonment. Even though Gorbachev has raised emigration levels, so that fewer than 2,000 refuseniks remain in the Soviet Union, the refuseniks' situation has come to represent the plight of Soviet Jewry in many eyes.

It is important to recognize, however, that refuseniks are not representative of the overall condition of Soviet Jews—that in fact the majority of Soviet Jews are not even would-be émigrés. As leaders of the Moscow Jewish Association—a new, as yet unofficial group—put it, "Even by the most liberal estimates hardly a quarter of Soviet Jews

George Perkovich, "Soviet Jewry and American Foreign Policy," *World Policy Journal*, Summer 1988. Reprinted with permission.

want to leave. Three-quarters of us have resolved to stay here." . . .

When Gorbachev told NBC interviewer Tom Brokaw that he was concerned about the "brain drain" of Jews from the U.S.S.R., he meant it. As a highly educated, hard-working, Russian-speaking group, Soviet Jews are uniquely valuable to the Soviet economy—hence Gorbachev's desire to keep them there. In 1987, the Kremlin formalized emigration regulations, attempting to do away with the earlier system's capriciousness. The new regulations state that only people with "first degree" relatives abroad—parents, siblings, or spouses—qualify for emigration. According to Western sources, if the regulations were to be uniformly enforced (which they aren't), they would reduce the eligible emigration pool by about 90 percent. The Soviets seem to calculate that this criterion for even accepting an application will hold down the numbers of applicants, thereby lowering emigration expectations among the Jewish community and reducing the number of times the state has to refuse applicants. The fewer the refusals, the less the international and domestic outcry over human rights abuses.

To justify their restrictive emigration policy, the Soviets point to the Helsinki Accords, which, in the section on "Human Contacts," obligate signatories to facilitate reunification of families but do not demand an unlimited right to emigrate. Of course, as Western observers argue, Basket I of the Accords also stipulates that participating states will act in conformity with the Universal Declaration of Human Rights and the International Covenant on Human Rights—documents that do pledge signatories to allow free emigration.

Moscow's Pledges

Yet Moscow's pledges are not always an accurate predictor of its actions. The Soviets waive the first-degree relative requirement when doing so suits their purposes, as in the cases of many of the refuseniks who have been permitted (or required) to leave the U.S.S.R. since early 1987. Indeed, of the 3,445 Jewish emigrants in the last four months of 1987, more than 80 percent were refuseniks, most of whom did not have close family abroad. The release of these individuals seems intended to weaken the leadership of the remaining activist Jewish community by getting rid of the most prominent leaders. It also meets the first-priority demand of Western governments and human rights activists.

In general, Soviet officials are fully aware that restricting Jewish emigration (or retaining refuseniks) does the society little good if it dramatically heightens Jewish discontent. Their goal is to diminish interest in leaving and to reengage the talented Jewish community in the Soviet economy. To accomplish this, the Soviets need to reduce the economic and educational discrimination that motivated many emigration applicants in the 1970s. Based on anecdotal evidence, the National Conference on Soviet Jewry believes that virtually all restrictions on education have been lifted. Less is known about hiring and promotion practices: although Soviet Jewish activists say conditions have significantly improved under Gorbachev, precise statistics are not yet available. . . .

"To serve Soviet domestic interests . . . Soviet leaders have allowed over 275,000 Jews to leave the U.S.S.R. since 1968."

The Kremlin will most likely tolerate Jewish expression only on an ad hoc basis. The state will not sponsor or finance these activities, but will simply allow Jews themselves to teach Jewish history and Hebrew and otherwise promote Jewish self-identity outside formal institutions. This unofficial policy will be half-hearted—a means to relieve internal and foreign pressure.

Yet if the prospects for full nationalist recognition are dubious, the potential for gains in other areas of nationalities policy is real. From the standpoint of the majority of Soviet Jews, the most significant formal step Moscow could take in nationalities policy would be to reestablish the primacy of merit in education and employment. A recent *Pravda* article argued that the essential question in evaluating nationalities policy should be: "Does a person's nationality have an effect on his status in society? In principle, *in socialist conditions a person's place, the opportunities for his development, etc., are determined not by his class or nationality but solely by his personal qualities, abilities, and labor.*" The author, A. Zharnikov, goes on to acknowledge that party policy is to establish a system of "proportional representation for . . . both indigenous and nonindigenous peoples . . . in bodies of power, agencies of economic management," and so on. He cites the failure to do this—the inadequate opportunities for nonindigenous minorities—as a cause of "discontent." And then, insinuating that the real problem is not the violation of state policy but rather the quota policy itself, he concludes, "The very fact of an official division of people into indigenous and nonindigenous could not help but have a corresponding impact on individual consciousness."

Whether or not meritocracy is soon to be reestablished, the fact that the subject is being raised in the pages of *Pravda* is cause for hope, and deserves further discussion between American academics and their Soviet counterparts. For Jews to prosper in the U.S.S.R.—especially in Russia, the Ukraine, and Belorussia—a shift away from nationality quotas is essential.

Another positive sign has been the recent efforts to publicly challenge the anti-Semitism of growing organizations such as Pamyat. An article in *Sovetskaya Kultura* stated: "We must not close our eyes to the remnants of anti-Semitism still surviving in everyday life in our country. Unfortunately, some publications also 'work' on them. One can still come across people who are inclined to blame errors in our economy, architecture, and urban development on some malevolent spirit guided from outside." *Pravda* has gone further and accused Pamyat of "attempting to stir up anti-Semitic attitudes in the Soviet people." Aside from the repugnance it provokes both within the Soviet Union and in the West, overt anti-Semitism is also attacked because it is a form of "extremism"—something Soviet leaders fear in any manifestation as a potential threat to public order.

Nevertheless, the campaign against Zionism is still waged with little effort to distinguish between Zionists and other Jews. There is no call for positive measures to protect Jews from the harassment engendered and encouraged by the anti-Zionist campaign. Certain newspapers name individual Jews who have applied to emigrate or protested to the government, knowing that anti-Semites take this as a cue to attack these individuals through letters, threatening phone calls, and vandalism. Indeed, even when the press criticizes Pamyat, it does so partly because overt anti-Semitism is exploited by the West and "impels Jews to unite on the basis of 'blood'; it makes a nationalistic opposition out of them" [Ye Losoto in *Komsomloskaya Pravda*, December 19, 1987]. In other words, anti-Semitism is bad because it fuels Zionism.

"Another positive sign has been the recent efforts to publicly challenge the anti-Semitism of growing organizations."

Nationalities policy, however, is not the only factor affecting Soviet Jewry. Also important is human rights or democracy policy—the official position on rights and opportunities extended to all citizens. Though the Soviet Union is far from institutionalizing extensive and legalistic regard for individuals and groups, current developments in the Kremlin's approach to law, human rights, and democracy could change the way Jews are treated despite their poor standing as a nationality. The greater the liberty given to Soviet individuals as a function of democratization, the better the future of Soviet Jews. Indeed, the only way to reconcile the desire of some Jews to assimilate and the desire of others to further their national culture is to see each as an expression of democratic rights.

Soviet tolerance of individual and group expression appears to be greater today than in many years past. Within the U.S.S.R., this tolerance is thus far attributed to *glasnost* and democratization rather than to formal changes in the legal system. . . . Since political rights, as opposed to economic rights, have always been of primary concern to intellectuals, and fairly meaningless to the average Soviet worker, the loosening of political control is seen as a way to enlist the intelligentsia in the reform process. By opening public debate and welcoming criticism of bureaucratism and other failings of the old guard, Gorbachev and his colleagues win allies to their cause.

Establishing Bona Fides

To establish their bona fides, the authorities have released roughly 350 political prisoners (close to 350 are known to remain) and allowed or even encouraged the formation of over 30,000 independent associations—everything from environmentalists to sports clubs to "rockers." Beyond the 30,000 registered associations, many other unregistered groups have been allowed to form, including human rights organizations and some nationalist organizations, such as Pamyat. The Soviets are clearly wary of these specific groups, as evidenced by *Pravda*'s denunciation of Pamyat and by the arrest of some leaders of the Democratic Union. Yet even in articles and statements critical of these groups, care has been taken to affirm that independent associations are integral to democratization. Writers say that the expression of "initiative" and the "explosion of social activity" take getting used to. It is predictable that the Russian-dominated leadership will not permit independent associations to become a threat to the Union or to Soviet socialism, either by fomenting separatism, by encouraging reactionary anticommunism (as Pamyat may), or by challenging the role of the Communist Party (as the Democratic Union did early in May 1988). These are the outer limits of *glasnost* and democratization; the authorities will not allow them to be transgressed.

In this regard, the crucial test for Soviet Jewry will come when the Moscow Jewish Association attempts to register officially as an independent group. The association's leaders have met with representatives of a nonauthoritative Russian cultural foundation (in which Raisa Gorbachev is involved) and were reportedly told the foundation would support their efforts. Several concessions to Jewish cultural and religious interests have already been made. . . . In May 1988 the Soviets agreed in principle to allow a Jewish rabbinical school to open in the U.S.S.R., under the direction of Israeli rabbi Adin Steinsaltz.

This yeshiva would reverse a 50-year policy of prohibiting the training of rabbis in the Soviet Union. Authorities have also approved Jewish culture clubs in Leningrad and Minsk, a Jewish museum in a Moscow apartment, and preparation of a Kosher take-out facility, also in Moscow. According to some recent visitors to the U.S.S.R., Hebrew classes are under way in many places, though Jewish leaders caution that mere toleration of classes is much less reassuring than official sanction: significant though humanitarian gestures may be, they fall far short of outright recognition that Jews are entitled to the same rights and dignity as non-Jews. Actual registration of the Moscow Jewish Association would be a breakthrough, signaling the legitimacy of "Jewishness" and inviting more Soviet Jews to become active. Refusal to register would cast the activists into the margin of accepted society, making their future uncertain.

"Beyond the 30,000 registered associations, many other unregistered groups have been allowed to form, including human rights organizations."

In many ways, the state's treatment of individuals will determine the fate of associations. If individuals, typically leaders of groups, are subjected to long-term imprisonment for their political activity, the associations will freeze and wither. For this reason, knowledgeable observers, such as former dissident Yuri Orlov, say that the key standard of Soviet human rights policy should be the elimination of all political articles in the Criminal Code and the release of all political prisoners. Orlov thinks these steps can "realistically be achieved through internal and international pressure for a genuine *glasnost*." A hopeful sign is the review of the Soviet penal code now being conducted by a party commission headed by Central Committee member Anatoly Lukyunov.

International Pressure

Though Western observers sometimes overstate the impact international pressure can have, it is true that the Soviet objectives of winning favorable West European opinion and smoothing the way for East-West arms control and trade agreements dictate closer adherence to Western human rights standards. More concretely, Soviet involvement in international fora such as the Conference on Security and Cooperation in Europe (the Helsinki process) obligates the Kremlin to engage with the West on human rights issues. Soviet treatment of its Jewish population complicates these interactions on many levels.

Just how to bridge the gulf between American and Soviet positions on human rights and the treatment of Soviet Jews is a key subject in U.S.-Soviet diplomacy. Unfortunately, since the issue gained prominence in the early 1970s, neither side has adequately advanced the cause of Soviet Jewry. Both have allowed the issue to obstruct progress in East-West rapprochement without substantially benefiting the Jewish minority in the U.S.S.R. Today, as a new Soviet administration is revamping the apparatus and objectives of domestic and foreign policy, it is vital that the United States also reappraise and perhaps revise its own objectives and practices in dealing with Moscow on human rights.

George Perkovich is a journalist and a fellow of the World Policy Institute in New York City.

"The entire Soviet system is being marshaled to prevent a distinctive, proud, sharply defined Jewish community from emerging."

viewpoint 17

Repression of Jews in the USSR Is Continuing

Thomas A. Idinopulos

Moscow is "crumbling and cracked, grimy, leaking, peeling and flaking," wrote columnist Richard Reeves recently, adding, "Soviet Communism doesn't work . . . and the Soviets know it themselves" (*International Herald Tribune,* May 21-22, 1988).

After visiting Moscow, I could add to Reeves's accurate description the word "hungry." First impressions: Muscovites standing in the snow outside a meat shop on Gorky Street across from Red Square; up Gorky Street more lines for bread, fish, fruit, vodka. A greengrocer's shack above the Metro station in central Moscow selling only carrots the length of a man's finger and potatoes the size of a baby's fist. Near Tolstoy's house a group of shoppers grabbing at tiny pouches of frozen raspberries that had just arrived. And persistent rumors that in many parts of the country a doctor's prescription is needed to purchase milk.

Only the soldiers look well fed. They are also smartly dressed in the finest winter wool coats of beige, acorn brown and navy blue, cut to the ankle, covering black knee-length boots.

The aim of *perestroika* is to clothe every Soviet citizen with a good wool coat and provide a chicken or two for every cooking pot. It is General Secretary Mikhail Gorbachev's goal to lift the U.S.S.R from Third-World status (somewhere near Argentina in per capita income, with one car per 22 people and one private phone per 16 people). To achieve his goal Gorbachev has called for a measure of economic, cultural and religious freedom (*glasnost*). At the same time he has made it abundantly clear in public speeches that the Communist Party apparatus will remain dominant and will not tolerate "chauvinism, nationalism and parochialism"—i.e., freedom or individualism or human rights, Western style.

Thomas A. Idinopulos, "Vanishing Jews and Visible Christians in Gorbachev's Soviet Union." Copyright 1988 Christian Century Foundation. Reprinted by permission from the October 26, 1988 issue of The Christian Century.

Is Gorbachev's *glasnost* cosmetic? Is it merely another counterpart of Potemkin's cardboard village which hid the ugly reality of Russia from the passing czarina? These were the questions on our minds as my wife, Leah, and I arrived in Moscow to talk with Jewish "refuseniks"—people whose requests to emigrate from the Soviet Union have been officially refused.

On March 11 [1988] at 5:00 P.M. we were among 13 Swissair passengers who arrived to a darkened and empty airport; only some 60-watters were lighting up billboard advertisements in the baggage claim area. Those in English: "Camel"; "Mastercard: Your Key to the Soviet Union"; "Pepsi Welcomes You to Moscow."

Billboard Lights

Twenty minutes passed without any sign of our luggage . . . 30 minutes . . . 40 minutes. I paced in the dark. Leah sat under the billboard lights reading *Russian Made Easy*. A tall young blonde woman, wearing huge gold loops in her ears—no doubt to offset the drabness of her customs uniform—crossed my path. I threw up my arms in mock despair. She smiled and said, "Payshoons, please."

After an hour the luggage arrived. Fortunately, the woman with the earrings was at the customs counter and waved us through without a check. I blessed her silently. Inside our bags I was bringing to the refuseniks a small library of Jewish books—history and fiction and books on the Bible, Zionism and Israel. Later I learned that books brought in by two Jewish professors on a similar mission were confiscated at customs and returned to them only as they left the country.

Because we were forewarned not to use our room telephone, we left our hotel for a public booth nearby; a two-kopek piece reached Yuli Khasarovsky, who in excellent Hebrew agreed to meet us the next evening. In preparing for the interview I'd learned that Yuli, 46, was educated in Moscow as an electronic engineer and worked in the Soviet rocket program until he applied for an immigration visa to Israel—whereupon he immediately lost his job. When he began to teach modern Hebrew, one of nine languages he was to learn in 17 years, he was hounded by the KGB. To spare his non-Jewish wife hardship, they agreed to a divorce. He then married Inna, a mathematician, a Jew and a refusenik. We would meet with Yuli on the fourth day of a hunger strike, started on the 17th anniversary of his having become a refusenik. Inna had joined him in the hunger strike.

Leah and I walked back to our hotel, the National, where Lenin slept. The line outside the meatshop on Gorky Street had shortened. A light powdery snow was falling; large snow crystals were illuminated and lovely under the arclights of the Kremlin walls across from the National.

The next day we took the light blue Metro line from central Moscow, and 40 minutes later were walking on icy sidewalks flanking block after block of identical six-story yellow apartment buildings. Leah used her Russian on the conveniently located street signs. We heard the sound of a jogger's feet in the snow, then a voice calling in Hebrew and English. It was Yuli in a dark blue running suit. His doctor, also a Jewish refusenik, had prescribed a half-hour of light jogging each day of the hunger strike.

Yuli's apartment, like nearly all apartments we saw, was tiny, shabby, crammed with books, bikes, clothes, appliances. The small, airless rooms of such apartments actually are the envy of 280 million Soviet citizens, some of whom will arrange marriage to a Muscovite in order to live in what they call "the center."

Yuli was short, slight, handsome, almost rakish in a trim beard à la Trotsky that I associate with Russian intellectuals. As we shook hands he asked me, "Have you come to see me starve?" I replied by asking him if he had read Franz Kafka's short story "The Hunger Artist."

The Starving Man

"Of course," he replied. "Every starving man deserves an audience."

Yuli was eager to talk, but our conversation was constantly interrupted by telephone calls. One caller asked, "Will you publicly demonstrate to call attention to your hunger strike?" "Already have," answered Yuli in Russian. Another call came from Oslo—a Norwegian diplomat was asking about Yuli's health.

Between telephone calls Yuli reminded me that in 1971 he was denied permission to emigrate to Israel because he was classified a holder of "state secrets."

"Is it true?" I asked.

"Nonsense. I haven't been able to keep up with advances in electronics or do any research for more than ten years. Whatever I know is dated, useless."

"Gorbachev takes the position that refusal to allow Jews to immigrate to Israel or the U.S. is linked to the brain-drain problem."

Yuli smiled contemptuously. "Gorbachev should rather speak of the brain-dead problem. At the moment I am one of more than 600 scientists who want to emigrate from here. All of us have been dismissed from jobs, cut off from professional societies; we are rapidly losing the capacity for productive technical work."

Official Refusal

"So what then is the real reason for the official refusal?"

Yuli looked at me thoughtfully before replying. "To show the world that the Soviet government will not bend to pressure from the U.S. You have to understand that the Soviet government wants to make deals with the West, particularly with America. 'Give us something and we will let your precious Jews go.' We are pawns. I am now the oldest pawn. A bigger pawn was Anatoly Scharansky. To improve relations with the U.S., the government let Scharansky out. I am confident that they will let me out, too, but only as a political gesture—something to make the West believe that a new spirit of détente, *glasnost* or whatever you want to call it prevails."

"The Soviet government will not bend to pressure from the U.S."

I could appreciate Yuli's feelings, but was he correct about Gorbachev?

"Are you telling me that *glasnost* is not a new spirit in this country? That Gorbachev is deceiving people? Trying to get something from Reagan and using human rights to do that?"

"Yes," he said, "I do think that. And something else you should understand. *Glasnost*, human rights, letting Jews out—these acts can only go so far. Russian leaders are terrified of the national minorities. The demonstrations going on now in Armenia prove that. Armenians, Jews, Latvians— most of the 100 ethnic minorities of the U.S.S.R. want their national independence. And they want their freedom to leave the country just like Jews do.

"Everyone is tired of living under the Russians and at the mercy of Moscow. Could you imagine what would happen if one day soon the Ukrainians would begin to demand a national state of their own, free from Moscow's control? It would be a catastrophe for the Communist Party, which seeks to control the whole country from Moscow. As I see it, the Jewish problem is not in itself a big problem for the Soviet leaders. But it can become one if the party agrees to every Jewish request for emigration and allows the non-Russian ethnic minorities to believe that they, too, can succeed in getting out of the country or getting away from Moscow's domination."

The Jewish Problem

The Jewish problem? I asked Yuli to be specific.

He replied: "The Jewish problem is what it has always been—the need for a scapegoat, a way for the Soviets to excuse their own mistakes and explain their own miseries. Jews are blamed for everything that goes wrong in this country; low work production, the food shortages, alcoholism."

"Alcoholism?"

"It is a false rumor now being spread by *Pamyat*."

Pamyat ("memory" in Russian), Yuli went on to explain, is a recently established organization dedicated to reviving traditional Russian cultural and religious traditions—evidently including the country's historic penchant for anti-Semitism. The supporters of *Pamyat* are politicians, writers, professors, Russian Orthodox priests and, surprisingly, a youth group called "the Hitlerites," who believe that Jews were responsible for Russian defeats in World War II.

As Yuli went on to explain, there is a contradiction in the official Soviet response to the Jewish problem. If Jews want to be educated, get decent jobs and advance through the professional hierarchy, they are supposed to suppress any inclination to express their national or religious traditions; they are to become assimilated into Soviet society. At the same time, active discrimination against Jews in universities, in the work place, on their internal passports (where the word "Jew" is prominently printed) makes it difficult for Jews to assimilate.

"Look," Yuli said, "if a Jew in this country wants to make something of his Jewishness, as I and others try to do—if he is proud of being a Jew, learns to speak modern Hebrew and identifies with the Jewish national renaissance, and is even willing openly to identify with Israel and Zionism—then in the eyes of the government he is a traitor. For in the eyes of the officials, Zionism and Hebrew are expressions of an enemy state, Israel. Iosef Begun was imprisoned for teaching Hebrew; so was Raul Solinchonik in Leningrad."

Attending Services

I interrupted: "Yuli, it can't be true that the government seeks to stamp out all expressions of Jewishness. I know that the Moscow synagogue has been restored and that many Jews attend services. By all reports the synagogue is well attended on Sabbath services. Also, I've learned that there are plans for opening more synagogues and a Jewish museum."

Yuli waited patiently for me to finish and then spoke carefully. "The government allows some Jewishness to be shown so that it can defend itself against anti-Semitism. But you should not be deceived by appearances. At the heart of Russian policies is the desire to end an independent expression of the Jewish national experience and hope."

Listening to Yuli, I knew that he had personally paid a price for his Jewishness, for teaching Hebrew, for writing letters to foreigners to dramatize the plight of Jews in the Soviet Union. One day the authorities came to arrest him for the "illegal" activity of maintaining contact with foreign agents. They took many of his books, including his prized Arabic dictionary. They wrote him a receipt for the books they confiscated. Some books were returned, but not the Arabic grammar. He was offered compensation—2,500 rubles—for the books they kept, most of them on political subjects or on Judaism or Israel.

"The government allows some Jewishness to be shown so that it can defend itself against anti-Semitism. But you should not be deceived by appearances."

"Did they consider these books subversive?"

"Who knows? You are never given reasons for state actions."

"Did you accept the compensation?"

"Yes, because I wanted to buy more books."

Leah and I left Yuli's apartment after making a phone call to Yuri Sokol, a retired Red Army colonel and a Jew who recently opened a library of Judaica in his home. Yuli Khasarovsky agreed to meet us the next day in Sokol's apartment-library.

The Six-Day War

"What brought you to Judaism, Colonel? After all, you are a military man—Russian infantry, fought with bravery against the Germans. You receive a good pension; you have a spacious apartment. Then you decide to collect books and open a Jewish library in your apartment, and from what I hear the anti-Semites are phoning you day and night."

"It is true. I placed an advertisement in the city's newspaper to announce the opening of the library and immediately I began to receive angry calls. But to answer your question: For many years I knew nothing about Jews. My father was a Jew, but he said nothing to me about it. Throughout the years in the army I thought not at all of Jews or being Jewish—even when I knew about the concentration camps and the Holocaust. For me these terrible things happened to a foreign people. But after the Six-Day War between Israel and the Arab nations, I began to pay attention to Israel. I read Leon Uris's book *Exodus*, and for the first time I began to realize that, as a Jew, I belonged to a real people. After that I read as much as I could about Jewish history. I began to associate myself with the Jewish people and to think of myself as a Jew."

"And the library?" I asked.

"I started the library to make it possible for other Jews to discover, as I've done, what it is to be a Jew. This library is now my dedication. I spend my entire pension on it."

"You are not wanting to emigrate, then?"

Sokol laughed. "I cannot. I must remain here for the library. To receive guests. Do you know that only last week your own Senators Levin [Democrat Carl Levin of Michigan] and Cohen [Republican William Cohen of Maine] came to visit the library?" . . .

As we said goodbye to Yuli and Colonel Sokol I told them that the next day Leah and I were scheduled to visit the old monastery town of Zagorsk, 90 miles northeast of Moscow. Yuli smiled broadly. "I must tell you that when the KGB arrested me they put me in a prison in Zagorsk, within the monastery, but not a religious place. Perhaps you will see it."

Active Religion

Promptly at 9:00 A.M., a car, a driver and an interpreter, Elena, appeared at the National Hotel. Elena is short, well groomed, a graduate of Moscow University in English literature, a "proper lady" who used English stiffly, completing each sentence with a period before beginning a new one. I found myself speaking to her in a grammatically correct way.

We drove through the heart of Moscow. A light morning rain melted the snow and turned the streets into streams. Under the blackened sky the buildings became an extended mass of gray stone. As we turned a corner I was startled by a flush of color: red, blue, green and gold—bright, joyous colors drawn from a child's paint box—were painted onto a Russian Orthodox church, which was like a wedding cake, topped by sugared eggs and chocolate turrets. "A museum?" I asked Elena. "No," she replied, "this church is active." The thought occurred to me that Russia clings to its Christian past the way a poor man clings to his one old, good coat. . . .

I contemplated the cruel fact that as the Russian church is given fresh visibility in the Soviet Union, so the Jewish community *as Jewish* is programmed for extinction through the process of enforced assimilation. Statistics tell the story. At present there are more than 2 million Jews living in the U.S.S.R. The majority are already assimilated to the secular Soviet culture, and were the word "Jew" eliminated from their internal passports, they would become even more assimilated. However, there is a sizable minority that wants to express its Jewishness in religious, traditional or cultural ways but cannot do so. Anti-Semitism and other sources of opposition to Jewish self-expression have created Gorbachev's Jewish problem. How he solves the problem will tell us much about his commitment to human rights.

"The doors to Jewish emigration will be shut tight."

We do not know precisely how many Soviet Jews seek Jewish self-expression; the figure may run as high as a half million. What is signficant is that from 1970 to the present more than 375,000 Jews have sought permission to emigrate. Approximately 250,000 were allowed to emigrate to Israel, with about half of those actually going to Israel and the other half to the United States. Today some 25,000 await permission to leave, including about 10,000 refuseniks. It is widely speculated that Gorbachev would soon like to convene an international conference on human rights in his country, in conjunction with which he will give the green light for emigration to the refuseniks and to most of the Jews who have made a first application for emigration.

After that Gorbachev seems bent on pursuing a complex policy on Soviet Jewry. Official permission will be given for the opening of synagogues, Jewish cultural centers and libraries in Moscow, Leningrad and Kiev, and there may be some easing of the restrictions against the teaching of Hebrew. All this will be used by officials to counter charges of anti-Semitism. Then the doors to Jewish emigration will be shut tight and government efforts will be made both to discourage anti-Semitism and to persuade Jews (perhaps by dropping the word "Jew" from passports) that their future lies in the U.S.S.R. and nowhere else.

In short, Gorbachev's policy toward the Jews will not be much different from his policy toward all other national minorities in the U.S.S.R. The relation of that policy to *glasnost*? Rabbi Arthur Hertzberg answers the question lucidly:

> In the days of glasnost, there is more freedom of choice than before, but the entire Soviet system is being marshaled to prevent a distinctive, proud, sharply defined Jewish community from emerging—just as the regime is trying to prevent comparable kinds of self-assertion on the part of its other national groups [*New York Review of Books*, October 22, 1987].

Thomas A. Idinopulos is a professor of religious studies at Miami University in Oxford, Ohio.

"Steadily but chaotically, with a lurching, creative energy, the transformation has cut wider and deeper into the rudiments of Soviet foreign policy."

viewpoint 18

Soviet Reforms Are Genuine

Robert Legvold

A revolution is under way in Soviet foreign policy greater than any in the postwar period, indeed greater than any since Vladimir Lenin in the early years of his regime accepted the failure of the pan-European revolution and allowed the Soviet Union to join the game of nations. The current upheaval is on a scale with the other dramatic foreign policy reorientations of the last half-century: comparable to the 1940s when U.S. foreign policy moved from isolation to global engagement; greater, in fact, than the 1950s when French policy passed from the modest aims of the Fourth Republic to the grand enterprises of Charles de Gaulle's Fifth Republic; and greater, too, than the 1960s in Chinese policy, a ten-year transition from a troubled alignment with the Soviet camp to an emerging realignment with the West.

Steadily but chaotically, with a lurching, creative energy, the transformation has cut wider and deeper into the rudiments of Soviet foreign policy. For three and a half years, changes have accumulated, spreading from one sphere to the next, altering not merely the workaday calculations that trapped Mikhail Gorbachev's predecessors in their Afghan imbroglio and in their leaden approach to the Euromissile challenge, but altering the assumptions by which the Soviets explain the functioning of international politics and from which they derive the concepts underlying the deeper pattern of their actions. Revolutions of this kind do not make states into saints nor do they remove them as preoccupations in the policies of other nations, but they do leave a vastly different challenge. Once understood by the outside world, such revolutions create new imperatives and often new opportunities.

Why now? Why, when only a few years ago Soviet policy seemed so menacing in its rigidity? A part of the answer lies in the fact that radical circumstance often stirs radical change, and the Soviet circumstance these days is surely radical. Rarely, if ever, has a leadership under the duress of a basic failure of its system attempted so much. It would be difficult to do what Gorbachev wants to do to the Soviet economic and political order and not also affect the foreign policy order, to focus on massive problems in one sphere and ignore those in another, to turn society upside down but leave the external stakes of the country untouched, or to reexamine the entire Stalinist experience but give no thought to the lessons of the last twenty years in foreign affairs.

When a foreign policy has diminished national welfare and weakened the state's ability to influence or control external change, as so many Soviet spokesmen now freely admit has been true of Soviet policy, the price of not responding mounts. Moreover, no country, least of all a superpower such as the Soviet Union, can disregard the constraints and requirements of a changing international environment, one less and less amenable to old formulas and presumptions. In the Soviet case, intellectuals and various parts of the foreign policy establishment have known this for some time, and over the last decade they have slowly created the foundation of a substantially different Soviet approach to international politics. When all these influences converge, especially in the presence of a leader like Gorbachev, great, even revolutionary, departures come more naturally.

Historic Change

Revolution is not a word to be used lightly. To qualify, change must be of historic proportions. It would not be enough for the Soviet leadership to alter its actions in this or that respect, even if some of those shifts represented important breaks with the past. Even far-reaching modifications in strategy would be insufficient.

Robert Legvold, "The Revolution in Soviet Foreign Policy." Reprinted by permission of *Foreign Affairs*, Volume 68, Number 1, 1988/89. Copyright, 1988/89 by the Council on Foreign Relations, Inc.

What must change is thinking. Real revolutions are, ultimately, conceptual. Unless the national leadership's understanding of the realities of the world undergoes a modification, no initiative, no matter how surprising, carries sufficient depth or conviction. Therefore, to assume that only deeds, and not words, count, as cautious Western audiences have so often done in reacting to Gorbachev, ignores what deeds owe to words, when words represent the concepts by which leaders come to terms with reality. Before behavioral revolutions come conceptual revolutions.

Since Gorbachev came to power in March 1985, Soviet ideas about international politics and how the Soviet Union should perform as a superpower have been in constant flux. No aspect of policy, no dimension of the intellectual underpinning of policy, remains untouched. In the process the tumult has slowly engulfed the whole of policy, from the mechanisms of its formulation to the core assumption on which it rests. Indeed, the sheer sweep of the drama is what should have first caught our eye.

There is, however, a good deal more. What gives such power to the conceptual revolution currently under way is its appearance on three different and critically linked levels. Change at any one level would be important enough. Take, for example, change in what might be called *basic concepts,* or the key notions by which the Soviet leaders and foreign policy elites make sense of the opportunities and problems posed for them by the world outside. These have not been so thoroughly reconsidered for more than sixty years—not since the wrenching adaptations to the Treaty of Brest Litovsk, the civil war and the Rapallo accords. Literally every dimension of Soviet policy is being touched.

Fundamental Questions

First, Gorbachev has radically altered the Soviet concept of national security, or, at least, the framework within which it is discussed. He has raised the most fundamental questions: What constitutes national security in these waning years of the twentieth century? How is a superpower like the Soviet Union to pursue it without becoming its own worst enemy? His answer, boiled down to its two essential parts, stresses, as the answer of no Soviet leader has before, (1) the insufficiency of military power as the way to national security, and (2) the link between national and mutual security.

As early as the 27th Party Congress in February 1986, Gorbachev began to convey an unusually complex appreciation of what constitutes national security. The military dimension, he has since said over and over, is but one aspect of the problem— almost certainly not the main one. It is not merely, to use his words from the party congress, that "the character of contemporary weapons leaves no country with any hope of safeguarding itself solely with military and technical means, for example by building up a defense system, even the most powerful one." More to the point, in the present era, according to Gorbachev, most threats to national well-being are not military but economic and political—and the possession of military power, let alone its use, provides little or no solution to these threats.

The second theme emerged in the fall and winter of 1985. After that year's Geneva summit Gorbachev went out of his way to emphasize his "deep conviction" that, were the United States to possess less security than the Soviet Union, only bad could come of it, because inevitably only mistrust and greater instability would follow. No nation's security, he has repeated often since, can be achieved at the expense of another country. Thus national security cannot be divorced from mutual security. "To think otherwise," he said in August 1986, "is to live in a world of illusions, in a world of self-deception."

"No aspect of policy, no dimension of the intellectual underpinning of policy, remains untouched."

Of still greater significance, Gorbachev has also helped to reorder a second basic concept. From Lenin's day it has been an article of Soviet faith that the struggle between two social systems, capitalism and socialism, creates the core dynamic of international politics. The notion is not simply hollow cant. What the Soviets have thought about the possibilities of East-West relations and what they have felt obliged to do for Third World revolutions derive from it.

No longer, say Gorbachev and the many who take their cue from him. Not the struggle between classes but the common plight of man forms the central imperative. Not a Manichaean contest between good and evil, but the entangling effect of interdependence, holds the upper hand. Aleksandr Yakovlev, Gorbachev's alter ego in the Politburo, spoke in August 1988 of a "planet compressed to an unprecedentedly small size," a world whose history can end with "the touch of a button," a world in which "any event becomes the property of five billion people within hours," a world needing not the primacy of "individual countries or classes, people, or social groups," but ways of countering "the forces of separation, of opposition, of confrontation, and of war, which have already delayed the development of civilization by whole centuries." The Soviet foreign minister, Eduard Shevardnadze, third among the most powerful Soviet foreign policy figures, views as "anti-Leninist" the

Khrushchev-Brezhnev thesis of peaceful coexistence as a specific form of class struggle.

The third change concerns the place of the Third World in international politics, and of the superpowers in the Third World. Soviet thinking in this respect no longer resembles what prevailed in the pre-Gorbachev era. Hardly anyone pretends any longer that the woes and turmoil in Asia, Africa, the Middle East and Latin America are part of some grand, heroic "national liberation struggle," once the excuse for Soviet commitments and intrusions. Instead, Third World conflicts are portrayed more as a vast drain on the pitiful resources of developing countries and a "catalyst to local and international tensions," [according to A. Kislov]. Or, as Gorbachev proclaimed in his speech before the U.N. [United Nations] General Assembly in December 1988: "The bell of every regional conflict tolls for all of us." There is a corollary: not so long ago Soviet leaders and elites treated their own country's role in the Third World imperiously (beyond reproach and none of the United States' business); now they agree that any future agenda of détente with the Americans must set limits to superpower intervention.

Finally, the concepts by which Soviet leaders order their relations within the world of socialism—with Eastern Europe, China and nonruling communist parties—are no less in flux. Considering the importance and scope of the conceptual categories already discussed, to add this fourth one is to say that no piece of the foundation of Soviet foreign policy remains unaffected.

From the late 1940s, when Joseph Stalin made over Eastern Europe in his own image, according to the Soviet catechism, the socialist world has been a universe unto itself: Soviet leaders have refused to admit that within it relations could be anything other than harmonious, built as they were on the "general laws" (or imperatives) of socialist development, laws validated first and foremost by the Soviet model. Assuming a natural, even preordained, unity, Soviet leaders and their proconsuls in Eastern Europe presumed not merely a need, but a right to discipline any serious deviation from it.

"Under Gorbachev, the catechism has changed."

Under Gorbachev, the catechism has changed. Those who reflect deeply on the power of the Soviet Union in its relations with Eastern Europe (and, in the long run, in Sino-Soviet relations), including Gorbachev, Yakovlev and Shevardnadze, now acknowledge that socialist international relations are no different from those of any other type of polity. They are as prone to conflicts, including armed engagements arising from self-interest and ambition, as are relations among and with other systems. In light of this, Soviet leaders now ask: Why pretend, let alone demand, that a "single truth," a single shared wisdom, should prevail within what until recently was called the socialist commonwealth?

Policy Concepts

The revolution in Soviet foreign policy is occurring on yet another level, where notions more directly inform practical choice, the level of *policy concepts*. The change is stunning and portentous. If Soviet leaders are rethinking the very notion of national security, they are also revising the concepts that guide their defense decisions and their negotiating posture in arms control settings. Three new ideas form the core of this transformation.

The first is the notion of "reasonable sufficiency," an idea Gorbachev himself first introduced at the 27th Party Congress in 1986. By these words, he and other nonmilitary commentators mean something less than parity, not to mention superiority. In simple terms, they are advocating that the Soviet Union cope with, rather than keep up with, the Joneses. Rather than imitate every new U.S. program, such as the Strategic Defense Initiative, it would be better, in their view, if the Soviet Union were to take the cheaper and simpler route of developing means of foiling the weapons the Americans field. And rather than match the capabilities of each and every country whose arms could threaten the Soviet Union, they would ask of Soviet defenses only that they meet threats that might be plausibly imagined.

Gorbachev has not provided specifics, doubtless because he does not yet have them in mind. But others, beginning with his foreign minister, are filling in the blanks, and their thoughts have far-reaching implications for the Soviet approach to the military competition with the West. In the strategic nuclear realm "reasonable sufficiency" would end the quest for a Soviet arsenal designed to overmatch the United States at every rung up the ladder of nuclear escalation—including, in the end, a force designed to devastate the nuclear arms of the other side—and replace it with a secure retaliatory force capable of ensuring some essential but minimal level of deterrence. In conventional arms the concept would leave the Soviet Union with forces capable of defending against a surprise attack but not of launching one or, more important, of conducting a large-scale, extended offensive. As for Soviet military power usable at great remove, according to the new doctrine there should be enough to help discourage outside interference in local crises, but not to make revolutions or save clients too feeble to defend themselves.

The other two ideas are strategic stability and defensive defense, the latter with its corollary of asymmetrical arms reductions. Strategic stability incorporates the technical, and narrower, American notion of crisis stability (namely, a structured nuclear balance that reduces the temptation for hair-trigger response in crisis situations) but goes much further. For more than a year, Soviet experts working on the problem have struggled to imagine a more stable nuclear regime at drastically reduced levels of armament, one that takes into account not merely the characteristics of weapons systems, but also the effects of strategic doctrine and even of political context.

Defensive defense embodies the simple idea that in no sphere of military power, conventional or nuclear, should either side be able to launch and maintain a vast frontal offensive. The idea is simple; figuring out how to achieve it is another matter. Gorbachev, however, in summer 1986 did introduce a new, albeit vague, guideline for proceeding, one that has since become a standard Soviet formula: let the side with an edge be the one to sacrifice more in order to create a more stable balance at lower levels.

Political Disadvantage

The knowledgeable reader is no doubt protesting: "But these notions have not been embraced by much of the Soviet professional military—and is that not a complication of some consequence?" Indeed it is, yet not one to be overestimated. First, to say that the military by and large does not use the same concepts is not to say they have consciously chosen against them. Second, where their preferences are clearly in conflict with the new ideas, that is not to say they will fight to have their way. And, third, in those instances where they do choose to fight, this is not to say that they will win, given their current comparative political disadvantage.

Other new policy concepts parallel Gorbachev's reformulated insight into the basic dynamic of contemporary international politics, an insight that exalts interdependence and devalues class struggle. Reduced to their essence, these concepts stress multilateralism in place of great-power unilateralism and substitute responsibility of the many for the arrogated duty of the two superpowers. This in turn means strengthening international institutions, such as the United Nations, to give them a larger role with all manner of tasks, from facilitating communication during crises to providing aid in environmental emergencies, from managing regional violence to policing the fragile settlements by which such violence is ended. However, it also means altering Soviet institutions and practices that make the U.S.S.R. an unfit participant in other international institutions, such as the General Agreement on Tariffs and Trade (GATT) and the International Monetary Fund.

The Soviet leadership has not been as successful at developing policy concepts to go along with shifts in its thinking about the place of the Third World in international politics. Since late summer 1987 Soviet speakers have begun favoring political over military settlements and suggesting the notion of "national reconciliation" as the way out of the chaos in places like Afghanistan, Angola and Cambodia—and this might be taken as a new policy concept. But it may only represent a recoiling from the ardors of these particular entanglements, rather than a more durable new approach to regional instability as such. However, Soviet academics have urged that the United States, the Soviet Union and other great powers begin designing an explicit code of conduct regulating their intrusions in the Third World. The outlines of such a code remain foggy and, at times, distinctly prejudicial to the far-flung basing of U.S. military power.

Of the transformations in basic concepts, the gravest and most traumatic is the process of rethinking Soviet relations within the socialist world, particularly with Eastern Europe. Not surprisingly, therefore, Soviet leaders are not having an easy time generating concrete concepts to guide policy in this area. Two departures, however, have enormous implications. First, the old notion of "socialist internationalism," for decades a euphemism for Soviet tutelage, has been replaced by something far closer to laissez-faire. East European regimes are to be left essentially alone to solve their own problems and make their own mistakes. Second, the Brezhnev Doctrine, while not actually lifted, no longer sets the same limits to change. Put differently, doubtless there are still circumstances in which the Soviet Union would intervene with force, but they would probably not include those of 1968 and 1981.

In sum, we are witnessing significant changes in basic concepts and operational policy. What makes all of these changes on the two levels still more momentous, however, is the passage occurring on a third level.

"Of the transformations in basic concepts, the gravest and most traumatic is the process of rethinking Soviet relations within the socialist world."

To a degree particularly difficult for Americans to understand, *fundamental assumptions,* on which the entire edifice of Soviet foreign policy beliefs ultimately rests, are at stake. Never, not even in the 1940s or as a result of the Vietnam War, have Americans been forced to reexamine the basic premises of their worldview. In the Soviet Union, today, people are engaging in such a reexamination. No two matters are more fundamental to the Soviet mind than revolution and capitalism, and the view of each has come to a remarkable pass.

Twice before, the Soviet conception of revolution has undergone profound change. The first time was in the years following 1917, when Lenin's rationalization of the Russian Revolution as the "spark" for a European revolution died, and Soviet leaders were left to fend for themselves. The second time was in the 1950s, when the advent of the nuclear era forced them to rethink the relationship between war and revolution, and, therefore, accept the argument for peaceful coexistence.

Now comes a third transformation: the end of revolutionary faith. Its last repository had been the Third World, but nothing any longer convinces most Soviet observers that revolution is the probable fate of most developing countries (not, at least, the kind of revolution that they would wish to see); more likely their fate is either political vagrancy or, for those that escape into the ranks of the newly industrializing countries, something more akin to capitalism.

The Durability of Capitalism

Capitalism, too, is coming to represent something vastly different for Gorbachev and his supporters. They are more attentive to the durability of capitalism, as the twentieth century draws to a close, than to its predicted doom. More of their sensitivity is concentrated on its dynamism than on its crises, a dynamism that some openly, others by implications, acknowledge has shamed socialism. For capitalism has successfully made the transition from the industrial to the technical-information age, while socialism has yet to prove that it can—an admission that one finds in Soviet journals these days. (Hence, not so incidentally, the "crisis" of communist parties in the West, to put it as Soviet commentators now do.) And the discovery that certain ills, such as militarism, are not in fact intrinsic to capitalism engages more attention now than do the features which the Soviets continue to regard as capitalism's flaws.

When Gorbachev can come to New York and deliver a speech in praise of tolerance and diversity and "the universal human idea," raise the revolution of 1789 to equality with that of 1917 as a source of "a most precious spiritual heritage," identify "freedom of choice" as "a universal principle that should allow for no exceptions," reject force or the threat of its use as an instrument of policy, and call for a more open international order, he may risk being "a little too romantic"—and Gorbachev has acknowledged that some of his own people think he is. But his words should not be regarded as mere bluster. Not when values, assumptions and prescriptions are being recast at every turn, at every level, in every dimension of policy....

Soviet actions suggest that the churning in Soviet minds is genuine. Some of the evidence lies in a wide range of what might be called symptomatic behavior. Releasing Andrei Sakharov from internal exile in Gorky in December 1986 was an early illustration. Paying long-owed obligations for U.N. peacekeeping operations in May 1988 was another. Handling the hijacking of a Soviet cargo aircraft in November 1988 as Washington itself might have was a third. This behavior is symptomatic because, while none of these actions is crucial, taken together they represent something qualitatively different from the Soviet Union's past demeanor.

"[Gorbachev and his supporters] are more attentive to the durability of capitalism, as the twentieth century draws to a close, than to its predicted doom."

By now the list is long: the end to the jamming of foreign broadcasting; the bid for observer status in GATT, the Asian Development Bank and the Pacific Economic Cooperation Council; collaboration with British law-enforcement agencies against drug trafficking; cooperation with the International Atomic Energy Agency investigating the Chernobyl disaster; the vote in favor of keeping Israel and South Africa in that agency; the creation of a commission to examine the so-called blank spots in Polish-Soviet history—and so the list swells. It is already too long and too diverse to be only a nondescript series of random occurrences.

Robert Legvold is the director of the W. Averell Harriman Institute of the Advanced Study of the Soviet Union, and professor of political science at Columbia University in New York City.

"Insofar as new reforms do give encouragement... they nevertheless must be understood as safety valves: i.e., measures designed to save the system."

Soviet Reforms Are Not Genuine

John Lenczowski

With all the news about proposed and actual changes in the Soviet Union, the realistic observer has some cause to be perplexed.

On the one hand, we have the record of seventy years of Soviet behavior. During this time, the regime has repeatedly demonstrated its basic nature and the limited degree to which it can accept change. On the other hand, we have been witnessing a dramatic thaw in Soviet political and literary discourse accompanied by a veritable cascade of economic and political reform proposals which have enjoyed enormous publicity.

President Reagan is assuredly impressed. When asked whether he still viewed the U.S.S.R. as an "evil empire," he stated that that was "another time, another era." When asked about continuing Soviet human rights violations, he blamed them not on the new leadership's policies but rather on bureaucratic inertia.

When the President tells his people that the moral character of our country's greatest adversary has changed so dramatically in such a short time, it is an event of enormous strategic consequence. The reason why the U.S.S.R. is an adversary in the first place has everything to do with its moral character. If that character has changed, then this might call for a wholesale restructuring of U.S. foreign and defense policies.

The moral differences between the American and Soviet political systems and the strategic objectives deriving from their respective moral visions constitute the fundamental source of tensions between them. However much one may point to Soviet nuclear weapons as a potential threat to U.S. security, it is the intentions underlying the use of those weapons which constitute the threat. If it were the weapons themselves, then we should long ago have wanted to seek arms control agreements with the British and the French, whose nuclear arsenals could inflict considerable destruction on our country.

Unfortunately, our society increasingly finds it difficult to grasp the moral differences between the two political systems. Several influences have contributed to this incapacity, including the rise of materialism, moral relativism, a decline in civic and moral courage, and a pattern of foreign policies which both reflects and nourishes moral confusion.

Marxism Lives

To make sense of the new developments in the Soviet Union, some perspective on the nature of the system is in order. It first must be understood that the entire system rests on Marxist-Leninist ideology. In spite of the media's repeated assurances that this ideology is "dead," the fact remains that people within the U.S.S.R.—and particularly those in the Communist Party—must behave *as if* they believed in the ideology. This is so because of the role ideology must play in the system: (1) as the only vehicle by which the Party can attempt to legitimize itself in power; (2) as the principal instrument to establish conformity, identify deviationists and therefore serve as the linchpin of the internal security system; and (3) as the sole foundation of ideals, morals, and therefore direction for society.

The ideology has been subject to manipulations and modifications over the years. But as a rule, these have been of a tactical nature and have never involved any change in the *strategic direction* of the regime's policy. There have also been times when ideological conformity has been less rigorously enforced. Inevitably, however, conformity must be restored if the regime is to survive in power. The Party's General Secretary, of all people, must be faithful to this standard. It was such faithfulness that elevated him to power in the first place. Any

---

John Lenczowski, "What Ever Happened to the Evil Empire?" *Crisis*, October 1988. Reprinted by permission from *Crisis*, PO Box 1006, Notre Dame, IN 46556.

deviation would be regarded as such a threat to the cohesion of the Party that his peers would be constrained to remove him from power—as Khrushchev was removed twenty-four years ago.

Any moral judgment of the Soviet system must take into account whether the moral-ideological foundations of this system have changed. The most important of these is atheism: Marxism-Leninism holds that human reason is the only creative intelligence of this world. Another foundation concerns human nature—specifically, the rejection of original sin and the acceptance of the perfectibility of man on this earth through changes in man's economic, social, and political environment. The communist thus diagnoses a severe illness within society, declares it must be changed, posits that it is within the power of man's reason to change it, and concludes that whatever is necessary to prosecute this change, including murder and mass destruction, must be undertaken if there is to be any hope for the future at all.

"Independent political activity continues to be harassed and repressed."

Since revolution and the creation of a new society are the highest objectives, all moral standards and determinations of truth or falsehood must be constructed around them. Thus, as Lenin taught, anything which furthers revolutionary advance is good while anything which impedes it is evil. Since the Communist Party has appointed itself sole agent of this revolution, anything which challenges its power must be considered a retrograde and evil force. The Party, therefore, establishes all truth, all law, all morality, and grants all rights. There can be no restraint on its power to do these things.

The communist need not believe in all the rosy promises about a classless society and the perfection of man for the Marxist-Leninist ideology to be operational in the U.S.S.R. All that is necessary is for him to accept its basic premises. He must simply believe that man and no higher authority is the source of all laws and morals, and that the men who establish them in fact belong to the Communist Party. Thus, to accept these premises and the system based on them is to live not according to the objective truth, but by precepts declared to be true by the Party. As Whittaker Chambers explained, this is the communist vision: the vision which challenges man to prove that he is master of a world without God.

Has the reform process in Gorbachev's U.S.S.R. changed these moral foundations? It is true that there has been a diminution of purely and overtly political prosecutions. Few new political dissidents have been jailed and there have been "show releases" of a few hundred prisoners of conscience and refuseniks. But independent political activity continues to be harassed and repressed. Editors of independent journals are consistently arrested, released, and rearrested. Four-and-one-half to five million people remain in the vast network of forced labor camps.

It is true that the Kremlin has sponsored an official celebration of the Millennium of Christianity of Kievan Rus'. It is also true that Gorbachev has made a pledge of non-interference in church affairs to the Patriarch of the Russian Orthodox Church (himself a Kremlin appointee)—a pledge given global publicity by the Kremlin's news management team.

Nonetheless, if a number of recent and, naturally, unpublicized events are any indication, these ostensibly favorable indicators of change will prove to be chimerical. For example, a few days before one of the new independent clubs called "Choice" had scheduled the first of a series of public lectures on historical and religious subjects relating to the Millennium, the KGB forbade the use of a legally rented hall for this purpose. The day before, the fire department arrived and shorted the fuses in the fuse box, depriving the hall of electricity. Then, due to the necessity of "electrical repairs," the hall was closed. Three hundred people came anyway—only to be met by a phalanx of police.

Attempts to open a new church in Moscow have recently been refused. The "legal" reason: the church in question is located near schools and the Party declared that it was not about to open a church for students. Similarly, attempts to open a church in Ukraine in recent months have also been rebuffed. The leaders of these church movements have all declared that, in spite of glasnost, believers are being forced to go back underground.

Real Democracy

It is true that among the various "theses" for political reform has been the proposal for multi-candidate elections at the local level. On the face of it, this looks to the Western eye like the possibility of real democracy. We have seen this "revolutionary" reform before: Khrushchev had such "elections" instituted under his regime. Now as then, only members of the Party can run for office.

Other new proposals call for greater rule of law, limitations on tenure in office, the rehabilitation of victims of Stalin and the strengthening of local "legislatures" (the "soviets"). In no case, however, has anything been done to diminish the "leading role of the Party." In no case has anything been done to change the basis for the determination of law, morals, or rights. In no case has there been any repudiation of Marxism-Leninism or its atheistic foundation. Steps toward such a repudiation would be the only meaningful sign of genuine reform in the U.S.S.R. Instead of religious freedom, we see repression.

It is true that we have been witnessing elements of a "thaw" in Soviet society. But Soviet history has already seen several "freezes," several "thaws." The reason for these fluctuations lies in the fact that communist governance consists of the Party's effort to force civil society into a mold into which it cannot fit. In its effort to remake human nature, the Party confronts the immutability of nature. Sometimes it appears to succeed, only to find human nature roaring back with a vengeance.

Remaking Human Nature

When the Party compels society to conform to its new and unnatural norms, when it forces everyone to mouth the nostrums and falsehoods of an ideology that increasingly demonstrates its failure to solve society's problems, when this regimen destroys people's incentives to work creatively and productively, human nature pays the Party its reward: public demoralization, slipshod service, mass alcoholism, corruption, sullen rebellion, economic collapse. As Soviet workers say: "They pretend to pay us, we pretend to work." In a sense, the failure of elements of Soviet society is the triumph of human nature.

So the Party must undertake a tactical retreat. It must loosen the controls on civil society to restore the productive capacity of the economy. If production sinks too deeply, then even the highest of production priorities, the instruments of coercion, will suffer. Therefore, it institutes a policy of "perestroika" (restructuring) which consists mostly of cursory and tangential "reforms" more in the form of proposals than actual actions.

> "Soviet history has already seen several 'freezes,' several 'thaws.'"

There are limits, of course, as to how much the Party can loosen up. A decentralization of economic decisionmaking means a decentralization of political power. Supply and demand can never be ceded too much influence, lest the Party lose its ability to make military production the highest priority. Insofar as new reforms do give encouragement to the spiritually starving people of the U.S.S.R., they nevertheless must be understood as safety valves: i.e., measures designed to save the system. Lenin called this tactic "two steps forward, one step back."

The economic situation, however, is not the only crisis faced by the Party. Simultaneously, it is facing a political crisis within its own ranks. For years, the Party has had to tolerate one element of civil society—the underground economy—since it is indispensable for the survival of the labor force. This private economy has co-opted and therefore "corrupted" ever-larger numbers of Party members into its operation. The result has been an erosion of those qualities required of good communists: Leninist asceticism, self-discipline, ideological and behavioral conformity, and "party-mindedness." Without these qualities, the Party risks losing its ability to maintain itself as a cohesive force, separate from society yet with a decisive influence over it. Once co-opted by civil society, the Party faces further degeneration, to the point of an inability to take those ruthless steps necessary to maintain a monopoly of power.

Gorbachev, like Andropov before him, has been as concerned with this political crisis as with the economic. As a consequence, the Party has taken major measures to reverse these trends: the reactivation of the courts, the arrest and prosecution of 200,000 members of the Party elite and a full-fledged attack on the private economy: 800,000 underground entrepreneurs have either been arrested or fled their jobs for fear of arrest in just the first two years of Gorbachev's regime.

Three Reasons for Glasnost

The principal measure designed to address both the economic and political crises has been "glasnost" (publicity or controlled openness), a policy with several purposes. One is to give vent to a stream of criticisms of various villains in the system (except the Party as an institution). This is a typical Soviet method of searching for someone to blame and distracting public attention from the real culprit. Such criticism simultaneously serves to terrorize mid-level bureaucrats, whom the Party has identified as a major obstacle to efficiency, and to invigorate a demoralized workforce by locating the alleged source of their problems. It also assists the anti-corruption effort by subjecting bribery and other underground activities to public exposure and Party censure.

Another purpose of glasnost is to revive the vast but moribund domestic propaganda apparatus. Despite the billions of rubles and man-hours devoted to the various organs of ideological indoctrination, political socialization, and mass mobilization, few people pay attention. After years of droning repetition, the public reaction to domestic propaganda had become one of numb indifference and boredom. What better way to revive audiences and readership than to insert smidgens of truth into the grey texts?

Finally, glasnost and its accompanying incantation, "perestroika," have their explicitly admitted foreign policy purposes. They are to erode the image of the enemy in the minds of the Western public for the purpose of disarming the United States and the NATO [North Atlantic Treaty Organization] alliance. As Gorbachev stated: "Our perestroika, with all its international consequences, is eliminating fear of the 'Soviet threat' with [U.S.] militarism losing its political justification." In other words, if we no longer perceive the U.S.S.R. to be a threat, why do we need a strong national defense?

In light of all this, haven't any of the reforms—especially in the realm of greater freedom to talk about previously forbidden subjects—had any beneficial moral components? Indeed some of the new discussion has involved iconoclastic elements which would seem to erode Party authority. Unfortunately, most of this discussion has been strictly controlled and limited to a few elite journals in Moscow. And as is the case with all the current Soviet reforms, nothing has been institutionalized or made irreversible.

The Party's policy of glasnost, with its literary thaw and its torrent of criticism and finger-pointing, have no doubt unleashed and emboldened various forces of civil society—most notably nationalist elements—and these forces may develop a momentum difficult for the Party to control. But the instruments of control remain intact, ready when needed. With the Party purging some of its corrupt cadres and regaining control of the others, it will likely be better prepared than before to call those instruments into service.

Continuity in Foreign Policy

Meanwhile, the foreign policy of the U.S.S.R. has not changed its strategic direction either. The beginning of a pullout from Afghanistan has been accompanied by the laying of tens of thousands of land mines which will kill and maim people for years to come. While the Soviets bask in the favorable publicity, they have been effectively annexing the Wakhan corridor of eastern Afghanistan and conducting an unprecedented wave of terrorist attacks on Pakistan.

In our hemisphere, Soviet military shipments to the communist regime in Nicaragua in just the first two months of 1988 were larger than the entire amount of military aid sent by the United States to the resistance in seven years. In spite of the warm glow of the INF [intermediate-range nuclear forces] Treaty, just the new Kremlin acquisitions of conventional arms in the three years since Gorbachev took office exceed the arsenals of France and West Germany combined. Meanwhile, the Kremlin continues to conduct a wide variety of virulent forms of political warfare against the United States around the globe: propaganda, disinformation, covert political influence operations, and support for terrorism. It is not clear that all this represents a moral departure from Moscow's strategic purposes.

Our ability to judge the moral direction of Soviet policy depends on our general ability to make moral judgments. And this ability is very much a function of how committed we are to certain moral principles ourselves. A firm commitment to principles is almost always a prerequisite to understanding the importance of any principles. A moral relativist for whom there are no standards of right and wrong is likely to be a poor judge both of the importance of moral distinctions and of the distinctions themselves. Yet the public policy debates of late twentieth-century America seem to be dominated increasingly by relativism....

"As is the case with all the current Soviet reforms, nothing has been institutionalized or made irreversible."

Relativism suggests that the United States and the Soviet Union are morally equivalent. Both are "superpowers" that pursue global strategic interests in a spirit of *realpolitik* bereft of moral scruples. Both sides have spies who read other people's mail. Both build enormous arsenals which can allegedly destroy the world many times over. If the Soviets use chemical weapons on Afghan villagers, don't forget that the United States used agent orange as a defoliant in Vietnam. Both sides support their respective allies whether they are corrupt dictatorships or not. Both sides, in other words, soil their hands in the mire of international political manipulations. How then, can the United States sanctimoniously criticize the Soviet Union and its domestic and international behavior?

Moral Equivalence

For all the transparent plausibility of this kind of "moral equivalence" thinking, it has major flaws. First of all, it equates all forms and uses of power in international politics and uniformly brands them as objectionable, without distinguishing between the purposes they are designed to serve. First of all, where the Soviet moral code has explicitly endorsed the doctrine of "the end justifies the means," the American system rejects it. Whereas there are no restraints on the state authorities in the U.S.S.R., American authorities are restrained by an election system, a system of laws, a system of checks and balances and the Higher Law (or, as it says in the Declaration of Independence, "the Laws of Nature and of Nature's God"), without which minority rights would be insecure under majority rule.

One form of the logic of moral equivalence may concede that various uses of power may be naturally expected of the U.S.S.R., yet still hold the United States to a higher standard. In such cases, this logic damns the United States and nourishes the instinct of "blame America first." In this case, ostensible moral equivalence is not moral equivalence at all. Its purpose is to damn the United States and thus to exonerate the U.S.S.R. "The U.S. is just as bad" means in practice: "The U.S.S.R. is okay."

Advocates of moral equivalence fail to understand the nature of power in international politics and the moral difficulties involved in its use. The various instruments of state power may or may not be used scrupulously. How they are used depends not only on the moral character of those in power but on the nature of the political systems in question; that is, on whether or not such systems encourage better moral behavior or can even distinguish moral from immoral behavior in principle.

Moral equivalence thinking may also assume another form. Insofar as it does not focus principally on holding the United States to a higher standard of conduct, it will tolerate Soviet power and purposes and accord them legitimacy. Here, the Soviet system is just like any other. The Soviets are "just like us." They love their children as much as we love ours. They long for peace just as we do. Didn't they lose 20 million during World War II? (What is never said here is that war deaths were six to seven million while the other thirteen million were murdered by their own government. This particular communist regime was even then more deadly than war.)

Legitimizing the Evil Empire

Unfortunately, U.S. policy toward the U.S.S.R. has systematically encouraged moral equivalence thinking both before and during the Gorbachev period. However much the rhetoric of American administrations has condemned Soviet foreign and domestic depredations, numerous U.S. policy actions serve to legitimize this behavior and to minimize its moral signficance.

The pursuit of arms control with the U.S.S.R. plays perhaps the most prominent role here. By focusing on arms as the principal cause of tension between the two sides, the arms control process precludes consideration of the disparate political purposes of armaments. No distinction is made between arms acquired exclusively for defensive and deterrent purposes *versus* those amassed for purposes of aggression and intimidation. With such logic, any attempt by the United States to acquire arms solely for defensive purposes must mean that we are equally responsible for creating tension.

Arms control theory, of course, stresses the importance of strategic parity. Arms control allegedly prevents destabilizing imbalances and blocks the temptation of preemptive strikes. Again, such theory takes no account of foreign policy purposes and gives no moral credit to powers who arm solely for defense. Instead, the theory presumes potential hostile intent on the part of defensive powers, thereby ascribing moral equivalence to both. In an analogous situation, such theory would stress the desirability of parity between the police, who are armed for defending society, and the mafia, who are armed for offending it: if both sides had equal levels of submachine guns, German shepherds, tear gas, and armored vehicles, then the community could enjoy "peace" resulting from the mutual deterrence afforded by the "strategic balance." There would no longer be any need for shootouts in the streets.

The very talk of the desirability of balance or strategic parity between the United States and the U.S.S.R. is to make a moral concession to Soviet communism and to denigrate morally Western democracy.

"The Soviets . . . stress their rejection of 'bourgeois international law' and the necessity of replacing it with a 'class-based' (i.e., communist) international law."

Diplomacy with other countries, whether friend or enemy, is a necessary and sometimes distasteful responsibility of statecraft. The approaches diplomacy takes, however, are many and are subject to the prudential choice of national authorities. There is no iron law that dictates that certain forms must be pursued. But for a variety of reasons, summitry has been chosen as one of those forms, in spite of the fact that, when conducted with leaders of totalitarian countries, it has rarely if ever served this country's national interest.

Summitry encourages moral equivalence thinking by placing the democratically elected president on a symbolically equal plane with the chairman of a totalitarian party. When the two "leaders" (must one be reminded that the *primus inter pares* of a collective dictatorship is not a national leader?) talk, shake hands, smile, offer each other champagne toasts, and sing popular songs together, while their wives conduct a tea and crumpets "summette," what is the Western public to conclude? That the party boss represents an aggressive and repressive empire which remains a threat to Western security? Or that he is an enlightened, moderate, and even liberal reformer who seeks nothing more than mutual understanding, a reduction of tensions, a new peaceful and cooperative relationship and perhaps nothing less than the wholesale transformation of relations between two traditionally adversarial powers? What are the citizens of the town to believe when they see the chief of police having lunch at city hall with Al Capone? Perhaps Capone is not the boss of organized crime after all! Perhaps he is what he has been saying all along: a legitimate businessman. . . .

It has been commonplace for recent U.S. administrations to describe U.S.-Soviet relations as a combination of "competition and cooperation."

Competition is admitted as one of the realities with which we must live. Cooperation and expanded involvement in fields of mutual benefit are said to be a requirement of the search for peace. Such descriptions serve to treat the United States and the U.S.S.R. as moral equals. Competition implies playing a game according to a shared set of rules. By describing the relationship as a "competition," we convey the image of a Soviet Union that shares with us a commitment to traditional morality when the opposite is true. The Soviets, when talking among themselves rather than disseminating propaganda to the West, describe East-West relations as a "struggle" and stress their rejection of "bourgeois international law" and the necessity of replacing it with a "class-based" (i.e., communist) international law.

John Lenczowski is strategic studies consultant at the Council for Inter-American Security and adjunct professor of National Security Studies at Georgetown University in Washington, DC.

"The time of astonishment at changes in the Soviet Union is over. No subject seems sacred."

viewpoint 20

Soviet Reforms Are Easing Repression

Abraham Brumberg

A visit of several weeks in Moscow makes one aware that the time of astonishment at changes in the Soviet Union is over. No subject seems sacred, even at public meetings where stone-faced policemen and the familiar contingent of plainclothes KGB [Soviet secret police] agents stand by, watching. And what is spoken is sooner or later likely to be published. In December 1988 I heard rumors of suppressed chapters in Marshal Georgi Zhukov's memoirs describing Joseph Stalin's executions of Soviet officers in 1938, and his disastrous behavior as chief of the Soviet Armed Forces during World War II. No one was able to predict whether these pages would be published. Then on January 20, 1989 they appeared in *Pravda*.

Some skeptics in the West, and in the Soviet Union, say that documenting the atrocities of the Stalin era (or, as the more venomous term *Stalinshchina*, has it) has become a "safety valve" to divert the public from criticizing current realities. But in fact those realities are constantly the subject of attack. The Soviet press contains many reports on ecological blight, on declining living standards, the awful state of the country's public health system, housing shortages, and the power of "mafia" gangs that specialize in extortion and "protectionism," and demand a percentage of store sales or steal goods for sale on the black market. In addition, hardly a week passes without a news story about how Soviet *chinovniks* (officials) are conspiring to sabotage Mikhail Gorbachev's reforms.

Nor should one underrate the effect of disclosures about the past (including the "period of stagnation," or *Brezhnevshchina*) in opening the present to public scrutiny. The most interesting forum for such disclosures is the Memorial Society, of which Andrei Sakharov is chairman. The society was founded in 1987, when a group of young people began to collect signatures on petitions to erect a monument to the "victims of Stalinist repressions." Despite police harassment, the group won the support of *Literaturnaia gazeta* and in July 1988 the official approval of the Party at its Nineteenth Conference. By then more than 50,000 people had signed the petitions. Shortly thereafter, *Literaturnaia gazeta* and the weekly *Ogonek*, together with the USSR Unions of Cinema and Theater Workers, Architects, Artists and Designers, formally set up the society, which was headed by a "Public Council," with Sakharov as chairman.

The society holds frequent public meetings that are addressed by historians and by surviving victims of the Stalinist terror and their relatives. "How was it possible," the historian Leonid Batkin asked at a meeting of the society that I attended, "for a mediocrity like Stalin to defeat such infinitely more gifted people like Leon Trotsky, Grigori Zinoviev, and Nikolai Bukharin?" Only if we study how Stalin rose to power, he said, can we begin to understand how a "grayocracy" (*serokratiia*) of aging mediocrities has been able to rule this country for over half a century. Similar speeches followed, and the five-hour meeting adjourned after passing a resolution denouncing Stalinism for "having brought our country to ruin" and calling for the opening of all archives and the publication of the names of Stalin's accomplices, extinct and extant.

Opposition Groups

A few evenings later, at the suggestion of the young critic and historian Boris Kagarlitsky, I attended a rally sponsored by the Moscow "Popular Front" (Narodnyi Front), a coalition of opposition groups that now has several thousand members. The meeting was held in one of Moscow's many nondescript "Houses of Culture." Unlike the

---

Abraham Brumberg, "Moscow: The Struggle for Reform," *The New York Review of Books*, March 30, 1989. Reprinted with permission from *The New York Review of Books*. Copyright © 1989 Nyrev, Inc.

audience at the Memorial meeting, the five hundred or so men and women who packed the hall were mostly in their twenties and thirties. Many of them were students, but some were unmistakably workers.

On the walls were posters with hand-printed slogans like "Put the KGB under the Supervision of the Soviets!" One speaker after another (not all of them members of the Front) rose to denounce the government for tolerating attacks on the Armenians in Azerbaijan, for withholding "basic information" such as accounts of the Supreme Soviet proceedings, and for its failure—"despite all the talk about freedom"—to do away with the articles in the Criminal Code dealing with "anti-Soviet agitation and propaganda." Another demanded "an international tribunal such as the one in Nuremberg" to try those responsible for "*Stalinshchina* and *Brezhnevshchina.*"

"The criticisms . . . go to the very heart of the Soviet system and Communist ideology, and thus far beyond the limits that Gorbachev has set."

When a Party official then stood up and called for a vote of thanks "to our Communist party and the Soviet Army" for their part in "defending peace," and to Gorbachev for "bringing democracy to the Soviet Union," the audience erupted with derisive laughter, and there were shouts of "demagogue!" (At every public meeting I attended Party speakers were shouted down. When I mentioned this to a Russian friend, he said: "Now you can see why Gorbachev insisted that a third of the deputies to the Congress of People's Deputies be elected by the Party and other 'public organizations.' Without that, God knows how many apparatchiki [members of the Communist apparatus] would be elected!"

Deep Criticisms

The criticisms I heard in Moscow go to the very heart of the Soviet system and Communist ideology, and thus far beyond the limits that Gorbachev has set. The question of a multiparty system is a case in point. Although Gorbachev has called for greater social and political "pluralism," he has made it clear that this does not mean more than one party. The "leading role" of the Communist party, which is to say its political monopoly, is still central to the Soviet political order.

Yet in the climate of glasnost the words of the General Secretary no longer seem to carry the same weight as before. At the Popular Front meeting, several speakers called for "the rule of the people and not of the Party." An elderly worker denounced Marxism as "the apotheosis of force," the Bolshevik Revolution as an "unmitigated tragedy," and the Leninist principle of "democratic centralism" as "having paved the road to Stalin's rise to power" and to the creation of "our monstrous one-party state." During the intermission, a number of young people flocked around him as he continued to expound views that in 1985 could have landed him in a camp.

The merits of a multiparty system had also become a legitimate subject of scholarly discussions. On November 15, 1988, for instance, *Izvestia* ran articles by two prominent legal scholars, both members of the Institute of State and Law of the USSR Academy of Science. The first, Professor B. Lazarev, claimed that "pluralism of interests can be fully expressed, by a one-party political system." The other author, Dr. Boris Kurashvili, disagreed. "A socialist multiparty system," he asserted, "is a major component of a developed socialist democracy."

When I went to see Dr. Kurashvili at his Moscow office, he told me, "I consider myself a democratic socialist. All the forms of socialism we've had in this country so far—from 'war communism' of 1918-1919 all through Brezhnev's brand—have been soaked in authoritarianism." Unlike some of his Soviet colleagues (and some Western scholars), Kurashvili is not an uncritical admirer of Lenin's New Economic Policy, which granted considerable scope to private business. "True," he said, "in 1921 the Red Terror came to an end when the NEP was put into effect, but elections to the Soviets were still undemocratic. Practically everyone who could be labeled as a member of the old ruling class was stripped of his civil rights, and power stayed entirely in the hands of a single ruling party. Democracy inside the Party virtually disappeared." For Kurashvili the time has come to work out a new model of socialism, in which

> the existence of many parties, including one of a bourgeois-liberal type advocating the private ownership of industry, would not be seen as a danger, but a guarantee for the further development of a genuine socialist democracy. By the same token, it would provide a safeguard against the bureaucratization, corruption, complacency, servility, and mania for self-glorification that have taken root in our country because of the absence of a real political arena.

Kurashvili is by no means the most radical of the dozens of prominent intellectuals who are talking openly about a "new model of socialism." In fact, it is just this topic—in Gorbachev's words, "the philosophical and political principles of the renewal of Soviet society"—that the Central Committee has announced it will take up. . . . In a recent speech, he emphasized that the Soviet "people made their choice—they are for 'socialism' and for 'a one-party system.'" Neither on this nor on any other occasion, however, has he ruled out discussion of a multiparty system. Those who advocate such views, he said, are "mistaken."

As the search for a new basis of Communist legitimacy—both within the Party and without—continues, the wisdom of Karl Marx and Vladimir Lenin is for the first time being challenged. "Is Marx Necessary for Perestroika?" is the title of an article by the historian G. Lisichkin in a recent issue of *Novyi mir*. Only in the most general terms, is the reply. (Among other heretical views the author says that "there is more socialism in countries which officially are not socialist—for example, Sweden.")

As for Lenin, the editors of even the most outspoken journals are not likely to print any outright attacks on him; Gorbachev's reforms are claimed to derive from his teachings. A journalist showed me passages from one of his articles that had been cut out by his editor (himself a staunch *"perestroishchik"*), in which the journalist referred to Lenin's dissolution of the Constituent Assembly in 1918, the trial of Socialist Revolutionaries in 1922, and to the link between Leninism and Stalinism.

"You can say that Lenin committed mistakes," the journalist said, "provided you also say that he had come to correct them. This is sheer sophistry. First Lenin brings this country to the brink of disaster, then he's forced to change his policies. What kind of genius is that who can't foresee the consequences of his actions?"

"Marx and Engels, it now can be said, were not infallible. Lenin was frequently wrong. Stalin was psychotic."

The most damning comments on Lenin are made by implication in the revised histories of the revolutionary years. In an article *"Istoki"* ("Sources"), published in *Novyi mir*, for example, the economic historian Vasili Seliunin disputes the orthodox interpretation of the terror against the peasants in 1918, as a response to the famine that was caused by the peasants' refusal to turn over their grain to the state. Seliunin writes:

> It wasn't the famine that caused the grain requisitions, but rather the opposite: it was mass requisitions [ordered by Lenin] that caused the famine. The peasants were told to feed the country free of charge.... The evidence clearly points to the fact that the mass liquidation of kulaks [wealthy peasant farmers] took place precisely in the years of "war communism," and not in the early 1930s.

Thus, though paying lip service to Lenin for having abandoned the "erroneous" policies of "war communism," the author presents him in effect as Stalin's ideological and political precursor. Another historian, Nikolay Popov, has gone even further, clearly stating in one of his articles (*Sovetskaia kultura*, April 26, 1988) that Lenin lay the foundations of the Stalinist state.

Marx and Friedrich Engels, it now can be said, were not infallible. Lenin was frequently wrong. Stalin was psychotic, Brezhnev corrupt, Khrushchev tried to change the system but was done in by his rivals, Andropov had no chance to prove what he could do, and Chernenko was nothing but an insipid historical footnote. Who, then, truly belongs in the pantheon of Soviet heroes? The most obvious candidate is Nikolai Bukharin, "Lenin's most faithful disciple" and champion of the New Economic Policy, who was murdered by Stalin in 1938, and whose conception of a liberalized economy and political order is the basis for many of the recent discussions of reform. But as Lenin's policies themselves come under scrutiny, a hidden history is being uncovered, not only of his long-suppressed allies, such as Trotsky, but of his opponents as well.

Soviet History

At a meeting with students at the Historical-Archival Institute, arranged by its rector, the outspoken historian Yuri Afanasev, I asked them what they thought of the official syllabus, which lists as "required reading" on the October 1918 Revolution only works by Lenin and selections from Gorbachev's *October and Perestroika: The Revolution Continues* (Moscow, 1987), while, for the 1920s, it recommends articles by Bukharin, Zinoviev, and Lev Kamenev—under the heading of "Supplementary Reading."

I said to the students that this was just more Party-line history. Why was there no mention of Trotsky? And what of works by Mensheviks and Socialist revolutionaries? How could a course on Soviet history overlook the March 1917 Revolution?

Both the students and their teacher at once agreed. They pointed out that in 1986 the very mention of Zinoviev would have been unthinkable, but that they now see his books and documents, although in special sections of libraries and archives that cannot be entered without special permission; they expected they would soon be able to read the works of Trotsky....

To Professor Afanasev, one of the most respected and most radical of Soviet historians, the word "rehabilitation" itself is despicable. "The business of a historian," he said, "is to write history, not to hand out certificates of good behavior. Most of our historians still regard history as an ideological instrument. And there is still no sign that the authorities will accept the demand for a law allowing access to archives. You have to stand on your head to get permission to see certain materials, say at the Ministry of Foreign Affairs. It's all part of our daily struggle—and it must go on."

Borba idyot. "The struggle goes on." "The struggle has just begun." The phrases I heard every day of my visit in the Soviet Union suggest that nothing—not the latest Party pronouncement, not a decision by a local bureaucrat, or a government decree—can be taken as the final word. More than anything else, these words, optimistic and uncertain at the same time, define the atmosphere in Moscow. One day I heard that the director of a popular television show, *Dobryi Vecher, Moskva* (Good Evening, Moscow), had just been fired for approving news reports that were "distortions of Soviet reality." I asked Natalia Ivanova, the poetry editor of the monthly *Druzhba Narodov* (Friendship of Peoples), if he had no chance to get his job back. "Oh, no," she laughed, "the struggle has just begun. The staff will do everything to have this decision reversed—you can be sure of that." In late February 1989 I was told he had returned to his job.

The controversy over the publication of Aleksandr Solzhenitsyn's writings is another example. Early in December 1988 the new Party chief in charge of ideology, Vadim Medvedev, announced that Solzhenitsyn's books would not be published in the Soviet Union. A week later, there were two well-attended meetings in Moscow in honor of Solzhenitsyn's seventieth birthday. *Novyi mir*'s editor, Sergei Zalygin, says he still intends to publish Solzhenitsyn; so does Julian Semyonov, the author of spy thrillers who is president of the International Association of Crime Writers and now edits a new literary magazine. In the meantime, yet another work by Solzhenitsyn has been published—his 1967 Letter to the Fourth Congress of Soviet Writers, demanding the abolition of Soviet censorship and protesting the persecution to which he had been subjected. Whether more of Solzhenitsyn's work will be published has become a symbolic issue and an intense one. . . .

"The current attempts at reform may well amount to the last chance in our time for the country to emerge from the poverty and backwardness that are the legacy of a succession of corrupt and repressive regimes."

At stake in such controversies, I was told again and again, is the very future of the Soviet Union. The current attempts at reform may well amount to the last chance in our time for the country to emerge from the poverty and backwardness that are the legacy of a succession of corrupt and repressive regimes. But just who is fighting whom is a more complex question. The formula, so popular in the West, that Gorbachev and his allies are on one side and their foes are on the other—"Gorbachev vs. the conservatives"—is misleading. It is true that during the past few years Gorbachev has had to fight continually with opponents of perestroika in the Politburo and Central Committee, and he still has enemies in both groups. But according to nearly everyone I have talked to, his personal power is now more secure than ever before. Although he has thus far not been able to pack the four hundred-member Central Committee with a majority of perestroika supporters, he has succeeded in gaining control of the ruling Politburo. This means, according to Shmelev, that Gorbachev for the time being does not have to worry "about challenges from contenders for power." . . .

What I found most striking, however, is that not even his most radical critics are ready to give up on Gorbachev. They give him credit for starting the most extensive process of change in the history of the USSR, and for some large achievements. Shmelev, for instance, for all his criticism of the new cooperative system, regards it, with its nearly million members, "as the single most successful step in setting up market incentives in the Soviet Union."

The Profit Principle

More than a few enterprises, ranging from shoe factories to photographic processing plants, have already begun to work on the profit principle. Joint ventures with foreign investors (which now allow most of the shares to be controlled by the Western partners) are increasing, particularly with West Germany. . . . A number of "free economic zones" have been created, in which deals with foreign firms are allowed without interference from the state. (Estonia has just signed a contract with Aer Lingus—the first of its kind in the history of the Soviet Union.) The long-promised reform to bring prices in line with the demand for products has been delayed, thus threatening one of the central tenets of perestroika, but several plans for a new price mechanism have been drafted and vigorously discussed in the Soviet press. And although the proposals of economists such as Shmelev and Popov to import food in order to satisfy immediate consumer needs have been rejected by Gorbachev, many economists agree with his view that the country must reorganize its production and distribution system and not rely (as it did under Brezhnev) on the West to bail it out of its troubles.

Indeed, many of the radicals do not blame Gorbachev personally for all the compromises and setbacks they have experienced, or ascribe them to sinister motives. But they criticize him publicly for "obtuseness" and for "lack of sensitivity" in dealing with the grievances of nationalities such as the Baltic peoples and the Armenians. Gorbachev, practically everyone agrees, should have acted much more decisively at the time of the first protests on behalf of the Armenians living in the enclave of Nagorno-Karabakh in Azerbaijan who wanted to become part of the Armenian Republic. Still, on January 19, 1989 the Soviet government announced that Nagorno-Karabakh would be placed under the direct rule of the Supreme Soviet—a clear concession to the Armenians, who will in effect be administering the region.

Nor is Gorbachev's move to combine the positions of Party Secretary and Supreme Soviet Chairman seen necessarily as an opportunistic, vulgar attempt to gain power; as Sakharov has said, it is a dangerous step intended to prevent Gorbachev's opponents from challenging the entire process of perestroika. Both the "centrists" and the "radicals" emphasize that despite all its problems and setbacks, perestroika has already had considerable successes. While the Supreme Soviet is not what the *perestroishchiki* had hoped for, for the first time in the history of the Soviet Union there will be a continuously active legislature, whose deputies can be replaced at regular elections, and whose Chairman's tenure is restricted to two five-year terms. With all the talk and protest accompanying the elections, the electoral fever has been spreading; and while the Party apparatchiki are trying as hard as they can to contain it, Soviet citizens themselves, . . . are no longer cowed by them.

> *"The hopes are based on the prospect that major institutions are being transformed . . . and that citizens will continue to be able to advocate more changes and more reforms."*

On February 12, 1989, *The New York Times* carried a remarkable account by its Moscow correspondent, Bill Keller, of a woman who was able to persuade the voters in one electoral district to defeat the local Party candidate. When the Party leaders tried to stop the debate, a seventy-four-year-old pensioner, Vladimir Lovin, "stepped up to the microphone and silenced the crowd with a burst of indignation: 'We have waited 70 years for this and now they want to shut us up!'" This, Keller wrote, "turned the tide." Similar stories about stormy election meetings in factories and enterprises appeared in the Soviet press throughout December 1988 and January 1989. They suggest something of the hopes one encounters in Moscow. The hopes are not expectations that life will suddenly improve. Gorbachev himself has said that there will be no clear economic improvement for at least four years, and meanwhile the continuing shortages of food and consumer goods remain a source of anger and irritation. The hopes are based on the prospect that major institutions are being transformed, however slowly, and that citizens will continue to be able to advocate more changes and more reforms. . . .

Degrees of Freedom

I left Moscow both exhilarated and apprehensive: it is exhilarating to watch the gradual disappearance of fears, lies, and hypocrisy, and to see a degree of freedom that no one—not I, not a single Soviet expert I know—had predicted would emerge so swiftly and so dramatically in so short a time. Yet the process has uncovered such appalling realities that one is apprehensive about the still more staggering problems ahead.

It has become increasingly fashionable in the West either to pronounce eulogies over the imminent demise of the reforms and of Gorbachev himself or to dismiss the changes as "much glasnost and hardly any perestroika." It is difficult to imagine, however, that the process could be reversed, although it could be halted. No counterrevolution ever succeeds in obliterating all the traces of a revolution. And what is going on in the Soviet Union today is surely that: a glance backward to conditions in 1948 or even 1968 makes this clear.

While everyone agrees that the most spectacular change has been made in glasnost, it is also true that without the freedom to expose the misdeeds of the past as well as of the present, no attempt to undo them, and no search for different solutions, could possibly take place in the USSR. Conversely, perestroika encourages criticism. It is precisely because of the hopes raised by the law on cooperatives . . . that the latest decree about them has provoked so much spirited protest: and the protest may lead to the annulment of the decree's most objectionable features.

In my view, no one, either in the West or in the Soviet Union, can predict the outcome of what is taking place in the Soviet Union. No one can assess the weight of the forces conspiring against the reforms on the one hand, and those (including both "radicals" and "centrists") determined to push ahead on the other. Frequent speculations by Western observers about Gorbachev's political future are for the most part senseless, if only because there are no precedents for what is happening and there is no way of measuring the shifting sentiments for and against his reforms. For the moment, *borba idyot* seems a good short summary of how things stand.

Abraham Brumberg is a visiting fellow at the School for Advanced Studies at Johns Hopkins University and has written widely on the Soviet Union and Eastern Europe.

"Gorbachev has been waging [a campaign] to turn back the clock on human rights and seal them off from outside intrusion."

Soviet Reforms Are Not Easing Repression

I.F. Stone

In surrendering to Mikhail Gorbachev's demands for a Moscow human rights conference in 1991, the American government shut its eyes on two key issues. The first is that the USSR will be able to hold the conference without changing the laws and practices that were responsible for past human rights abuses and that choked off surveillance from within by Soviet activists.

Washington has also chosen to overlook the campaign Gorbachev has been waging to turn back the clock on human rights and seal them off from outside intrusion. Though little noticed, this campaign would nullify the UN [United Nations] Declaration of Human Rights and the similar provisions of the Helsinki Accords. No one knows better than Ronald Reagan, as we shall show, how hard Gorbachev has been trying and how determined he is. Yet Reagan, in endorsing the Moscow conference, did not exact any promise to give up this "new thinking" or any assurance that Gorbachev will not use the Moscow forum to further his goal.

What Gorbachev has been proposing is a revolution—or, more exactly, a counterrevolution—in the sphere of human rights. On three major occasions he has tried to sell an old doctrine under a new name to the world community. He calls it "freedom of choice," or "freedom of socio-political choice." But it is really the old and anachronistic dogma of absolute national sovereignty and noninterference in so-called domestic affairs. This has always been the Soviet response to human rights criticism, and remains the basic argument of all authoritarian regimes accused of violating the rights and liberties of their subjects. Gorbachev would turn the struggle for human rights upside down. Although he and other Soviet officials speak with several voices, the main emphasis in his statements is on guaranteeing not the right of individuals against state oppression but the right of each state to treat its subjects as it deems fit.

Oddly enough, though these efforts have been made under conditions ensuring maximum publicity, they have evoked little discussion, and indeed attracted little attention. Perhaps this is because they were presented as part of what appeared to be offers of greater Soviet cooperation in international affairs. Another reason may be that the cult of personality around Gorbachev has grown so great outside the Soviet Union that it fosters a tendency to overlook whatever he says that does not fit the mythic image of this energetic and gifted but often contradictory Russian ruler who has aroused so much hope at home and abroad.

Thus while he often talks in One World terms, his proposals on human rights would go far toward sealing off this topic from international criticism and pressure as matters—so he affirms—of strictly domestic jurisdiction. This not so new example of what he terms "new thinking" appeared in the lengthy appeals he made to . . . the UN General Assembly and between them at the press conference he called in June 1988 at the end of his Moscow summit with Reagan.

New Rules for Coexistence

On the first occasion, September 17, 1987, in an appeal published in the pages of *Pravda* and *Izvestia* and addressed to the forty-second session of the UN General Assembly, Gorbachev presented his human rights doctrines as "new rules for coexistence." On the second, at the Moscow summit, Gorbachev expressed disappointment because the American president had refused to sign a joint accord shifting the emphasis from human rights to the rights of nations. This would have affirmed the right of each

I.F. Stone, "The Rights of Gorbachev," *The New York Review of Books*, February 16, 1989. Reprinted with permission from *The New York Review of Books*. Copyright © 1989 Nyrev, Inc.

nation to make its own "free choice" of domestic regime, and pledged both superpowers not to interfere with the internal human rights policies these choices entailed. When Gorbachev himself addressed the forty-third session of the General Assembly in New York on December 7, 1988, he not only argued that this "principle of free choice" was "mandatory," but warned that its "nonrecognition" would be "fraught with extremely grave consequences for world peace."

This sounded almost like a threat. The threat was not spelled out. Gorbachev escalated his tone and tried to elevate this "principle" into an international First Commandment. "Denying that right to the peoples under whatever pretext or rhetorical guise means jeopardizing even the fragile balance that has been attained. Freedom of choice is a universal principle that should allow for no exceptions." Even in that forum, he offered no exception for the UN's Universal Declaration of Human Rights, although he did endorse the declaration toward the end of his speech. It is strange that such sweeping and contradictory language should have provoked no probing questions or challenge in the General Assembly. The delegates seem to have been rendered numb.

Gorbachev's doctrine, if accepted internationally, would be a historic step back from the notion embedded in the United Nations Charter of a new world order based not on unfettered national sovereignty but on a new world law which seeks to safeguard certain elementary rights everywhere on the planet from cruelty and oppression.

This was the chief difference between the Charter of the United Nations and the Covenant of the League of Nations which preceded it. The covenant emphasized disarmament—not just that equivocal phrase "arms control" favored by the Pentagon—and the peaceful resolution of disputes between nations to prevent another world war.

The charter struck a new note. For the first time it added human rights to the international vocabulary. It sought to transcend national boundaries and mentalities, emphasizing the protection of human rights within nations, whether the rights of majorities or minorities or individuals. This change reflected the lessons of the Second World War, which demonstrated that internal regimes were not just a domestic matter but could themselves become a menace to world peace.

Thought Control

This amnesiac and unhistorical generation needs to be reminded that Nazi Germany, Fascist Italy, and the Japanese military dictatorship began by thought control at home. They gagged peace movements, stifled dissent, forbade a free press, and glorified war, turning their peoples into submissive zombies for aggressive leaders. The nightmare of the crematoria—and the other horrors of Axis occupiers in Europe and Asia—were still fresh in the mind of mankind when the charter was adopted and its new concept of crimes against mankind was applied at the Nuremberg trials. Need Moscow be reminded now that these fundamental changes in international law were intended to prevent a repetition of what cost the USSR alone some 25 million lives?

Three years before the General Assembly voted for its Universal Declaration of Human Rights in 1948, the charter's preamble affirmed human rights as a foundation stone of world peace, and the charter itself contained eight articles for their implementation.

"This amnesiac and unhistorical generation needs to be reminded that Nazi Germany, Fascist Italy, and the Japanese military dictatorship began by thought control at home."

This may be "history," but history repeats itself in strange and unexpected ways. The sinister relationship between internal abuses of human rights and external policies is once again evident—and threatening to international stability—in the way the iron-fisted Libyan, Syrian, Iranian, and Iraqi regimes covertly foster abroad the terrorism with which they subjugate their own peoples at home. It is not reassuring that all four of these regimes are led by grim charismatic Pied Pipers, miniaturized clones of *Il Duce* and *Der Führer*. Should they be sealed off from human rights criticism on the ground that they represent a "social choice" or "freedom of choice"? When did they count ballots in a free election?

In these efforts to turn back the clock on human rights, Gorbachev has varied his arguments and his tactics. At one point in his first appeal, in September 1987, he startled the reader by seeming to throw in the sponge and accepting the basic premise of the Universal Declaration of Human Rights. This appears at the bottom of page 7 of the official [Soviet news agency] Tass English translation. There Gorbachev suddenly said, "I agree: the world cannot be considered secure if human rights are violated in it."

But this turned out to be a debater's trick like that of the wrestler who throws his opponent off balance by an unexpected recoil. What follows this welcome admission is simply a bald effort to change the subject by changing the definition of human rights. This has been a standard ploy of Soviet propagandists in dealing with Western human rights criticism. I heard the same apologetics on CBS's *60 Minutes* from a Fidel Castro spokesman.

"I will only add," Gorbachev added with what he seemed to consider great cleverness,

> if a large part of this world has no elementary conditions for a life worthy of man, if millions of people have the full "right" to go hungry, to have no roof over their head and to be jobless and sick indefinitely when treatment is something they cannot afford, if, finally, the basic human right, the right to life, is disregarded. . . .

The sentence was left unfinished, but the message implied was clear enough. He seemed to be suggesting that so-called human rights were of little importance when these more elementary "rights to life" were ignored. But who proposes to ignore them? Gorbachev never explained why there was any contradiction between striving for human rights and striving for peace and decent standards of living. Everywhere on the globe, the Soviet block included, the same activists strive for both. Andrei Sakharov has been the foremost leader and symbol of both campaigns.

Human Rights

Gorbachev's argument will probably be a major theme of the coming Moscow conference on human rights. But in the context of the human rights debate, it could be diversionary, an effort to change the subject from the evils of authoritarianism to the "evils of capitalism." This is what logicians used to call the *tu quoque* argument or in barfly parlance the "you're another" clincher.

Without political or human rights it is impossible to struggle for wider socio-economic reforms and for peace. The best witness against Gorbachev on this point is Gorbachev himself. In his own evolution as Soviet leader, Gorbachev has said many times that he soon discovered that economic reform of the stagnant Soviet system could not be brought about without political reform, without democratization, without a freer press, without giving the Soviet peoples a voice in their own destiny. He might have added, but didn't, that the main obstacle was the new ruling class entrenched by the one-party system.

A dramatic example: How many Soviet and Afghan lives might have been spared, how many billions of rubles might have been saved for urgent needs at home if Sakharov instead of being exiled to Gorki by Gorbachev's predecessors for criticizing the Afghanistan invasion—Russia's Vietnam—had been allowed to lead a public debate to curb the headstrong military and bring about earlier withdrawal? Housing and hospital facilities in the Soviet Union were bled to keep that stupid and cruel war going. Now, in the wake of the Armenian earthquake, we learn that many hospitals in the rural areas of the USSR do not even have hot water! That is the price Soviet peoples paid for a secretive and undemocratic regime. Stale propaganda may try to play one off against the other, but in the real world political and economic rights are Siamese twins. They add up to human rights, which in the UN context includes both political and economic rights. The relationship is acutely visible in the third world, where so much of foreign aid is wasted by military dictators or stolen by the new native elites allied with them.

Gorbachev took a different tack on human rights when he met Reagan in Moscow in 1988. Gorbachev didn't have to be a genius to know that there was no sense in lecturing Reagan (or Margaret Thatcher either) on the shortcomings of capitalism. As for trying to turn America's homeless into an advantageous debater's point, there was the danger that Reagan might whip out a three-by-five card explaining that the homeless were either rugged individualists who preferred sleeping in the streets or canny entrepreneurs saving the rent money for investment.

With Reagan, Gorbachev tried to reduce human rights controversy to a question of some individual "cases" which the Soviet Union had shown itself ready to resolve in bilateral negotiations. He seemed to prefer the word "cases" to the more usual Soviet term "mistakes." The latter does imply, however faintly, that something was done wrong, though it still avoids any admission that this was a consequence of the authoritarian system itself.

Internal Abuses

The confrontation in Moscow was an odd bit of pantomime. Though Gorbachev likes to call himself a revolutionary, and is indeed a reformer, at least up to a point, he wanted Reagan to sign a joint accord freezing the status quo on basic rights and insulating internal abuses from international criticism. This proposed accord has not been given the study it deserves, although Gorbachev disclosed part of the aborted agreement in his press conference in Moscow the day the summit ended.

"Gorbachev . . . wanted Reagan to sign a joint accord freezing the status quo on basic rights and insulating internal abuses from international criticism."

Gorbachev complained that when he first showed the text to the President (in Russian as well as English!) Reagan read it and said, "I like it." But when they met again the next morning on the last day of the summit, Reagan, after consulting his advisers, had changed his mind. "And that," an exasperated Gorbachev told the press on June 1, 1988 "is what we were debating this morning." It is a pity their debate was not made public. Some day it may provide delicious tidbits for the historians on both sides.

Perhaps one reason Reagan first agreed so readily is that he is notoriously fatigued by fine print and the first half of the text sounds as uncontroversial as motherhood used to be. "Both of us," the joint statement said,

> proceeding from an awareness of the obtaining realities in the present day world believe that no problems in dispute are insoluble and that they should not be solved by military means, that peaceful coexistence is something that we resolve as a universal principle of international relations. . . .

So far this was indisputable. Everyone would hope that no problems are insoluble. And no one would be so uncouth—or *nekulturna*, as the Russians say—as openly to suggest that they should be solved by military means, though Moscow just tried it in Afghanistan and Washington has been practicing it by proxy against Nicaragua. But then the fine print begins. The proposal went on to shut the door not only on military action but on peaceful political efforts to deal with human rights abuses.

The text continued by saying " . . . and that the equality of all states, noninterference in domestic affairs, and freedom of socio-political choice should be recognized as inalienable and mandatory for all." That is the Brooklyn Bridge an innocent visitor from America was on the verge of acquiring.

Declaration of Independence

The vocabulary seductively echoes a word hallowed by the US Declaration of Independence and the English Revolution of 1688 before it. The word is "inalienable." But the Gorbachev proposal turned its meaning upside down, reversing its purpose and direction. The "inalienable" right stressed by John Locke and Thomas Jefferson were the rights of individuals, not of governments. That citizens had inalienable rights implied an end to the divine right of kings and other autocrats. It was the answer to Louis XIV's "L'état c'est moi" [I am the state]. That formula has also been the basic premise of Russia's autocratic rulers from both Greats, Peter and Catherine, through Vladimir Lenin and Joseph Stalin. Gorbachev would have made it a universal law to protect a plague of dictators, right and left, in today's world. The inalienable rights of Gorbachev's proposal were to become the rights of the states whose helms they had seized and not of individual citizens fighting to regain their basic freedoms. In the long historical perspective this is counterrevolution on a grand scale. From the same perspective, our Declaration of Independence reads like the original declaration of human rights. The faded phrases from our schoolbooks spring forth with a fresh sharpness and a reinvigorated relevance.

Jefferson and his fellow Framers sought to justify the overthrow of the onerous British yoke by affirming as "self-evident" that "all men"—men, not states—"are created equal" and "endowed by their Creator with certain inalienable Rights" and that "among them are Life, Liberty and the pursuit of Happiness." Locke's phrase was "life, liberty and property." Jefferson changed "property" to "the pursuit of happiness," subordinating property rights to human rights and aspirations. Here Jefferson took a great leap forward and made the classic phrase as applicable today when used by rebels in Moscow and Beijing as it once was in Philadelphia.

"The inalienable rights of Gorbachev's proposal were to become the rights of the states . . . and not of individual citizens fighting to regain their basic freedoms."

The words in which the right of revolution were spelled out would be regarded as inflammatory in much of the third world as well as in the Soviet orbit from Hanoi to Havana. Governments derive their legitimacy from "the consent of the governed," and "whenever any form of Government becomes destructive" of life, liberty, and the pursuit of happiness, it is the right of the "People" to "alter or abolish it." This may be old hat to us. But try reading that aloud today in Pushkin Square.

It is a tremendous turn in the dialectic of history—to borrow a favorite Marxist concept—that the greatest revolution of the twentieth century would end up seeking to preserve the status quo, no matter how oppressive. The final irony is how easily Gorbachev's sullen hard-line opponents could turn this against him. They see glasnost and perestroika as alien serpents in a Soviet paradise.

Declaration of Human Rights

When the Declaration of Human Rights was put to the UN in 1948, the vote in favor was unanimous. But Stalin, despite a plea from Eleanor Roosevelt, who mothered it as the American delegate, led the Soviet block into abstention, along with South Africa and Saudi Arabia. South Africa abstained to protect apartheid; Saudi Arabia did so because the declaration outlawed slavery—it still had slaves in 1948. Stalin never explained why he abstained. It would have challenged his monolith.

Stalin's hostile abstention set Soviet policy until the Leonid Brezhnev years, which in this respect were not wholly stagnant. At that time, 1976, the USSR ratified two major UN covenants intended to implement the Human Rights Declaration—the International Covenant on Economic, Social, and Cultural Rights, and the International Covenant on Political Rights. These, as the titles indicate, protect the entire range of human rights, including economic rights. But under Brezhnev these obligations were ignored.

The human rights landscape in the USSR has changed dramatically over the last thirty-five years. The first mass outpouring of politicals from prisons and labor camps began spontaneously after the death of Stalin and continued under Nikita Khrushchev. Then the Gulag began to fill up again under Brezhnev. The two covenants Brezhnev accepted not only remained dead letters but his legal reforms became new, though milder, authorizations for repression.

The ferocious law against counterrevolutionary crimes, for example, was repealed under Khrushchev. But two products of the slow and sticky legal reform mills turned out to give the KGB [Soviet secret police] equivalent tools against the outspoken—section 70 against "anti-Soviet agitation" and 190.2 against "anti-Soviet slander." Both are so vague they invite abuse. And the prospect of their repeal grows dimmer.

Glasnost and Perestroika

Under Gorbachev the atmosphere was changed by the magic prospects of glasnost and perestroika, though no one, including Gorbachev, seems to know exactly what they mean. He has freed most if not all the political prisoners whose very existence he had sedulously denied. Every few months over the past few years—and again in Gorbachev's address on December 7, 1988 to the UN—legal reforms have been promised to prevent future abuses. But the apparatchiks [members of the Communist apparatus] hate to give up the arsenal of future intimidation, and with Victor Chebrikov moved up in 1988 from KGB chief to head of the legal reform commission, the first products of the promised reforms are disturbing. . . .

I.F. Stone is a well-known journalist and author. He is a former editor of The Nation *and* The New York Post *and has written over ten books including,* The Trial of Socrates *and* The War Years: 1939-1945.

"Gorbachev could clear the atmosphere of suspicion by a single stroke. He could invite exiled activists . . . to come home and invite them to resume monitoring human rights abuses."

Of course Gorbachev could clear the atmosphere of suspicion by a single stroke. He could invite exiled activists like the heroic Soviet psychiatrist Dr. Anatoly Koryagin to come home and invite them to resume monitoring human rights abuses, with the promise of no interference by the police or the postal authorities. But that would indeed be a revolution.

"What we found was a virtual cornucopia of new political groups and initiatives all born under glasnost and perestroika."

viewpoint 22

Soviet Reforms Are Succeeding

Jim Wallis

I was visiting the Soviet Union with a small group of journalists from the United States. Ten days of dialogue with Soviet dissidents had been arranged to discuss the reality and future of the changes taking place in their country. The Americans were all from "dissident" publications as well, and it was thought that we might have some things in common.

What we found was a virtual cornucopia of new political groups and initiatives all born under *glasnost* and *perestroika*. Out of the frozen ground of Soviet society, new and still-fragile shoots of cultural and political life are breaking through to herald what all those involved fervently hope will be a Russian spring.

Each day in Moscow, we had almost non-stop conversations with a wide range of people and groups having a great variety of experiences and perspectives. While they seem to run the entire ideological spectrum, they all appear to want the same thing—a more democratic, pluralistic, and open political system and society. Most seem tolerant of each other and even supportive of the different opinions and roles among them.

"That's what democracy means," they would tell us. The groups have names like Civic Dignity, The Club of Social Initiative, Democratic Perestroika, Democratic Union, Moscow Popular Front, Obschina (Community), *Glasnost* magazine, The Trust Group, and more.

I was the only "religious" journalist in our group, but many of the others joined me in visiting churches and seeking out both church leaders and religious dissidents. We met with human rights activists and those who, until recently, had been in prison, some for many years.

Some of the groups seem quite "establishment," with respected members from the Academy of Sciences. These groups are made up of political scientists, physicists, historians, journalists, and filmmakers who met with us in comfortable conference rooms where portraits of Mikhail Gorbachev and Vladimir Lenin adorn the walls.

Grassroots Movement

But most of our meetings took place in crowded apartment living rooms with more ordinary people who work at the grassroots level. These walls are more commonly covered with art, political posters, Russian icons, and, in one instance, a picture of Robert Redford.

Our guide was Viktor Zolotaryev, a 28-year-old activist who, for me, symbolized the best of the hopeful but realistic idealism many of these new groups represent. His group, Civic Dignity, is mostly made up of young people who believe politics should be "moral," but they are quick to admit that most people think that is impossible. They started as a human rights group but soon realized that such concerns inevitably lead to political involvement.

The night we met with Civic Dignity, the group was wrestling with the dilemma of how to stay faithful to their belief in law when the authorities act in lawless ways. They and other groups recently had public meetings and protests blocked by the police. Mohandas Gandhi's name came up in the conversation, and a discussion ensued about civil disobedience.

Viktor is committed to nonviolence and has become a vegetarian. While riding the Moscow Metro to the next meeting or walking back and forth from our hotel on Karl Marx Square, Viktor and I would often get into long talks about moral philosophy and political strategy.

There is a freshness and sincerity in Viktor and his friends which bodes well for the political health of the nation. They aren't really sure where they are headed or, for that matter, what lies ahead for them

Jim Wallis, "Dialogue and Dissent," *Sojourners*, February 1989. Reprinted with permission from *Sojourners*, Box 29272, Washington, DC 20017.

or their country. What is clear is how deeply they care about the future and how much integrity they are bringing to the questions.

"The most terrible thing is that people have had no choice," said one of the members from The Club of Social Initiative. Their president, Grigory Pelman, told us that these political clubs became a means of getting people into active social life again "when most were still living with the memory of stagnation." The groups help people to find each other, discover new resources, and create the new initiatives necessary to reconstruct the country, according to their members.

These activists don't want a monochromatic society with no autonomous spheres but a "multicolored future with many ways of living." In place of a totally planned economy in a unitary society, they speak of "economic democracy." Some talk of replacing bureaucratic management with worker self-management, while others speak of introducing a "free market," and many favor both.

A movement toward a multiparty system is critical for most, but some believe more genuine political discussion is possible within the one-party system. Pelman feels the most important task is the realization of new economic conditions and social activities. He said that the need for pluralism would lead to "tensions and contradictions," a price they seem willing to pay for greater freedom.

But regardless of the issues under debate or the opinions held on all sides, the real change in the Soviet Union is the introduction of political discussion itself. There were many times when we found ourselves in the midst of a room where fervent political dialogue was under way. But even if we couldn't understand the conversations in Russian, it was the changed political atmosphere that became the significant thing to see. We were witnessing, as Viktor put it, "the first growth of political life" in the Soviet Union.

> *"Even if we couldn't understand the conversations in Russian, it was the changed political atmosphere that became the significant thing."*

While we were there, a "democratic fraction" was announced within the Young Communist League and, much more significantly, we learned of a new effort by 50 prominent members to create the same inside the Moscow Communist Party. Such party "fractions" have always been illegal, but under *perestroika*, permission has been granted.

For many, however, the real obstacle to genuine political reform was the absolute power of the party itself. Until the Communist Party was willing to surrender its monopoly on political control, there would be no fundamental change in Soviet politics. The dissidents' strategy, said one member of Civic Dignity, is "to use openness to create more openness without provoking reactionary forces." Many are still very wary of the old bureaucracy and conservative bureaucrats resistant to change. Some even spoke of the danger of civil war.

Democratic Perestroika is a club formed by a new generation of social scientists. They hope to produce alternatives to one-party monopoly socialism, which, according to them, is "not socialism at all." Democratic socialism is the movement they want to build. Gorbachev's pluralism isn't enough, they say, and the concentration of power in one man should give way to mechanisms of control from below.

Real Socialism

"*Perestroika* must not be ruled by one man," said a club member. Another favored "real socialism" and the "greening of civil society in Moscow." There was a humorous moment when one member of the group called for a "fourth revolution—a peaceful revolution." He was interrupted by another who pleaded, "Please, no, say *evolution*. There have been enough revolutions in this country."

We quickly saw the political differences between various groups. One observer described the spectrum between traditionalists, liberals, democratic socialists, and new leftists. But American-style political labels and categories really don't fit here, in a country with such an entirely different history and experience.

For example, the capitalist-socialist debate doesn't really exist in the Soviet Union, though the words are used in political conversations. Those realities and choices are simply not part of people's situations.

The only system that the Soviet people know is the one that has failed. Gorbachev's bold experiment in reform comes not because of U.S. strength, as Ronald Reagan has claimed, but rather because the new Russian leader had no choice. The totalitarian and stagnant system that many of the people we met describe as "70 years of terror" simply could be sustained no longer. In this unitary state, creativity had been made illegal and continued political repression made necessary social progress impossible.

To conceive of "socialism" apart from their experience of it is more than many we spoke with can imagine. It is natural for many Soviets to look to the West for alternatives, even though they have never been there or read a foreign language newspaper. The West is simply the only alternative to their own system that they know.

Among the dissidents, we often found a mirror image of the historical tendency of American radicals to idealize the Soviet Union or other socialist revolutions as preferable alternatives to U.S.

injustice and violence. After awhile, we realized that when many dissidents spoke of "capitalism" or the "free market," they were referring more to the political system of pluralism they imagined in the West than to anything else.

Civil Disobedience

One of the most strongly pro-West groups is the Democratic Union. One irony is that its members are perhaps the most activist, regularly committing civil disobedience and going to jail. We had interesting conversations comparing the conditions of Soviet prisons with the U.S. jails some of us have known. Their analysis of Gorbachev's reforms is the most negative, and their demands the most radical. Utilizing quite provocative and confrontational tactics, they are in continual conflict with the authorities.

Some of our most interesting discussions were with veteran human rights activists like Lev Timofeyev, an economist, journalist, and recently released political prisoner, who is now with Press Club Glasnost, a civil rights coalition. Related to Helsinki Watch, the club is a sort of Soviet ACLU (American Civil Liberties Union) working in defense of human rights and political prisoners. He confirmed the fact that many political prisoners had been released, and it was from Timofeyev that I learned that an imprisoned Russian Orthodox priest I came to ask about was soon to be set free.

"Day by day, the process of democratization is harder and harder to reverse," Timofeyev said. "I'm an optimist. The powers of resistance have less and less chance of going back." But he is also cautious in pointing out that the resistance to change is very great, and, therefore, change should be made very carefully.

Like others we spoke to, this experienced political observer is concerned about the dangers of instability. He mentioned the realities of nuclear power stations, bandits, and a political underground of reactionary forces that others likened to a Soviet mafia. But any democratization of "hard and official structures" is useful, according to Timofeyev.

When asked "What kind of society do you want?" Timofeyev's answer was unlike the theoretical visions we had heard from many dissidents. In tempered realism, he replied, "No, I want to be active in this society. . . . We cannot predict the development of history. . . . I was surprised by how fast *perestroika* came."

A fascinating discussion developed with Timofeyev after he expressed the view that any interference with the free market was incompatible with democracy. He cited Milton Friedman, the ultraconservative economist from the University of Chicago.

When it was clear that he wanted to discuss the matter, I described the dynamics of the free market in the area of housing and their consequences for the poor in inner-city Washington, D.C. That was terrible, said Timofeyev, who recommended that the government make provision for low-income housing. When we pointed out that such proposals often draw the accusation of "socialism" by the free-market economists he admires, the human rights activist frowned. "Well, then, I support that kind of socialism." It was yet another example of how the terms and language of debate in the United States cannot be superimposed on the political dialogue in the Soviet Union.

"Many political prisoners had been released, and . . . an imprisoned Russian Orthodox priest . . . was soon to be set free."

Sergei Grigoryants, editor of *Glasnost* magazine, provides the perspective of the independent movements in the Soviet Republics, whose rapid growth and emerging militancy add yet another explosive element in an already volatile political crucible. After many days of hearing so many varied and conflicting assessments of the political situation, I became convinced of Grigoryants' assertion that "the organization of democratic initiatives is the only real hope for changing the country."

The role of Gorbachev himself is one of the greatest ironies. The method he has chosen to democratize his country requires the consolidation of more and more power in himself. Some say that is the only way it could have happened, while others contend it is the ultimate contradiction that could become the most formidable obstacle to true political democracy. "Democracy will have come when Gorbachev himself can be criticized," one dissident said to us.

The official line now is that Lenin was a true socialist and so is Gorbachev. Every leader in between "distorted" true socialism. Such a simplistic and self-serving analysis relegates more than 60 years of the 70-year experiment to the period of distortion. More important, it fails to acknowledge the roots of Stalinism that were already present in Leninism. And it does not allow for a climate in which the policies and practices of Gorbachev the reformer can come under real democratic scrutiny.

While there is undeniably much more cultural and political space now in the Soviet Union, the economy remains largely untouched by the reforms thus far. Unless that problem is resolved, it may prove to be the Achilles' heel of *perestroika*, and Gorbachev knows it.

However, there is another more troubling political dilemma just under the surface of every conversation. A basic contradiction remains. How can democratization really take place on the foundations of a system that is essentially undemocratic? Before the 1917 Revolution, there was czarist Russia, which means that no popular democratic tradition really exists in the Soviet Union. Upon what will a democratic future be built?

The first night we arrived, even jet lag couldn't keep a few of us from a walk to Red Square. We entered through the high-arched gate and made our way up a steep cobblestone walkway to the most famous public place in the Soviet Union. Finally we reached the top and saw one of the most spectacular sights any of us had ever seen. The breathtaking expanse, brightly illuminated, quickly roused us from our travel-induced stupor.

On the left is displayed an unbroken line of huge and dramatically colored flags, and they were rippling in the cool night breeze. On the right is the massive Kremlin Wall, standing behind the impressive starkness of Lenin's tomb and the enormous reviewing stands, where communist officials watch hundreds of tanks thunder through the endless expanse of Red Square on important political occasions. We learned later that we had arrived on "Constitution Day," and the square was all decked out and lit up for the celebration.

Red Square

But it was something at the far end of Red Square that caught my eye, almost as if everything else simply led up to it. We quietly approached and felt almost overtaken with the beautifully colored onion domes of St. Basil's Church, reflecting almost mystically in the night's illumination. It seemed as though everthing else in the square pointed to this Russian Orthodox church that had been closed by the revolution and made into a museum.

Later in the week we visited the Kremlin. On the inside, the Kremlin is filled with churches. The irony of that never left me during the entire trip. Most of the inner sanctums of Soviet political power are off-limits to the long lines of tourists that daily stream into this old fortress that has become the worldwide symbol of communist power. But inside the Kremlin, what the people are doing is viewing religious icons in Russian churches.

Beautifully painted representations of Christ, Mary, the disciples, and saints—the icons are much more than a principal Russian art form to the millions of Orthodox Christians and anonymous believers who revere them as sacred objects of worship and devotion. Some people just stand and meditate for a long time, and the atmosphere of prayer is clearly discernible—inside the Kremlin.

The churches themselves are wonderful to behold, and there are five of them within the Kremlin walls. They have survived the 70 years of atheistic propaganda and persecution, and it almost seems as though these churches and all the extraordinary faces in their icons are keeping a careful eye on their communist adversaries, rather than the other way around.

The Russian Christians have suffered grievously, especially during the terrible Stalin years. It is said that most active Christians were martyred or sent to prison. I met with Christians who had known the pain and purging of persecution.

Zoya Krakhmalnikova and her husband, Felix Svetov, are ex-political prisoners recently released from exile. Their only crime was their faith. Both are writers, and she was the editor of a religious journal named *Hope*. Zoya spent five years in prison before being exiled to Siberia where, eventually, she was joined by Felix, after he too was released from prison and sent into exile.

Mystical Experience

It was a "mystical experience" that led to her conversion from atheism. The magazine she edited concerned itself with spirituality and theology, but that was enough to put her in jail. During Zoya's prison years, it was her "thirst for Christ" that enabled her to survive. The KGB [the Soviet secret police] tried repeatedly to break her through interrogation and intimidation, but she refused to submit to their demands. She says that she "really experienced hell" but learned that "only a strong faith can save us—a faith that goes until the very end."

"Perestroika may be ushering in a new era of church-state relations in the Soviet Union."

Today, Zoya believes that Christians are "rather taken with the comforts of life." She thinks the problem in the West is just as great because "Christianity has become a comfortable way of life—well-established, rich, and safe." There is a powerful fervency and determination about this woman. She outlasted her persecutors, and it's easy to see why.

At the same time, Zoya possesses a very gentle spirit and a mature faith that has been tested and purified. Her piety is very natural and real. "Christianity is madness," Zoya said. "It is the madness of the cross. Only by returning to the true source of Christianity is there hope." She firmly believes that the persecution the Russian church has lived through can be a true gift and grace to the world.

Epiphany Church is the "largest working Russian Orthodox Church," according to the tour book. I wondered what a "working" church is, compared with one that doesn't work. A friend of mine knows a priest there, so I went on my first Sunday morning in Moscow. A number of our delegation came along.

I have never seen anything like it in my life. The inside of the church is absolutely radiant, with gold-colored walls literally covered with icons. The smell of incense curled through the air, while wonderful music wafted up to the brilliantly crafted ceilings. It actually sounded like the singing of angels, so when I couldn't see the choir, I wasn't surprised.

It was standing room only in the church, and that is because everyone stands all through the Orthodox services, which typically last at least two to three hours and are held at various times throughout the day—every day. As I had often heard about the Russian churches, this one was very full.

Men were there, along with some families, and everyone says that the number of young people is increasing. However, it was the women who made the lasting impression on me. They appear to be simple women, even poor, working-class, and peasant mothers who look and dress the same way they have for decades.

At one point in the service, a "babushka," as these women are often called, was having difficulty getting through the crowd of worshipers to where she wanted to light her candle. She poked my companion, Adam Hochschild from *Mother Jones* magazine, handed him her candle, and pointed to the place he should take it. Adam gracefully weaved through the worshiping throng to the candle stand of flickering hopes and prayers, where he graciously completed his assignment.

Church-State Relations

Alexi Bytshkov is pastor of the Moscow Baptist Church and president of the Union of Evangelical Christians. Proudly displayed on his office wall is a large, framed photograph of Billy Graham delivering a sermon in the church on the occasion of its 100th anniversary. Bytshkov is a respected Russian church leader who believes that *perestroika* may be ushering in a new era of church-state relations in the Soviet Union.

The liberalization extends to the churches, according to the Baptist pastor, and his church is now allowed a freedom to do things hardly imagined possible just a few years ago. The Baptists are now holding open-air meetings in Moscow. He reported a great interest in church teaching, music, and literature. Formal dialogues and debates are occurring between students on the meaning of being a believer. He said many are "thirsty and eager to hear."

For the first time, they now have a great supply of Bibles. From the Scandinavian churches have come 150,000 Bibles, in Russian and with commentaries. On the day before, 50,000 had arrived from Finland. The Baptist World Alliance has sent 180,000 Bibles and hymnals, and more seem to be coming all the time. Before *perestroika*, only a small number were allowed. "The Bible is a great treasure for us," said Bytshkov, and he told me the story of how his old family Bible was carefully passed down from generation to generation.

When the revolution came, the church was completely shut out of all the social services it had carried on for many years; from then on, only the state would be needed, was what church people were told. Now that is changing. In a dramatic turn of events, Christians are being welcomed back into social service by the communist state.

"A more ecumenical spirit seems to exist now, and most feel that perestroika *is part of the reason for it."*

Bytshkov told the story of a government official addressing a group of Baptists who were volunteering at a state hospital. "I never thought that I, as an atheistic scientist, would be standing before Baptists to say thank you for your help. We provide the chemistry, and you provide the love."

Children's education, once strictly forbidden, is becoming more possible again. Much of the new church activity is still illegal, but the authorities are "indulgent" now. New "freedom of conscience" provisions are being drafted to cover all groups, including the churches. The Baptists are even part of the process of writing the sections which apply to them. Their three most basic concerns are evangelism, education, and unity; and they believe that progress is being made on all three fronts.

There is still tension between "official" churches, like Bytshkov's, and the "unregistered" churches. The historical animosity between the Orthodox Church and the rest of the churches is not yet gone. However, a more ecumenical spirit seems to exist now, and most feel that *perestroika* is part of the reason for it.

Jim Wallis is the editor of Sojourners, *an independent Christian monthly magazine.*

"There is the real possibility...that Gorbachev's current reforms will fail."

viewpoint 23

Soviet Reforms Are Failing

George Feifer

When I was a student in Moscow almost thirty years ago, I thought how I might one day be the John Reed of Soviet reform. I would record the demise of the Communist party's stranglehold on the Soviet people, the unleashing of creativity and productivity that would follow, the flowering of the instinctively Russian socialism that would replace Marxism-Leninism. I longed for reform more than for journalistic glory, for I loved Russia deeply, and still do. And if that sounds forced or high-flown, know that most Americans who have resided there for any length of time, even those who have been imprisoned or otherwise maligned, love her too.

Two Russias alternate in the experience of long-term American residents: the oafish Kremlin of oppression and lies; and the sloppy, beguiling sitting room, or cramped, battered kitchen, where one is more alive and emotionally free than in the rational West. In these shabby rooms one feels surprising relief at having come home to one's emotional motherland—an odd thought, isn't it, in a country with such an alien political and economic system?

I recently returned to Moscow after many years away. Together with the city's smells of cheap diesel fuel and strong tobacco, I gratefully inhaled the old emotional exhilarations, as well as the sudden freshness, the "something new" in the heavy air. Some old friends were gone—to other countries and to cemeteries, for the Russian diet gets them young—but those who were still in Moscow received me warmly, as did new acquaintances. Straight to the drab kitchen and the food and drink, to heavy confidences relieved by comic gossip and dirty jokes. As in the Chekhov plays, the conversation bounced like a pinball from anguish over the human condition to the price of a proper manicure. Once again I felt blessed relief at not having to look successful, smile, pretend. Where else do people so nonchalantly drop every endeavor for talks, walks, and other ways of "wasting" a business day, never counting hours as if they were change in their trouser pockets? And this is not because my friends have money; though most are sophisticated professionals who live high on Moscow's scale, all remain simply *poor*, even from my perspective, on a lower rung of the American middle class.

Russian Repression

I wish I knew why I feel so "connected" in Russia, to my own feelings as well as to others'. Naturally, it is related to what makes Russian literature so moving. Living close to mankind's "tragic essence"—which prompts the need for thought and fun and dispensing with affectation—one feels in touch with fate and eternity. Maybe the spirit soars in Russia precisely because of the efforts to repress it; the closeness among the people sharing your table comes from nothing more exalted than the need to block out so much beyond it, especially the deprivation of choice. ("Westerners live; we talk about it," is how one Russian émigré I know explains the spell of those conspiratorial conversations.) Why then, in the midst of so much good feeling, did I become convinced that Russia is even worse off now than during my last visit in 1980?

Worse off? Despite the vivid signs of stunning change? Despite the remarkable Mikhail Gorbachev, who, at the nineteenth Soviet Communist party conference championed nothing less than radical reform of the structures of the state and of the economy—not with airy talk of the future, but with pragmatic insistence on confronting past failures? It's true that the rumors of what Soviet rule has done (and is doing) to its people are being documented

George Feifer, "The New God Will Fail." Copyright © 1988 by *Harper's Magazine*. All rights reserved. Reprinted from the October issue by special permission.

and discussed. It's even true that the terrible secrets about Soviet atrocities in Poland, and later in Afghanistan, are becoming known—*glasnost* is anything but another clever trick to bamboozle the West. *Novy Mir* charges that Lenin—the exalted Father himself—laid the groundwork for Stalin's savagery by introducing terror and founding the Soviet concentration camp. To my friends in Moscow, highly skilled in reading between the lines, the citing of Lenin's "concentration camps" amounts to an indictment of Leninism itself.

"Astonishing!" I kept saying to myself in Moscow. "Unprecedented!" "Unbelievable!" The many splendid changes filled me with hope—until my friends began telling me in detail of the things that will probably prevent anyone from becoming the John Reed of a brave Soviet rebirth, at least in this century. Simply put, more bad is rooted where we don't see it than good is happening where we do. This, at least, is the conviction of the Russians with whom I spoke during my visit.

My Moscow friends are for the most part Westernized cosmopolitans. No one in Russia wants to believe more in reform—in *glasnost*, and in the restructuring of the political system and the economy that Gorbachev calls *perestroika*—than they. For one thing, few would benefit more. Indeed, they are benefiting already. One artist I've known since the '50s has been on his knees for much of the past thirty years, begging the authorities for just a week in Paris. When I visited Moscow, he was away—in his second month of Left Bank ecstasy. My less lucky friends blessed the new absence in the Soviet papers of paeans to "glorious" socialism, and told me of the satisfaction they now find in reading of some of the abuses they'd told me about over the years. Instead of the old whispering about this and that outrage, they shoved newspapers and magazines at me. "There it is. Read for yourself."

Little Change

But these same grateful beneficiaries of the reforms are profoundly pessimistic about the chances for fundamental change in the society. My friends make no attempt to predict "inevitable failure"; they rail and criticize, I think, to express their anguish, and to prepare themselves for the worst. And although our newspapers sometimes quote voices like these, overall the press had prepared me to expect cheer rather than the gloom I found. Muscovites have an explanation for this. "Naturally your press seeks 'colorful' stories," said a theater manager. "So it runs article after article about change and cooperatives, just like it used to about dissidents. That makes good reading for you. For us, it's different."

I wish I could sketch portraits of these men and women, could describe their circumstances with a novelist's detail. But still fearing repercussion, they requested anonymity—itself an indication of what *hasn't* changed. So imagine if you can, while listening to what they have to say, the drab kitchen, the food and drink on the table, the conversation wandering in all directions. I too will bounce from big questions to ones that may seem small. I've organized the discussion in a way my Russian friends would not, but I trust they'll forgive me.

"The reforms are the work of one more powerful leader foisting radical changes on a cowed, passive people. Perestroika . . . is another party line."

Far from being the result of some popular movement, the reforms are the work of one more powerful leader foisting radical changes on a cowed, passive people. *Perestroika,* my friends insist, is another party line. This argument is clearly disputable: Gorbachev is hardly Peter the Great, and a small percentage of the passive people *are* involved in the reforms, at least to the extent of wishing they might come true. A wordly physics professor believes "totally" in Gorbachev, "because this is our last chance for a normal country, and last chances can't be lost. Don't tell me that's an illusion. Damn it, I *believe!*"

But when I asked others why, if the reforms can happen now, they didn't happen before, their answer was bafflement at the very question. *Of course* the bosses decide. Even relatively sophisticated Muscovites know they have nothing to do with such matters. "And if you'd asked in, say Gorky, the workers wouldn't give a damn," said my oldest friend. "Why *should* they, after all that's been done to them? Some workers may protest about food, wages, or vodka. But they're spectators in everything else."

The intelligentsia feel little more involved or responsible. Most are good at specifying and deploring Soviet "idiocy," but its remedies are nothing for them to decide or even influence, certainly nothing for which to risk any possible danger. The most eloquent spokesmen—in private— for fuller reforms lift not a finger for them in public.

Seize the Moment

A solid journalist, whom I will call Z, lectured me passionately on the need to seize the moment and act on Gorbachev's opening. "We may lose everything—meaning, we are doomed—if people remain frightened, *paralyzed,* and don't FIGHT this fight." But when a Swedish journalist asked Z for his reaction to a Reagan speech before Z had read the official reaction to it, this closet crusader ducked and ran, as if to prove his point about paralysis.

Not even the dissidents are much involved in the reforms. For all they did to draw attention to Soviet abuses, they probably had extremely little influence on Gorbachev—who, my friends agreed, launched his program, and will stop it, for *his* reasons. It's a Politburo show from start to finish.

In the conventional Western view, the Soviet worker should support reforms because they are his only way up, and the only way out for the stumbling Soviet economy—if restructuring succeeds, which could only be in many years. "Meanwhile they hear slogans about it," said a dentist friend. "And if the workers have learned *one* thing in seventy years of Soviet rule, it's not to believe a single new slogan, not to fall for one more trick, never give something now for a promise to be paid later." To which the dentist's wife added: "Painful experience has taught people that each new campaign takes another bite out of their asses. So while Gorbachev and company want to avert national economic disaster, the majority of people have only one concern: to avert personal disaster from another national con job. While *you* might know why we must restructure, our workers know that what counts is what you can steal *today* from your factory."

To understand this sentiment, you have to understand how deep and endemic the problems of the economy are. Gorbachev himself may not have known, when he began his reforms—which, some Muscovites say, explains why he now has begun to seek profound political changes. We in the West, I was told, don't know the half of it: "Last year, only World War II veterans could buy toilet paper—yes, the old cliché about *toilet paper* in our land of immense forests. Now toilet paper is back, which means you find it at the end of a long line in the twentieth store you try. Yesterday, I saw a distinguished-looking professor riding to work on the subway with a huge sack of his precious find. My God! I had to laugh."

Provincial Life

Or: "However bad Moscow has become, it's a cornucopia compared to the rest of Russia. I just left a small city in the Urals. Nothing to eat, nothing for sale. Hundreds of people waiting for days in the airport—no flights out, the usual mechanical problems—without even sighing: they're *used* to that kind of nakedness. It's the story of provincial life."

Or: "Almost everything people want is 'deficit.' Not enough clothes, cookies, frying pans. . . . Isn't it incredible that we still can't satisfy these simple needs? That our consumer products can't compete with those made almost *anywhere* in the world?"

Or: "A huge percentage of our industrial output is superfluous. We manufacture eleven times more tractors and combines than America—imagine this in a country that can't feed itself properly! And more huge factories are being started to build more of the same tractors that will break down daily, although many of the factories will never be completed. Thousands of construction projects are virtually abandoned. All this mind-boggling stupidity and chaos thanks to an economic system that is a gigantic machine for waste, now stretched to the limit of its inefficiency."

"While you might know why we must restructure, our workers know that what counts is what you can steal today from your factory."

People described maternity clinics with no running (let alone hot) water, families waiting for thirty-five years for self-contained (as opposed to communal) apartments, workers living in wretched barracks. They said lack of money for preventative maintenance is causing an increasing number of industrial accidents. They insisted a corner has been turned—not to reform and modernization, but to Third World status. I have no way of confirming these plaints except to say that some came from the first whisperers to me twenty years ago that the Soviet economy faced dire trouble, when it seemed to be racing ahead.

So is it any wonder that workers hold on to their scraps with a death grip and risk nothing? And there is this too: Khrushchev accused Stalin of gigantic mistakes, and Brezhnev accused Khrushchev of the same. Why shouldn't Gorbachev's reforms turn out to be colossal follies someday too?

Consider Perestroika

Or consider *perestroika* another way, one friend advised. Look at how it's been implemented so far: new, independent inspectors are returning defective goods to the 2,300 largest factories, and workers must repair them—actually tighten the nuts, replace the dud parts *without extra pay.* Having been programmed to goldbrick for peanuts ("If you pretend to work," goes the joke, "the state pretends to pay you"), workers are now asked to work harder for the same pittance or less (thanks to inflation). "Our workers aren't crazy," I was told. "Why should they do this?"

If the worker doesn't want *perestroika,* his boss wants it even less. This resistance goes even deeper, my friends say, than the conventional Western view that Soviet bureaucrats oppose change as a threat to perks and positions. It's more a matter of shareholders fighting for control of a company; in this case, we are talking about the hard men who "own" the state-run economy. And they have no intention of surrendering without a fight. For a regional or district party first secretary, *glasnost* is one thing, and wealth another, as a diplomat's son pointed out to me. "Our new Hyde Park—the people shouting all kinds of things in our newspapers—doesn't involve *money*," he said. "The real battle is for control of wealth. And that's where the old guard is deeply dug in, out in the mines and factories."

"Khrushchev accused Stalin of gigantic mistakes, and Brezhnev accused Khrushchev of the same. Why shouldn't Gorbachev's reforms turn out to be colossal follies someday too?"

Frequently, it seems, local authorities subvert reforms by pretending to adopt them. "The trick is to be seen 'actively participating,' without losing a shred of your power and privileges," is how one friend put it. Without having achieved mastery in such maneuvering, high Soviet officials would not have become high Soviet officials. Local kingpins determined to hang on while pretending to let go make good use of the inspections to which every factory is subject. In some cases, I was told, an enterprise may have 200 inspections a year, by city party authorities, regional party authorities, People's Control teams, the State Bank, the Ministry of Finance . . . The welter of controls, and the habits of submission they breed, allow countless opportunities for confusion, corruption, and the desired inertia. An inspector receiving a kickback sees no signs of reform but reports seeing "all reforms completed," said a man who spends much of his professional life in Volga cities. Of course, Gorbachev may understand the dodges, but he's working against time. If the bosses hold on for three, four years, and there is still little to show for all the reform (and the sacrifice entailed in implementing reform), the bosses are safe.

Literally Hungry

A young journalist I know is convinced the bosses will prevail. "Let some farmers try to build a cow shed on their own initiative. The approvals will be held up ten years—in a country that's almost literally hungry, where the national dairy herd is actually decreasing. But the local authorities care about power much more than food. Their tenacity is tremendous. The obstacles they're throwing up to the kind of economic independence necessary for real progress are horrendous."

Don't assume the 'new' and the 'old' are battling for ideas," an economist warned me. I should keep in mind that many of the ringing calls for reform have come from the same overweight men who just a few years ago ran an economy that supposedly didn't need reform. The reformers and the hard-liners, the conservatives and liberals, all went to the same schools, all came up through the same ranks. There might be generational differences—but there have been such differences before. Generations have always done battle; it's a matter of who will take power, and who will cling to it.

My sourest friend put it this way: "What's really happening is one clique trying to oust another. All right, the new one is less miserable, but it remains a mafia." When push comes to shove, they will act according to their own code. They will close ranks. They will look for scapegoats. They will suppress.

During the first three years of Gorbachev's campaign against drinking and alcoholism, the bootleg trade has exploded; 500,000 makers and sellers of illicit alcohol were arrested last year, according to official, probably understated, figures. And I was told that last year 11,000 fatalities were caused by drinking industrial alcohol. The list of what is guzzled—antifreeze, brake fluid, cleaning fluid, toothpaste (of which a severe shortage has developed), floor polish, shoe polish, old standbys such as Sterno and eau de cologne—startles even Russians. In Moscow, I heard of a new and potent cocktail: three shots of insect repellant in a bottle of beer.

Loss of Revenue

The near halving of state liquor production has brought about a huge loss of state revenue and, according to my friends, has provoked a great deal of resentment, especially among workers. "The Russian worker's only real freedoms were to curse in solitude and to drink," said an old friend's new wife. "He had no other freedoms, not to eat a decent cut of meat, to travel abroad, to pray in church"—though this may be changing a little—"to take a holiday in a hotel. Only the freedom to forget with a bottle when he came home from work, dirty and disgusted, and waited for a dinner barely fit for human consumption. He was a slave for centuries, but until Gorbachev, no one took his bottle away, so how can he care about a *perestroika* that *started* with that? On the contrary, he hates it."

"Brezhnev was considered a joke," my friend added. "Simple people told stories about the medals the hack pinned on his chest, and the intelligentsia told stories about the books the dodo supposedly wrote—but they laughed at him, whereas Gorbachev takes away their vodka and then tries to make them *work*—and they hate him for it."

Almost every worker I spoke to voiced anger, if not hatred, at his deprivation of vodka and the need to stand for hours in colossal lines—galling new ones, since alcohol was often the single commodity not in shortage—for a "Gorbachevka," the caustic nickname for the bottle that now costs a crushing fifteen rubles. (These lines have actually caused a few fatalities of their own; several Russians have been crushed by frenzied crowds as closing time approached.) This is why the same friends who ten years ago despaired of an alcoholic "plague" threatening the country now insist that Gorbachev's anti-alcohol campaign is worse. Mere national drunkenness is less damaging than the hatred that is making so many committed enemies of *perestroika*. (Some friends claimed the restrictions are already being quietly, unofficially eased, although Gorbachev is reluctant to retreat from the first campaign of his reforms.)

Private Cooperatives

My friends question the importance of the much-vaunted cooperatives—the experimental organizations of workers who, using their own pooled resources, have taken over workshops within state factories, or have launched small workshops of their own. The "private" cooperatives have in fact begun to fill huge gaps in the state's production of items such as trousers and boots, but they sell these new and sought-after goods at prices higher than imported goods found on the black market. "A man who sells a pair of private shoes for 100 rubles can afford a meal in a cooperative restaurant with the millionaires and foreigners," said an engineer whose husband is also an engineer. "And a man involved in the restaurant can afford to buy his wife a pair of 'private' shoes." The engineer can afford neither; is that what's meant by restructuring?

"Mere national drunkenness is less damaging than the hatred that is making so many committed enemies of perestroika.*"*

And even if the cooperatives do someday work as planned, can they and other "private" initiatives help reshape the mammoth Soviet economy? My friends believe that the freedom given to cafés, sidewalk refreshment stands, and arts-and-crafts pushcarts does not *perestroika* make. "Come on," I heard from one Muscovite, "our massive industries—steel, chemicals, railroads, *everything*—need total reorganization, and you're talking bras and panties, balalaika music at supper."

Many Russians wonder how much better things might be today if Gorbachev had started the reforms with a crash program to improve food supplies. If he would have stocked the stores for a while—a potent symbol—the skepticism might have eased. He didn't, it didn't.

"See that big grocery store?" an old friend asked as we strolled near the city's edge. "Workers in towns and cities 200, 300, 500 kilometers from Moscow get their trade-union committees to hire buses to visit Lenin's mausoleum. Only they never get to the mausoleum. They stop right there, at the first store inside Moscow's city limit—and load sometimes fifteen buses at a time with awful sausages and potatoes."

"People will never get off their asses until they see something to buy," said a party official's chauffeur moonlighting as my driver. "What they see now is less every day, understand?"

Reform or Not

The dream is over, reform or not—you hear this from everyone. The twentieth century, with its complexities and contradictions and the post-war information-technology revolution, has revealed Marxism-Leninism—essentially a reaction to the industrial revolution of the early nineteenth century—as simplistic, messianic, and useless, when not poisonous. It worked in a way (and, at any rate, with great sacrifice and pain) when economies were measured by tons of pig iron poured. It also worked, in the classroom, as a means to understand aspects of capitalism. But it doesn't work now; it has become irrelevant in Moscow.

"Our jungle is just at a lower level than the capitalist jungle," said a political journalist. "If moral and ethical standards are eroding in America, imagine what's happened where people have been lied to so long, where everyone has to steal to live, where it's dog eat dog for decent *cabbage*, for God's sake."

"People are developing an inner hostility," said a grade-school teacher. She fails to see how any "new generation" could deliver social progress. Many of the young, on whom Gorbachev is counting, are among the country's most cynical. "At least I'm willing to *talk* about the country's future," said a photojournalist. "My daughter and her friends won't waste the time. They simply don't care."

"She is convinced that nothing good is going to happen in her lifetime," said a gallery curator about *her* daughter. "So she devotes herself totally to her personal hobbies and passions; it's the Me Generation without Western consumer goodies."

I visited a couple whose wedding I'd attended twenty years ago. "The threat of labor camps and mental hospitals has eased a lot," the husband said, "but not our degradation and humiliation. A foreigner can't know a fraction of the constant hypocrisy and stripping of human dignity here."

No Change

But hasn't this too begun to change? Not as it must, according to my friends. The architect: "People have begun shouting that the roof leaks badly. Others yell that the sagging floor, flooded basement, timbers with dry rot, also need repair. So everybody joins the *glasnost* babble, which cures nothing by itself—and won't, because we can't remember how to make a good roof and how joists should fit. Meanwhile, we're supposed to 'restructure' without touching the rotten Marxist-Leninist foundation or the Politburo architects who designed the mess or the wormy socialist facade. But even with real plans and fine workmen, restoring a wreck costs much more than building something new, so all attempts to do it *their* hopeless way will only throw more good money after bad, and set us further behind. The only real solution is to abandon the wreck and build a new house on a fresh site. But where? How?"

The transportation manager: "Our weakening economy is gasping to keep its maybe 18 million anti-productive 'supervisors' in clover. But let them stay there, let them eat caviar, hold conferences, pin medals on each other—as long as they have nothing more to do with running the economy, nothing *whatsoever.* That's our only hope, but is it a realistic one?"

A physicist: "When Neville Chamberlain almost delivered England to Hitler, somebody in the House of Commons told him: Now get out. You've been here too long, done too much harm, and don't know how to correct it. In the name of God, *Go!* That's it exactly. We don't need them to confess their past mistakes and stay. We need them to *get out.*" . . .

Reformist Czars

But most of my friends give Gorbachev only two or three more years before his reforms are scrapped and he is reduced to a much more standard Soviet leader (like some of the initially most-committed reformist czars) or banished to his garden, like Khrushchev. "Two to three years," I was told, "after which it will be clear to everyone that there's no real improvement, you still won't be able to get soup meat twice a week or buy a tolerable suit. End of experiment."

The point is summed up in a play on Pushkin's poem to Pyotr Chaadaev, a philosopher who insisted that Russia's future lay not in pursuing its Russianness but in joining the great body of European civilization—and was declared insane.

> Believe me, Comrade,
> The star of our captivating happiness will rise;
> Russia will straighten from its sleep—
> And on the wreckage of the autocracy
> Will be written our names!

Now rendered (with apologies to Pushkin's graceful rhymes) as:

> We now all live in the era of *glasnost*—
> Believe me, Comrades, this will pass;
> And in the Committee for State Security [the KGB]
> Will be remembered our names!

In many Western eyes, what matters most about Gorbachev is that he is moving Russia in the right direction. Whatever his motives, he seems to have realized that real economic reforms are impossible without political reforms. But when I suggested that Western freedoms were formed by a long series of sometimes chance events—that our cherished civil rights evolved from property rights, once more sacred than mere lives—my friends denied that Gorbachev's changes might lead to a parallel development. "The whole point is, there *are* no real property rights in Russia; there's no refuge of any kind from state power that might serve as a springboard to genuine liberties." Besides, Westerners *fought* for their rights. Russians are once again being granted a few and ordered to make use of them.

KGB Crackdown

If few were optimistic about the events of the day, many foresaw greater severity in the near future. Some predictions of what will follow Gorbachev's "two to three years" were more ominous than a KGB crackdown restoring the status quo. There is much fear that his failure will open the way to a rush of reaction, militarization, and retribution, the old guard and its henchmen settling scores with the reformers and cursed liberals—and the economy plummeting even more rapidly. Then rebellion, anarchy, and civil war will follow, with the likes of my relatively well-off friends running for their lives or being swallowed in an orgy of fury by workers whose patience will have snapped at last. "Or a foreign war—with China, America, it doesn't matter. Because appeals to help Mother Russia in a military crisis will be the only way to 'save' the country."

"My friends give Gorbachev only two or three more years before his reforms are scrapped and he is reduced to a much more standard Soviet leader."

In other words, liberalization will have been discredited, reaction will cripple the economy even more severely, and the something that will need to be done can only be good old adventurism. I don't know, and I think no one else knows, how to take these apocalyptic predictions, or whether a much more straitened Russia would represent a greater or a lesser danger to her more successful rivals. But there is the real possibility of the former, and a greater possibility that Gorbachev's current reforms will fail.

George Feifer is a regular contributor on the topic of Soviet affairs to Harper's Magazine.

"The first and very significant victory of perestroika is that the voice of the people has gotten much stronger."

viewpoint 24

Perestroika Benefits Ethnic Minorities

Indrek Toome, interviewed by Yekaterina Kozhukhova for *New Times*

New Times. We often hear today that perestroika is a social revolution. How applicable is this formula to what is taking place in Estonia? What are the distinctive features of the present political climate in the republic?

Indrek Toome. The policy of perestroika, as you know, originated at the top. But it released a large and powerful driving force—initiative from below. In our republic, this process was swift. In Estonia people are saying: in 1985 we learned to think boldly, in 1986—to speak boldly, and in 1987-88 came the time for bold action. The first and very significant victory of perestroika is that the voice of the people has gotten much stronger. That shows that the ideas of perestroika have found both a response and understanding in our republic.

The Leaders of Perestroika

The press was one of the leaders of perestroika. Next came the Cultural Council—a public organization uniting members of all the creative unions. Its investigations and conclusions influenced the adoption of important economic decisions. And many of the points made in the letter sent by the participants in the joint plenum of the boards of the creative unions to the Party leadership and government of Estonia formed the basis for the platform with which the republic's Communist Party delegation went to the 19th Party conference. In the spring of 1988, during the "three weeks of stagnation," the TV programme "Let's think again" acted as organizer of the Popular Front in support of perestroika. And in June at the meeting marking the opening of the 19th Party conference, Popular Front activists assembled 150,000 people out of a total Estonian population of one-and-a-half million.

The issues on which the Cultural Council, Popular Front, Green Movement and many other unofficial groups in Estonia are concentrating their attention are questions of national policy, relations between different nationalities, environmental protection and restrictions on excessive immigration. Speaking of the trends as a whole, it must be admitted that the intellectual forces in Estonia have put forward ideas so revolutionary that they have alarmed, and continue to alarm many people. But I am convinced that the time has come for radical changes, not half-measures. And if there is anything that should alarm Communists today it is the perceptible disparity between the revolutionary ideas put forward by the Party, and the evolutionary approach to their implementation. This disparity leads to a rift between words and action (and sometimes between words), to greater opposition from the different social forces. Because even at the first stage of perestroika everyone interpreted the concept of "changes are imperative" in his own way: supporters of stagnation had their interpretation, progressive politicians theirs. Everyone wanted some sort of change! But now, when from "recognition of the need" we are moving to concrete action, this contradiction between aims and methods is becoming deeper and more acute.

Today it is clear that perestroika, like any social revolution, has to resolve the question of power. The redistribution of power. And as you know from history, there has never been a case when people approached those in power and asked them to relinquish it, and the holders of power gave it up without a word. Power always had to be won. Let's call a spade a spade.

N.T. But it is not merely a question of replacing certain officials with new ones, albeit more progressive?

Indrek Toome, interviewed by Yekaterina Kozhukhova, "All Want Change," *New Times*, September 1988, No. 39.

I.T. It is a matter of creating genuine democracy. So if today we want to get anywhere, our first job must be to decentralize power: in politics, in the economy and in culture, so as to give society the opportunity to create freely. Perestroika must restore to all citizens, public organizations and enterprises the right to *initiative*. Restore the democratic popular essence of the power of the Soviets—that was how the matter was expressed at the 19th Party conference.

People and Party

N.T. For many long years the thesis "the people and the Party are one" was never doubted. It was beyond criticism. But when perestroika began and the people awakened, it turned out that this was far from being axiomatic, but was rather a theorem that required proving. Isn't that borne out too by the events in Estonia? What I have in mind in particular is the period of preparations for the 19th Party conference. On the one hand—as you have noted—the unofficial associations made a significant intellectual contribution to preparing the platform of the Estonian Communist Party's delegation. On the other hand, among delegates to the conference there were people in whom the public had expressed no confidence. I should like to hear your views on this.

I.T. The elections in our republic were held in the same way as in most cities and republics. Work collectives and the creative unions nominated 600 candidates, and from this number, plenums of district and town Party committees recommended 80. Then the Bureau of the CC CPE [Cultural Council of the Communist Party of Estonia] chose 32. It's true that it had been suggested that all 80 candidates be discussed. But the plenum rejected this by a majority vote (80 per cent) and voted for a list of 32 candidates.

N.T. In other words, 80 per cent of those participating in the Party plenum voted against the views of the public. But, as it turned out, the grievances voiced by the unofficial associations proved well-founded.

I.T. I must say that the investigations and proposals drawn up by the informal associations contained no new questions of principle which the CC CPE was not aware of. Everyone was talking about these problems. However, they had not been stated so radically and boldly. It was thought that it was too early, that the time had not yet come to bring them up, as they were too serious and problematic.... And so they were posed by the intellectuals, the public. For this wait-and-see policy, for its conformism, the CC CPE and the government of the republic were justly criticized by the public.

N.T. Let's be more concrete. What are these issues?

I.T. This concerns a whole series of problems connected with the work of the central departments and orientated to the extensive and pollution-risky development of the Estonian economy, which have led to excessive and uncontrolled immigration into the republic. It is also about the fact that many paragraphs and articles of the Constitutions of the Union republics remain inoperative, since both the U.S.S.R. Council of Ministers and the central departments time and again adopt decisions that violate the principles of the sovereignty of the republics set out in the Constitution. Also, there is the bureaucratic diktat that strangled the country in the past decades and has had, as it were, a redoubled effect on the Union republics, since the U.S.S.R. ministries and departments pursued their own aims and completely disregarded local economic, socio-cultural and ecological interests. On the territory of Estonia, which had an acute labour and raw materials shortage, industries that required a great deal of labour and materials were developed. Hence the uncontrolled immigration, which in turn could not fail to affect the satisfaction of the socio-cultural requirements of the people and the relations between the different nationalities. As a result of the uncontrolled immigration processes, almost half of the one-and-a-half million strong population of the republic—forty per cent—are non-Estonians (most of the immigrants were invited by industrial enterprises). And in the town they are better supplied (1.5 times better) with comfortable housing than the local residents. That too speaks of the omnipotence of the departments, doesn't it? If one adds to that that the U.S.S.R. departments were far from being concerned about training skilled cadres, improving production, creating favourable conditions for the adaptation of immigrants—studying the culture, language and traditions of Estonia—then you can easily imagine what a hard knot of problems they bestowed on the republic. According to sociologists, 74 per cent of the immigrants don't care where they live. Often they are people who cannot share the anxiety of the basic population for the fate of their culture, their "small homeland."

"The value of the individual was denigrated during the period of stagnation and the cult."

Now many of these problems are being solved. A general plan for the national economy of the republic has come into force and it restricts departmental arbitrariness, while extending the rights of local bodies of power. The next step will be to switch the republic to cost-accounting, an idea that was recognized as promising at the 19th Party conference. The Institute of Economics of the Estonian S.S.R. Academy of Sciences has set up a special group to develop the concept of regional cost-accounting. And the general public has been drawn into this work. But it is a very difficult job and can't be done at a gallop. However, we can already submit for discussion the first versions of such a concept.

N.T. You believe that these measures to resolve the problems of the economy will help untie the knot of contradictions between the various nationalities.?

I.T. To a great extent, yes. But of course so far there are not enough such measures. The question of relations between nationalities needs profound revision. A special commission on nationality problems, which I head, has been set up under the CC CPE. Its job is to make a profound study of the contradictions that have accumulated in recent years, get rid of false preconceived notions and the complexes based on them, like the common argument that the development of national culture could hinder the development of internationalism. We proceed from the belief that Soviet culture is a matter of integration and that it is only as strong as the national cultures that make it up. But it also has to be recognized that just as the value of the individual was denigrated during the period of stagnation and the cult, so other moral values in society were devalued, and national sentiments were levelled and denigrated. The existence of national traits were permitted only as something exotic.

Today we have to find effective means to treat the disease of lack of national identity. Despite all the complexity of the task, it is clear that the solution of the problem does not lie in the artificial merging of nations, as was claimed at one time by those who sought to unify culture, nor through assimilation, but through mutual enrichment on the basis of language, cultural exchanges and knowledge of each other's history.

For instance, one of the first priorities—and this was decided by the 11th plenum of the CC CPE—is the introduction of a state language in Estonia (it will be the language of the basic nationality), a statute of citizenship of the E.S.S.R., amendments to the Constitution of the E.S.S.R. and on this basis the adoption of a law on languages. Each person living in Estonia shall have the right to conduct his affairs in the Estonian or in the Russian language. Knowledge of both languages will be regarded as one of the criteria of the professional suitability of a specialist, especially if he has to work with people.

International Movement

N.T. How should one regard the setting up in July [1988] of an International Movement in Estonia? As an ideological counterweight to the Popular Front? As a sign of the diversity of the democratic processes which we are observing today and a warning not to engage in euphoria prematurely? Remember how only a short time ago, a couple of days before the opening of the 19th Party conference, the Estonian public welcomed the Popular Front at a meeting attended by thousands. You were one of those who took part. And now another meeting is hearing and discussing the appeal of the International Movement to all citizens of Estonia in which the Popular Front is warned that unless it hastens to give a rebuff to those who seek to fan national differences in the republic, the International Movement will do so. . . .

"We have to find effective means to treat the disease of lack of national identity."

I.T. At the meeting of the International Movement on July 19, in the numerous—and so different—speeches the following idea was voiced: "It is not the Russians who are giving no peace to the Estonians, nor the Estonians who are giving no peace to the Russians in Kohtla-Jarve, Narva, Maardu, Sillamae. . . . It is the administrative-bureaucratic system that is installing harmful production techniques with complete disregard for the health of the people, no matter what their nationality." But the prevailing theme of supporters of the International Movement was the need to give equal rights to all nationalities living in Estonia. You will agree that sounds very nice. No one rejects that idea (the narrow-minded don't count!). However, the International Movement does not recognize that priority should be given to the development of Estonian culture, the language of the Estonian people on its primordial homeland. That can cause nothing but anger and hurt. The International Movement is right in those cases when priorities are demanded only for Estonians because of their nationality. That indeed is not humane. But it is equally inhumane and undemocratic to refuse the priority development of, I repeat, the Estonian people and their culture. What would help resolve many difficult problems we haved inherited from the times of stagnation and the cult would be wider constitutional rights for territories, real sovereignty for the republics, the development of federalism in the sense in which Lenin understood it (greater rights for local bodies of power in the economic and social spheres, in the development of culture and decentralization of power)—everything that was spoken of at the 19th Party conference and the 11th plenum of the CC CPE. The contradictions between nationalities can be overcome. The very difficult situations that arise at present on these grounds are not a cul de sac. There are ways out. But only through democratic solutions of problems, on the basis of the ethical principle of profound mutual respect and mutual understanding between people. No mistake, whether belonging to long past history or made only yesterday, should be allowed to serve as a pretext for national insults—that is something we always have to remember. And if somebody does that or even an entire public movement is guilty of it, under no circumstances should one reply in kind.

Party Authority

N.T. I should like to go back to what has been said about the Party's authority. To what extent do its bodies today control the socio-political situation in the republic, and to what extent can they influence the orientation of the new democratic structures? How much was said in the past about the "low political awareness of the population," who are therefore in need of wise shepherds, but it turned out that it was not the "flock" who lacked political awareness, otherwise why is it that so often it is the Party propagandists who can't stand up to their opponents at spontaneous meetings or discussions?

"What would help resolve many difficult problems we have inherited from the times of stagnation and the cult would be wider constitutional rights for territories."

I.T. I quite agree that on the whole in the present day public movement (it has its scum—but that's not what we are talking about) there exists a sufficiently high level of understanding and responsibility for the common cause. We have to do a colossal job among Party members in order to restore the Party's vanguard role, in order that it be represented by wise, intelligent people capable of keeping their finger on the pulse of society, all its sections and layers, capable of analyzing the processes at work in it, being the brains behind all these processes, drawing up the strategy and tactics for their development, in other words, hearing, understanding and putting into practice what the people have become conscious of, as Lenin put it. To carry out in practice, not words, the wishes of the people.

I am confident that the 11th plenum of the CC CPE can be regarded as the beginning of this colossal job. Preparations for it were made very carefully: the times required that answers be given to many extremely important questions for the republic. The ideological situation on the eve of the plenum was acute, and what was needed was a realistic approach, responsibility in assessing public phenomena. The plenum lasted two days, there was a business-like constructive discussion, different views were expressed on the existing situation, and different ways out of it were proposed. There were controversial topics. And people argued—they argued, but all views were listened to and taken into account. The response on the next day indicated that in its significance for the republic the plenum could justly stand comparison with the 19th Party conference. I must admit that the support given to the programme of action proposed by the plenum makes us happy. At the same time we realize that no little effort and time will be required to return, this time by deeds, the lost confidence of the people. One wrong step is enough to lose one's authority. But to win it back is some job. But we have no alternative.

N.T. What, in your opinion, should in future be chosen as the instrument for influencing the public and public processes?

I.T. Only the mechanism of a law-governed state, which rules out the possibility of the abuse of power, the usurpation of power. For what have we had until now? The force of power assumed the right to appoint a Communist to one post or another, even though he was poorly prepared and had no authority with the public, but satisfied superior officials or bodies.... Now, when each one of us is being asked to display not imaginary but real merits, knowledge and ability, we have been compelled to admit the weakness of many Party cadres. They are afraid to go to the people. They are unprepared to talk to them. They are accustomed to getting away with generalizations and the cast-iron formulas of poorly learnt and greatly cut-down Marxism. Yet until recently none of this stood in their way. Such people were automatically given power and the authority of their position. The right to leadership should not automatically follow from Party membership—the failure to abide by this principle has done too much harm to the people and the state. Today this is the question of questions.

N.T. But how does one stand up to this syndrome of mistrust, this back-sliding into administrative command methods in internal Party life and other spheres? At the beginning of this interview you yourself said that history knows of no instance when those in power have given up their prerogatives of their own free will.

I.T. We must move more determinedly and radically towards the setting up of a law-governed state. Concrete measures are needed, many instructions have to be cancelled, and changes and amendments have to be made to the Constitution, to the Party Rules, as was said at the 19th Party conference. The conditions should be removed which make it possible for Party functionaries in the executive apparatus of the Soviets to stand above the electorate.

For a long time we believed that all our troubles stemmed from the fact that we say too little, that all our shortcomings are those of education, that we should talk more, talk better, send good lecturers and Party workers to talk to audiences and then everything will be all right. No. Experience has shown that we have to get down to finding the root causes of our troubles. And when we've found them, see that conditions have to be changed. But conditions can't be changed by explanations and elucidations. Radical measures are needed. The entire electoral system has to be democratized. The strength of Soviet power, that is, people's power, depends on this. What kind of people will head the bodies of power? Will they have the support of the people or will they become mere ritual names on the edifice of socialist democracy? A new sociopolitical situation will already give the opportunity to operate democratically.

> *"We must seek to renovate the apparatus of power.... That... is the only way we can advance along the revolutionary course that we call perestroika."*

N.T. But how do we go about "changing the conditions"? What should be done first—should we first amend the Constitution and the Party Rules, or make changes in the system of our representative bodies, which will decide the fate of these and other changes? Or do you think it doesn't matter?

I.T. I think it extremely important and opportune. In my opinion, these problems should be solved simultaneously, which is far from being a palliative. For the minds of the people have been awoken and you can't stop them thinking more deeply and broadly. And society, its state and political systems, cannot, must not allow the gulf between ideas and actions, between the revolutionary posing of a question and evolutionary methods, to expand—efforts must be made to eliminate the disparity mentioned at the beginning. But at the same time we must seek to renovate the apparatus of power, to ensure that the problems really are resolved by new people, with new outlooks, new understanding, new criteria. That, in my opinion, is the only way we can advance along the revolutionary course that we call perestroika.

Indrek Toome is the secretary of the Estonian Communist Party. Yekaterina Kozhukhova is a correspondent for the Soviet weekly New Times.

"Gorbachev's economic reforms are likely to exacerbate the ethnic crisis. Perestroika is already producing unemployment, inflation, and recession."

viewpoint 25

Perestroika Harms Ethnic Minorities

Workers Vanguard

In mid-September 1988, Soviet leader Gorbachev, appearing in public for the first time in six weeks, was confronted by angry working people in the Siberian town of Krasnoyarsk. "Go to our stores, Mikhail Sergeyevich," they shouted at him, "there is nothing there!" "Lines everywhere! For meat, for sausage, for everything!" A few days later the Soviet news agency TASS reported that in the southern Caucasus mountain republics "mass-scale fighting" had broken out between Armenians and Azerbaijanis in the disputed region of Nagorno-Karabakh, this time with guns and knives. Faced with communal rioting and general strikes, virtual martial law was declared in Karabakh while Soviet troops cordoned off streets in the Armenian capital of Yerevan. Now in the Baltic republic of Estonia, anti-Russian nationalist forces have founded a "popular front" aiming ever more openly at secession from the USSR. Such are the bitter fruits of *perestroika*.

Perestroika (restructuring) was supposed to spur economic productivity, leading to more harmonious socialist development. Instead it has produced intensified social and national conflict as various groupings are out to get a bigger piece of the economic pie and political power at someone else's expense. The turmoil in Soviet society is reflected in the upheaval in the upper echelons of the Kremlin oligarchy. In a dramatic move Gorbachev purged or downgraded his conservative critics in the Politburo. Yegor Ligachev was ousted as ideological overseer, Andrei Gromyko as Chairman of the Supreme Soviet and Viktor Chebrikov as head of the KGB. Supposedly Gorbachev now has a more effective, *perestroika*-minded team. But it will take more than a shakeup at the top of the bureaucracy to overcome the food shortages or resolve the festering national conflicts such as the Armenia crisis.

Workers Vanguard, "Soviet Union: Perestroika Fuels Nationalist Turmoil," October 7, 1988. Reprinted with permission.

It will take a proletarian political revolution to return the Soviet Union to the road of workers democracy and revolutionary internationalism, the road of Lenin and Trotsky....

Up to half a million people thronged the center of Yerevan in July 1988 to protest the USSR Supreme Soviet's decision maintaining the status quo. The capital of Karabakh, Stepanakert, has been gripped by an off-and-on general strike since the spring. In late September 1988, an Armenian rally (called by local bureaucrats) degenerated into a riot. After reports that Azeris had ambushed a bus filled with Armenians, mobs left the Armenian rally and attacked Azeris in the nearby town of Khadzaly; in the fighting nearly 50 people were wounded, one of whom later died. In Stepanakert, Armenians roamed the streets for two days setting fire to homes abandoned by Azeris.

Nationalist Retribution

A deadly cycle of nationalist retribution has been set in motion that threatens the internationalist foundations of the Soviet state. Khadzaly came after the heinous anti-Armenian pogrom in the Azerbaijani city of Sumgait in February 1988 in which Azeri mobs brutally murdered at least 26 Armenians and six Azeris. As communalist violence escalates, Azeris long resident in Armenia have fled in fear of their lives to Azerbaijan, and vice versa. At the time of the October Revolution, the fate of the Caucasian peoples was closely linked to each other and with the working class of Petrograd and Moscow. The Baku Soviet of 1918 was led by Armenian, Azeri and Russian Communists. Prodigious economic growth based on socialist economic relations led to an increasing interpenetration of peoples. But now the net result of more than six decades of Stalinist bureaucratic rule is forced population transfers whose ultimate logic is genocide.

Several days after the outburst of Armenian chauvinism, on September 28, 1988, riot police with truncheons broke up a demonstration in the capital of Lithuania, Vilnius. Protesters reportedly shouted at the police, "Occupiers, get out of here!" The Baltic republics of Estonia, Latvia and Lithuania have been rocked by an explosion of anti-Soviet nationalism which, unlike the communalist feuds in the Caucasus, is more or less explicitly directed against the Soviet central power. On the occasion of the anniversary of the Hitler-Stalin pact, tens of thousands marched in Tallinn, Riga and Vilnius. Marching under the flags of the interwar bourgeois states, notorious for their persecution of Jews and Communists, many of the protesters carried placards which obscenely showed a hammer and sickle joined to the Nazi swastika. This is the language of the CIA's [Central Intelligence Agency] "Captive Nations" crowd.

What the Baltic republics and Armenia have in common is that they are among the most advanced parts of the Soviet Union, and they are playing out the dog-eat-dog logic of *perestroika* with its market-oriented reforms. A recent article in the *San Francisco Chronicle* (31 August 1988) made the perceptive observation:

> In addition to this political turmoil, Gorbachev's economic reforms are likely to exacerbate the ethnic crisis. Perestroika is already producing unemployment, inflation, and recession....
>
> But its most worrying legacy may be regional economic disparity. Variations in regional patterns of employment will produce economic inequalities between ethnic groups. Machine tool builders in Russia will soon race ahead of cotton growers in Central Asia. These differences are certain to create resentments.

Decades of mismanagement by the Kremlin bureaucracy have undermined the belief that there can be equality between the Soviet peoples on an increasing plane of material well-being. Much of the intelligentsia throughout the USSR identifies social and national equality with economic stagnation and leveling down. So they're going for increasing material well-being by the *inequality* route—decentralization and market competition.

National Oppression

Stalinism has been synonymous with national oppression of non-Russian peoples in the Soviet Union. Under Stalin (himself a Georgian) this meant Russification of the non-Russian republics of the USSR, the state which had been conceived by the Bolsheviks as a genuinely free union of peoples. (A contemporary analogue to Stalin is the "solution" to the national question in Romania by the ultra-Stalinist Ceausescu, who has ordered thousands of Hungarian villages in Transylvania razed from the face of the earth.) But once the iron lid of repression has been lifted by Gorbachev, you get the flourishing of national particularism and chauvinism as the result. And the most dangerous of these is the emergence of the blackshirted *Great Russian Nazis of Pamyat*, which has been staging weekly provocations in Leningrad. A massive, organized demonstration of Leningrad workers and youth to *crush Pamyat* would be a decisive signal that there is no place for nationalist chauvinism in the homeland of the October Revolution.

What's needed is the Marxist program which animated the Bolshevik Party of Lenin and Trotsky. It is necessary to reforge in the Soviet Union an authentically Bolshevik party committed to central planning under workers democracy, social egalitarianism and equality between peoples, and proletarian internationalism. Only such a program can liberate the creative energies of all Soviet peoples, overcoming the potentially fratricidal national conflicts which loom ever more ominously in Gorbachev's Russia.

"The intense nationalist agitation... underscores the historic bankruptcy of Stalinist bureaucratic rule and the dangerous effects of Gorbachev's efforts to 'reform' it."

The intense nationalist agitation in Armenia and the Baltic republics underscores the historic bankruptcy of Stalinist bureaucratic rule and the dangerous effects of Gorbachev's efforts to "reform" it. For the Armenians have traditionally been the most pro-Russian of Soviet nationalities, while in the era of the October Revolution Latvia and, to a lesser degree, Estonia were strongholds of Bolshevism.

As a small Christian people in the Near East, the Armenians have long looked to Russia as a protector against their hostile Islamic neighbors, especially Turkey. The Armenian Dashnaks were the only nationalist party in the Russian empire to support the tsarist autocracy. At the outbreak of World War I, the Dashnaks formed volunteer regiments to fight for Russia against Ottoman Turkey. Partly in response, the Turks massacred over a million Armenians the following year.

Amid the anarchic conditions in the Caucasus created by the Bolshevik Revolution and ensuing civil war, Armenia achieved a short-lived independence under the Dashnaks, who collaborated closely with the White Russian general Denikin. Yet even then a majority of Armenians regarded unity with Russia as the only permanent basis for military security and economic stability. To save themselves from an invading Turkish army, in late 1920 the Dashnaks negotiated an agreement with the

Bolsheviks which de facto incorporated Armenia into the Soviet state.

Armenia has subsequently become one of the most prosperous regions in the Soviet Union. With its well-educated working class and large intelligentsia, it is a center of high-tech industry and scientific research in the USSR. Under Gorbachev's *perestroika*, with its emphasis on rewarding competitive superiority, the Armenian bureaucrats and intellectuals had expected to gain even more, particularly at the expense of less developed Azerbaijan. Thus Armenians are in the vanguard of "market socialism" in the Soviet Union. The idea of *perestroika* in Yerevan is that Armenians will be the factory managers, Russians the production workers and Azeris the janitors.

Beginning [in 1987], Armenian intellectuals launched a campaign to transfer the Nagorno-Karabakh Autonomous Region, a mountainous enclave of 150,000 inhabitants, from the jurisdiction of Azerbaijan to Armenia. As we wrote, "Since a majority of inhabitants of Nagorno-Karabakh are Armenians who want to be part of the Armenian republic, that is their democratic right." But the Karabakh movement is only part of an irredentist program for consolidating Greater Armenia. Next on their agenda is the Autonomous Republic of Nakhichevan, once a part of Armenia but now with a majority Azeri population. The demand to transfer Karabakh has been rejected by the Kremlin bureaucracy for fear of opening the door to endless territorial claims and counterclaims by the various Soviet nationalities.

Frustration over Nagorno-Karabakh has produced a wave of rabid chauvinism in Armenia. The *Washington Post* (12 September 1988) quotes as typical an Armenian fruit merchant:

> Azerbaijanis are just Turks, the same lot, and if I see a Turk, I'll kill him. They killed our grandparents, and now they want to kill us. We could live with them if they were only human beings. But they act like animals.

A *New York Times* report from Yerevan cites a prominent Armenian intellectual offhandedly commenting "we are a nation surrounded by barbarians," while in the streets an agitator "loudly called for Christian nations to band together against the predominantly Moslem Azerbaijanis, who, he declares, 'breed like cockroaches'."

Easy Prey

The Armenians, a few hotheads notwithstanding, do not want to separate from Russia. They know that as a small, independent state of some three million people in the Near East they would be easy prey for stronger Islamic neighbors, especially Turkey. Traditionally they have appealed to the Russians as a fellow "Christian people" to unite against the Muslim infidel. Armenian bureaucrats, intellectuals and petty-capitalist entrepreneurs also understand their relative prosperity stems from being a culturally and technologically advanced section of the Soviet economy. They just wanted a better deal in partnership with the Russians. But when Moscow didn't give them what they wanted, the mood turned dramatically against the central government. Back in February-March 1988 demonstrators in Yerevan carried portraits of Gorbachev and hailed *glasnost*. No longer.

"Gorbachev's perestroika *has unleashed a new round of communalist bloodletting in the Caucasus."*

Gorbachev's *perestroika* has unleashed a new round of communalist bloodletting in the Caucasus. Yet the Stalinist regime *cannot* resolve the myriad national disputes, claims or aspirations in a democratic and equitable manner. Under a regime of workers democracy the borders of the various republics and autonomous regions could be adjusted according to the will of the peoples involved. Moreover, if the Soviet Union were carrying out a program of revolutionary internationalism, smashing the reactionary CIA-backed mullahs in Afghanistan instead of temporizing and then pulling Soviet troops out, if the USSR were promoting the program of proletarian revolution in Iran, . . . rather than capitulating before the anti-Communist Khomeini—then the Soviet peoples would not be consumed by feuding over age-old national grievances at home.

In the Western media the Soviet Baltic republics are presented as hotbeds of anti-Communist nationalism. Mass demonstrations have taken place in Riga and Tallinn and Vilnius, under the flags of the independent bourgeois Latvian, Estonian and Lithuanian states of the interwar years. Yet these "independent" states were created through the direct intervention of Western imperialism after crushing the pro-Soviet revolutionary workers of Estonia and Latvia. Historically, this region was a stronghold of Bolshevism. . . .

Today, Latvia and Estonia are the most economically advanced, Westernized parts of the USSR. The nationalist bureaucrats and intellectuals now want to retain control over every rouble generated in these republics. Activists in the Latvian and Estonian Popular Fronts—supposedly formed to promote Gorbachev's "reform" program—are demanding that self-financing be applied not only to individual enterprises, but also want full control of all foreign trade in the hands of the republics, including trade with other parts of the Soviet Union. A petty-capitalist entrepreneur in Estonia quipped:

"We'll have our own currency. The rate'll be three Soviet roubles for an Estonian rouble."

On October 1, 1988, the Popular Front of Estonia held its first national congress in the Lenin Palace of Culture in Tallinn. Reportedly, a quarter of its leaders are members of the Communist Party. But CP approval or no, where this is headed is toward a breakup of the USSR. "Naturally, independent Estonia is the aim of each Estonian," said one Popular Front organizer. Among other things, they are demanding the power to stop immigration of non-Estonians (some 40 percent of the population and half of Tallinn is now Russian), and call for the exclusive use of Estonian as the official language.

"The roots of the present Soviet crisis lie deep in decades of Stalinist bureaucratic misrule, now aggravated by Gorbachev's perestroika.*"*

These demands amount to an attack on the very foundations of the Soviet Union. The language question in particular was seen by Lenin and the Bolsheviks as a key aspect of the struggle for national equality in the tsarist prison house of peoples. The Bolsheviks fought against the imposition of the Russian language on non-Russian nationalities, but they also opposed the bourgeois and petty-bourgeois nationalists who demanded "national-cultural autonomy" and official sanction for their language. Lenin insisted: "The national programme of working-class democracy is: absolutely no privileges for any one nation or any one language. . . ." As was proven in practice through the October Revolution, a program of consistent democracy among the mosaic of nationalities under the tsarist empire could *only* be implemented through the proletarian seizure of power and the creation of a centrally planned, collectivized economy.

An Internationalist Program

And only on a thoroughly *internationalist* program could the working masses seize power. It was under Stalin and the nationalist dogma of "socialism in one country" that Bolshevik internationalism was reversed and Great Russian chauvinism and anti-Semitism again reared their heads in the Kremlin. Lenin's last political struggle, in 1922-early '23, was against Stalin's drive to impose on the Union of Soviet Socialist Republics the old tsarist principle of "Russia, one and indivisible." Lenin insisted that "freedom to secede from the union" was fundamental, not a paper clause to cover the Russifying bureaucracy. At the same time, class-conscious Soviet workers of all nationalities must oppose movements for secession which are in reality a cover for bourgeois counterrevolution. While the Latvian Soviet Republic of 1919 was an independent workers state closely allied with Soviet Russia, the forces now pushing for an independent Latvia and Estonia are increasingly anti-Soviet and anti-Communist. Thus Western imperialism welcomes and foments Baltic nationalism as a hoped-for first step toward the disintegration of the Soviet Union.

The roots of the present Soviet crisis lie deep in decades of Stalinist bureaucratic misrule, now aggravated by Gorbachev's *perestroika*. Wherever "market socialism" has been introduced, it has generated widening social, regional and national inequalities. These tendencies have reached an extreme point in the country which originated "self-management" and "self-financing" 40 years ago, namely, Yugoslavia. Today, Yugoslavia is wracked by a 200 percent inflation rate, mass layoffs, a savage austerity program imposed by world bankers, and violent hostility between the various national republics and autonomous regions. Nonetheless, practically all parts of Yugoslavia have seen militant workers strikes and protests against the increasingly desperate economic conditions.

On at least three occasions workers have stormed the parliament in Belgrade. Both the rising working-class anger and growing national hostilities were dramatically demonstrated in a rally of 70,000 in the central Serbian town of Kraljevo. Officially, the rally was to be a Serbian nationalist protest over the exodus of Serbs from the predominantly Albanian region of Kosovo. However, the rally turned into a bitter attack on bureaucratic parasitism. A union leader at a railroad car factory exclaimed:

> Return all you have taken from the working class! You with your privileged pensions, which are bigger than the pay of entire brigades of steelworkers, do you ever blush when you collect them?
>
> We demand the right to dispose of the proceeds of our work.
> —*New York Times*
> 23 September 1988

Such sentiments could lay the basis for a struggle against the parasitic bureaucracy uniting the proletarians of all the diverse nationalities. But that requires an internationalist communist leadership.

Market Socialism

Yugoslavia has experienced "market socialism" for four decades. In the Soviet Union, the very introduction of *perestroika* has produced a deepening economic and political crisis. There exists among Soviet working people a deep reservoir of egalitarian and collectivist values, the belief that what is produced in society should be available to all of its members more or less equally. Soviet workers have been told for decades, and they believe, that the productive resources of their country belong to them. Thus *perestroika* is bound to produce massive popular resistance which can open the road to proletarian political revolution to shatter the Stalinist bureaucracy.

After coming to power in 1985, Mikhail Gorbachev enjoyed what in American parlance would be called a "political honeymoon." The confrontation over food lines in Krasnoyarsk and the nationalist uproar in Armenia and the Baltic republics indicates that Gorbachev's "honeymoon" with Soviet working people is over. For Soviet workers to take back political power requires the leadership of a revolutionary Marxist party, a new Bolshevik party. And like the Bolshevik Party of Lenin and Trotsky, it would be based on the inextricable link between the struggle for authentic workers rule in the Soviet Union and the fight for world socialist revolution.

Workers Vanguard *is the biweekly newspaper of the Sparticist League, an organization that advocates a revolution of the working class to establish socialism in the US.*

bibliography

The following bibliography of books, periodicals, and pamphlets is divided into chapter topics for the reader's convenience.

Afghanistan

Harry Anderson and Fred Coleman	"Leaving the Quagmire," *Newsweek*, February 13, 1989.
Arnold Beichman	"No Reparations for the Afghans," *The Washington Times*, February 27, 1989.
John F. Burns	"With Soviet Weapons To Lean On, Kabul Is No Pushover," *The New York Times*, March 19, 1989.
Department of State	"Afghanistan: Soviet Occupation and Withdrawal," *Department of State Bulletin*, March 1989.
Edward W. Desmond	"We Really Must Go," *Time*, February 22, 1989.
Shireen T. Hunter	"In Afghan Act II, Let US Be Wary of Friends' Aims," *Los Angeles Times*, April 3, 1989.
Vasily Izgarshev	"What Will Spring Bring," *New Times*, no. 8, February 21/27, 1989.
Robert D. Kaplan	"The Afghan Ayatollah," *The New Republic*, November 21, 1988.
Robert D. Kaplan	"Afghanistan Postmortem," *The Atlantic Monthly*, April 1989.
John Lofton	"Tender, Loving Care for the Departing Bear," *The Washington Times*, February 22, 1989.
Donatella Lorch	"Target: Kabul," *The New York Times Magazine*, February 12, 1989.
Emily MacFarquhar	"After the Soviets Go," *U.S. News & World Report*, February 13, 1989.
Newsweek	"Inside a Frightened City," March 13, 1989.
Revolutionary Worker	"Afghanistan on the Brink of Civil War," February 13, 1989. Available from the Revolutionary Worker, Box 3486, Merchandise Mart, Chicago, IL 60654.
Barnett R. Rubin	"Afghanistan's Uncertain Fate," *The Nation*, February 27, 1989.
Radek Sikorski	"Still-Life by Shellfire," *National Review*, April 7, 1989.
Soviet Military Review	"Hopes and Concerns of Afghanistan," November 1988.
Yuri Tyssovsky	"Hopes and Apprehensions," *New Times*, no. 11, March 14, 1989.
Mary Williams Walsh	"The Veil Descends Again on Afghanistan," *The Wall Street Journal*, January 19, 1989.
Workers Vanguard	"Battle for Afghanistan," February 17, 1989. Available from the Spartacist League of the US, Box 1377 GPO, New York, NY 10116.

Glasnost

Abel Aganbegyan	*The Economic Challenge of Perestroika*. Bloomington, IN: Indiana University Press, 1988.
David Aikman	"One Bear of a Soviet Politician: Interview with Boris Yeltsin," *Time*, March 20, 1989.
Phyllis Berman	"Unloosing Demons," *Forbes*, February 6, 1989.
Fred Coleman and Russell Watson	"Perestroika Isn't Working," *Newsweek*, March 13, 1989.
Padma Desai	"Soviet Farm Plan: Gorbachev Takes Chinese Lessons," *The Wall Street Journal*, March 27, 1989.
Esther B. Fein	"Glasnost Is Opening the Door on Poverty," *The New York Times*, January 29, 1989.
Ernest Gellner	"Stalin Takes the Stand," *The New Republic*, March 20, 1989.
Leonid Goldin	"Initiative Versus Inertia," *New Times*, no. 47, November 1988.
Mikhail Gorbachev	"Gorbachev Meets with Representatives of Trilateral Commission," *News and Views from the USSR*, January 19, 1989. Available from the Soviet Embassy Information Department, 1708 18th St. NW, Washington, DC 20009.
Mikhail Gorbachev	*Perestroika: New Thinking for Our Country*. New York: Harper & Row, 1988.
David Holloway	"Gorbachev's New Thinking," *Foreign Affairs*, vol. 68, no. 1, 1988/89.
Moshe Lewin	*The Gorbachev Phenomenon*. Berkeley, CA: University of California Press, 1988.
Yegor Ligachev	"With Enemies Like This, Who Needs Friends," *New Perspectives Quarterly*, Summer 1988.
Roy Medvedev	"What Soviet Are We Rebuilding," *Soviet Life*, January 1989.
Michael Meyer	"A Message to Moscow," *Newsweek*, April 10, 1989.

Joshua Muravchik	"Glasnostrums," *The New Republic*, January 30, 1989.	*Los Angeles Times*	"A Carrot for Moscow," January 6, 1989.
Thomas H. Naylor	*The Gorbachev Strategy*. Lexington, MA: Lexington Books, 1988.	*The New York Times*	"Excerpts From East-West Agreement on the Protection of Human Rights," January 17, 1989.
Newsweek	"Talking to Gorbachev," May 30, 1988.	Richard N. Ostling with Ann Blackman and Cathy Booth	"Giddy Days for the Russian Church," *Time*, June 20, 1988.
Roger Rosenblatt	"The Altar of a Broken Idea," *U.S. News & World Report*, April 3, 1988.		
Time	"The New USSR," April 10, 1989.	Michael Parks	"New Soviet Code Will End Banishment, Internal Exile," *Los Angeles Times*, December 17, 1988.
Henry Trewhitt	"Responding to Gorbachev," *U.S. News & World Report*, December 19, 1988.		
Jeff Trimble	"Power to the People?" *U.S. News & World Report*, April 10, 1989.	Robert Pear	"Shultz Accuses East Bloc on Rights," *The New York Times*, January 18, 1989.
Robert C. Tucker	"Giving Up the Ghost," *The New Republic*, October 17, 1988.	Alexander Podrabinek	"Soviet Psychiatry: A Message from Moscow," *The New York Review of Books*, December 8, 1988.
The Wall Street Journal	"Glasnost Without Disclosure," April 5, 1989.	Irina Ratushinskaya	*Grey Is the Color of Hope*. New York: Alfred A. Knopf, 1988.

Human Rights

Jean-Pierre Barou	"An Interview with Andrei Sakharov," *The New York Review of Books*, March 2, 1989.	A.M. Rosenthal	"Prisoner at the Window," *The New York Times*, February 7, 1989.
Raissa Berg	*Acquired Traits*. New York: Viking Penguin, 1988.	Andrew Rosenthal	"US Explains Move on Rights Parley," *The New York Times*, January 5, 1989.
Department of State	"US Commemorates 40th Anniversary of Universal Declaration of Human Rights," *Department of State Bulletin*, March 1989.	William Safire	"Baker's First Blunder," *The New York Times*, January 5, 1989.
		Natan Sharansky	*Fear No Evil*. New York: Random House, 1988.
Michael G. Herlihy	"Gorbachev, Glasnost and God: New Thinking About Religion," *America*, January 9, 1989.	George Shultz	"Vienna Meeting: Commitment, Cooperation, and the Challenge of Compliance," Current Policy no. 1145. Available from the United States Department of State, Bureau of Public Affairs, Washington, DC 20520.
Bill Javetski	"Human Rights Get Their Biggest Boost in a Decade," *Business Week*, January 30, 1989.		
Bill Keller	"US Psychiatrists Fault Soviet Unit," *The New York Times*, March 12, 1989.	I.F. Stone	"Another Betrayal by Psychiatry?" *The New York Review of Books*, December 22, 1988.
Morton M. Kondracke	"Gulag? What Gulag?" *The New Republic*, February 13, 1989.	Elie Wiesel	"The Sun Rises for Soviet Jews," *The New York Times*, February 26, 1989.
Anthony Lewis	"A Better World," *The New York Times*, December 25, 1988.	Lev Yelin	"A School of Human Rights," *New Times*, no. 11, March 14, 1989.

index

Afghan Alliance, 20
Afghan refugees, 8, 28-29
Afghanistan
  agriculture, 2-3
    destruction of, 8-9
  communism in
    advantages of, 1-4
    disadvantages of, 5-9
    economic growth under, 2
  cost of war in, 1-2
  culture of, 6
  failure of peace talks, 15-16
  human rights violations, 5
    by secret police, 6, 7, 9
    treatment of intelligentsia, 7-8
  interim government, 20, 23-24, 28
  Kabul government, 23, 41
    and Geneva Accords, 35
    Soviet aid to, 19-20, 21
    UN relief for, 29
  relief efforts, 29-30
  self-determination necessary for, 27-30
  Soviet involvement in, 7, 27, 36
    benefits of, 31-34
    efforts to maintain control, 15-18, 24
    reasons for intervention, 39-40
    Soviet troop withdrawal, 27-28
      sham efforts, 16, 36
      US reaction to, 25, 28
      will end Soviet involvement, 11-13, 23-25
      myth of, 15-18, 19-21
  US aid, 33
    "day one deal," 20-21
    policy failures, 35-36
    should continue, 36-37
      con, 39-41
Arbatov, Georgi, 35
Armacost, Michael H., 20, 27, 35, 37
Armenia, 113
  Gorbachev's response to, 86-87
  nationalist agitation in, 114-115
arms race, 73, 81
atheism, Soviet, 51, 57, 60

Batenin, Gely, 41
Bloice, Carl, 39
Bolshevik party, 114, 117
brain drain, Soviet, 64, 68
Brezhnev, Leonid, 92-93
Brumberg, Abraham, 83
Bukharin, Nikolai, 85

capitalism, 72, 75
Catholic Church, 55, 57
communism
  absolute power of party, 96
  in Afghanistan
    benefits, 1-4
    disadvantages, 5-9
  in Estonia, 110-111
  Soviet criticisms of, 84
Council for Religious Affairs (Soviet Union), 52, 55, 59
cultural assimilation
  in Estonia, 109
  of Jews, 69, 70

defense, 72-74
  and perestroika, 80
  Soviet view of, 17
democracy
  and free market, 96, 97
  and socialism, 84, 96
  chances of establishing Soviet, 78-79

education, 44, 64
Eliot, Theodore L. Jr., 23
emigration
  laws under Gorbachev, 48, 63
  of Soviet Jews, 63, 64, 68
Engels, Friedrich, 85
Estonia
  conditions in, 108-109
  economy of, 115-116
ethnic minorities
  effects of perestroika on
    beneficial, 107-111
    harmful, 113-117
  Soviet fear of, 68-69

Feifer, George, 101

Geneva Accords, 19-20
  failure of, 37
  Soviet troop withdrawal, 27
  violations
    Afghan, 8
    Reagan administration, 40
    Soviet, 37
glasnost
  and Afghan withdrawal, 35
  as genuine, 71-75
    myth of, 77-82
  freedom of speech under, 48, 65
  improves quality of life, 95-99
    con, 101-106
  promotes freedom, 83-87
    myth of, 89-93
  purposes of, 12, 79-80
Gorbachev, Mikhail
  and Afghanistan, 11-13, 40
  and glasnost, 84, 97
  human rights doctrines, 86, 89-90
  Jewish policy, 63, 70
  religious tolerance, 51
Grachev, Andrei, 43

Hekmatyar, Gulbaddin, 21
Helsinki Accords, 48, 64
human rights, 90
  and political prisoners, 93
  conference in Moscow, 89, 91
  in Soviet Union
    activist organizations, 65, 97
    and Jews
      repression of continuing, 67-70
      repression of easing, 63-66
    desire for noninterference, 89, 91-92
    government supports, 43-45
      con, 47-50
    religious freedom, 51-54
      government violates, 55-57
        con, 59-62
    under glasnost, 65
  international support for, 66
  violations in Afghanistan, 5, 6, 9
Humphrey, Gordon, 20, 21

Idinopulos, Thomas A., 67
Intermediate Range Nuclear Forces (INF) treaty, 35, 80

Jews, Soviet
  assimilation in society, 69, 70
  characteristics of, 53-54
  repression of
    as continuing, 67-70
    as easing, 63-66
  Zionism of, 65, 69

KGB, 16, 47
Khan, Prince Sadruddin Aga, 24, 28, 29
Kharchov, Konstantin, 52
Khruschev, Nikita, 47-48
  release of political prisoners, 93
  religious suppression under, 52
Kriegel, Henry, 35
Kurashvili, Boris, 84

Laber, Jeri, 5
Latvia, 115-116
Legvold, Robert, 71
Lenczowski, John 77
Lenin, V.I., 43, 78, 85
  and Stalinism, 97, 102
  war on religion, 51-52

Marx, Karl, 85
Marxism-Leninism, 77-78, 105
Moscow Jewish Association, 63, 65
Moscow Popular Front, 83
mujahideen, 7, 19, 28
  internal fighting among, 20-21
  strength of, 15-16
  US aid to, 21-23, 36

Najibullah, 1, 8, 23-24
nationalism, 113-114
New Times, 107
Nicaragua, 80

Orlov, Yuri, 66

Pakistan
  Afghan policy, 24-25, 41
    and Geneva Accords, 20, 40, 41
    and *mujahideen*, 16
    refugees, 5-7, 30
  US relations, 25
Pamyat, 65, 69, 114
peaceful coexistence, 34
People, The, 39
People's Democratic Party of Afghanistan (PDPA), 1, 9, 33
  faction infighting, 3-4
  role of, 41
perestroika
  and church-state relations, 60, 98-99
  and ethnic minorities
    benefits, 107-111
    harms, 113-117
  effect on workers, 103-105
  foreign policy purposes of, 79-80
Perkovich, George, 63
Peshawar Alliance, 23-24
Phillips, James A., 15
Pimen, 52, 59

Rehimi, Lea, 19
religion, Soviet
  control of clergy, 52
  freedom of, 51-54, 59-61
  laws governing, 56, 57
  possibilities for reform 56-57
  suppression of, 55-57

Rosenthal, A.M., 21
Rubin, Barnett R., 5
Russian Orthodox Church
  government suppresses, 51-52
    con, 59-62

Sakharov, Andrei, 83
Satar, Abdul, 20
Seliunin, Vasili, 85
Sestanovich, Stephen, 11
Sharansky, Natan (Anatoly), 47, 68
Shevardnadze, Eduard, 12, 21, 40, 72-73
Shultz, George, 20, 35
socialism, 4, 60
  democratic, 84
  Lenin's views on, 43
  market, 115, 116-117
Solzhenitsyn, Aleksandr, 86
Sorokowski, Andrew, 55
Soviet Union
  activist groups in, 95-96
  Afghan policy
    atrocities committed, 6-7
    future role, 31-34
    lessening of control, 11-13, 23-25, 41
    retaining control, 15, 18
  alcoholism in, 104-105
  economic policy
    and per capita income, 67, 103
    Gorbachev's effect on, 50
  foreign policy of, 71, 80
  human rights in
    are denied, 47-50
    are supported, 43-45
  reforms in, 49
    as genuine, 71-75, 83-87
      con, 77-82
    as successful, 104
      con, 101-106

    Western response to, 50
  religious suppression in, 55-57
    anti-Semitism, 65, 69, 70
    myth of, 59-62
  Stalinism, 52, 83, 114
    Soviet elimination of, 43-44
Stone, I.F., 89

Third World
  and international politics, 73, 74
  Soviet military aid to, 12
Toome, Indrek, 107

Ukraine, 53, 57
United Nations
  Afghan policy
    failure of peace talks, 15-16
    relief and resettlement program, 29, 30
  need for strengthening, 74
  Soviet ratification of covenants, 92-93
United States
  Afghan policy, 27, 32
    role in relief effort, 30
    should aid *mujahideen*, 35-37
      con, 39-41
  improved Soviet relations, 25
Universal Declaration of Human Rights, 48, 64, 89, 90, 92-93

Wallis, Jim, 95
Williamson, Richard S., 27
women, Afghan, 32, 33
Woodward, Kenneth L., 51
Workers Vanguard, 31, 34, 113
World Marxist Review, 59

Yaklovev, Aleksandr, 72
Yugoslavia, 116

Zinoviev, Alexander, 49